# They Said This Day Would Never Come

## CHASING THE DREAM ON OBAMA'S IMPROBABLE CAMPAIGN

### CHRIS LIDDELL-WESTEFELD

HODDER &
STOUGHTON

First published in Great Britain in 2020 by Hodder & Stoughton
An Hachette UK company

1

Copyright © Chris Liddell-Westefeld 2020

A CIP catalogue record for this title is available from the British Library

Hardback ISBN 9781529308235
Trade Paperback ISBN 9781529308242
eBook ISBN 9781529308259

Printed and bound in Great Britain by Clays Ltd, Elcograf S.p.A.

Hodder & Stoughton policy is to use papers that are natural, renewable
and recyclable products and made from wood grown in sustainable
forests. The logging and manufacturing processes are expected to
conform to the environmental regulations of the country of origin.

Hodder & Stoughton Ltd
Carmelite House
50 Victoria Embankment
London EC4Y 0DZ

www.hodder.co.uk

*To Grace*

# They Said This Day Would Never Come

# CONTENTS

# AUTHOR'S NOTE

In the years since Barack Obama was first elected president, dozens of books have looked back on his time in office—some that go behind the scenes of Obama's White House, some that dissect the inner workings of his administration, some that analyze the broader Obama era. There is even a best-selling Obama-Biden detective novel series.

This is something different. In this oral history, you'll find well-known names from the Obama for America leadership. But you'll also hear from former field organizers and volunteers as they share what it was like to work deep inside the organization—the moments of joy and terror, inspiration and anxiety, loneliness and fellowship that remain seared into memory more than a decade later. Their voices are only a narrow slice of the six thousand staff, tens of thousands of neighborhood leaders, and millions of volunteers who, not so long ago, in the shadow of an unpopular president, banded together to move the country in a new direction. It would be impossible to include them all, but my hope is that this book offers a portrait of this grassroots movement, one forged when few expected Obama to prevail.

A few standard disclaimers: Because roles evolved as the campaign progressed, the title listed next to each speaker corresponds to the months covered in that chapter. The quotes here are drawn from more than two hundred interviews recorded between September 2013 and June 2015 as well as follow-up sessions in 2019. I've removed verbal placeholders ("you know," "like," "just," etc.), condensed quotes, and arranged stories chronologically so the narrative is as clear as possible.

My own voice appears in italics, a reflection of the fact that on this subject, I cannot be neutral. Many of the people included here were strangers when I began this project. Some were former coworkers, roommates, and close friends. One even officiated my wedding.

The common thread was having devoted themselves to the election of America's most unlikely president when the outcome was far from certain.

I chose to present their stories this way in the hope that a constellation of voices might best reflect what so many stressed to me about Obama for America: on every level, the whole was greater than the sum of the parts.

# INTRODUCTION
*January 2014*

"So, Chris, I want to hear more about this project," Barack Obama said as Marine One lifted off the runway.

Staring back at the forty-fourth president of the United States, seated in his helicopter, I felt a familiar anxiety set in. When I first started organizing for Obama in 2007, the campaign leadership drilled into everyone that our most precious resource was the candidate's time—every minute he attended to staff could mean one less minute persuading an undecided voter or inspiring a potential volunteer. If you wanted to contribute to the organization's success, you should never divert focus from those two goals. This lesson had been so deeply ingrained in me that even after nearly seven years of working for Barack Obama, I never felt at ease interacting with him.

So I always tried to keep my interactions as brief as possible. My job at the White House was to handle "the Book"—a black leather binder embossed with a gold presidential seal that functioned as the president's nightly homework assignment. The Book contained all the memos, national security directives, draft remarks, schedules, constituent letters, and other documents deemed worthy of the president's attention. Upon delivery, President Obama would confirm receipt with a nod, thanks, or sometimes—referencing the intense expression I wore nearly every time I entered his personal space, my attempt at professionalism—"you're still looking really serious, man."

I had never expected to have a front row seat to the Obama presidency. When I signed up to volunteer for him in my hometown, Iowa City, on the day then-Senator Obama announced his campaign, I assumed he would lose. Nearly two years later, I joined hundreds of other former organizers in following the new president to Washington, looking to be a part of the administration we had played a small, collective role in bringing about.

Through a mix of timing, luck, and privilege, I had landed this West Wing position, where I saw up close how the government documents a president's time in office. Every staffer's email is public record, every photo is archived, and every piece of paper is preserved under the Presidential Records Act. These materials are eventually administered by the National Archives and Records Administration and become primary sources for future generations. Sometimes I would imagine historians reading the Book decades later, trying to reconstruct Obama's eight years.

But as he entered his second term, it occurred to me that comparatively little had been done to document the campaign that put Obama in the White House. Aside from memoirs by the campaign leadership, few had recorded what it felt like to live through the experience in their own words. The reflections of organizers and volunteers—the majority of the people who made up the effort to elect America's first Black president—would likely be lost to history.

Only five years after his inauguration, the victory that had seemed so improbable at the outset was becoming more inevitable in the retelling. The outcome of the 2012 campaign had already reshaped the meaning of 2008, a trend likely to accelerate with each passing election cycle. Friends' oft-told campaign stories began to strain credulity, omitting moments of hardship or doubt. It was easy to see how decades of nostalgia might erode the details and reduce their recollection of the experience to "2008? It was great . . . we changed the world."

That's why this was my final trip as a White House staffer. With no other appointments demanding the president's attention, I'd been given a chance to tell him about the project that compelled me to leave three years before the end of his term.

"Well, sir, it's an oral history project to document your 2008 campaign," I said. "I'm leaving to collect interviews with alumni, starting in Iowa."

*        *        *

In the early days, presidential campaigns attract dreamers.

Every four years, ordinary Americans invest their hopes for the future in a new candidate for president. Despite the stereotype that politics is a cynical quest for power, for thousands of volunteers and activists, campaign fieldwork is an earnest act of blind faith—the belief that your labor might alter the trajectory of the most powerful country on earth.

Nowhere is that sense of possibility greater than in Iowa. The Iowa caucus is an election process different from other states. The caucuses reward grassroots activism, local organization, and community deliberation while offering everyday people the chance to rigorously vet each candidate. Although its predominantly white, older, and rural population doesn't much reflect the diversity of the national electorate, as host of the first primary contest, Iowa is where presidential dreams take root or die.

It was in Iowa, during his first trip as a presidential candidate, that Obama referred to himself as "an imperfect vessel for your hopes and dreams." That was especially true for a group Obama called "the kids"—the young volunteers and staff who joined his campaign from far-flung parts of the country in 2007 when he was still an underdog down twenty points in the national polls.

I was one of them. Over the course of eleven months, more than two hundred of us embedded across ninety-nine Iowa counties to build an organization of local volunteers. Our mission was to finish first in Iowa in hopes of proving that Obama could remake the electorate by attracting new voters and that an overwhelmingly white state would support a Black candidate for president.

On January 3, 2008, Obama's victory in Iowa shocked the country, validating a risky campaign strategy and providing momentum for the remaining primary contests. But to Obama, the experience was more than just another campaign win. It was a test of his most fundamental belief about democracy: that in the face of long odds, ordinary people can bring about change.

Primaries are often covered as national competitions, but they are also sequential, and each one counts in its own way. When the Iowa caucuses ended, Obama's organizers took what we had learned and went national. Most of us joined up with counterparts in other early states—New Hampshire, Nevada, and South Carolina—hopscotching across the country every few weeks through a new primary.

That summer, transitioning to the general election, volunteers and staff set up shop in areas uncontested by national Democrats for decades—longtime conservative strongholds like Indiana, Virginia, and North Carolina—to register new voters and build neighborhood volunteer teams. By the end, six thousand organizers were managing tens of thousands of trained volunteer leaders. And on November 4, 2008, that work culminated in Barack Hussein Obama—a Black man campaigning to lead a nation founded, in part, on the principles of white supremacy—earning more votes for president than any candidate in American history.

When President Obama is asked about his 2008 campaign, this is who he talks about: his volunteers and his organizers. Many of the people I met over those twenty-one months were natural organizers. I was not. I would equate long hours with productivity, skipping meals only to binge on cinnamon rolls and cake when my blood sugar dropped. The basic duties of a campaign organizer—cold-calling strangers and showing up at their door—made me deeply uncomfortable.

But the cause was all-consuming. Raw enthusiasm eventually infused me with a self-confidence I'd never had before, and it proved contagious around volunteers. "We're making history," Iowa state director Paul Tewes, a veteran campaigner, kept telling us. I believed him. Later, when I was working in North Carolina during the general election, I would tell volunteers that knocking on twenty doors could be one of the most important achievements of their life. Every action carried outsize weight. Nothing seemed small.

In the years that followed, I met hundreds of staff and volunteers whose path to joining up had required more sacrifice than mine. It had been easy for me to sign on because it started in my backyard, but I wanted to understand what inspired so many other people to uproot their lives on behalf of an unlikely cause. To know what lessons their experience could offer future generations and how these bit players formed the foundation of the most successful grassroots campaign in modern American history.

So I set out to track down the alumni—the staff and the volunteers, the young people and the young at heart, those who toiled in the campaign's Chicago headquarters and its local field offices. I wanted to document how they went from wanting something to be different to pulling it off. To capture their spirit and their effort as proof that what happened once could happen again.

*     *     *

As Marine One touched down on the White House lawn, President Obama turned to me and said, "Well, if you want, when you're ready, let me know and I'll do an interview with you."

More than a year later—after nearly two hundred interviews—I took him up on that offer. In the Oval Office, he described what kept him going during the early months of the campaign, when he was widely expected to lose:

> *It was really the team on the ground—and I would include the volunteers with that—those staff and volunteers that carried us in those early months at a time when we were still honing our message and I was still finding my way as a candidate.*
>
> *When I was their age, I had become a community organizer, not even really knowing exactly what that meant and not necessarily being as good at it as any of them were. But it was based on a premise that drew from my reading of the civil rights movement and my reading about the union movement and the women's suffrage movement. This vision of a politics from the bottom up. And so often electoral politics was something completely removed from that. It's money, and it's TV ads, and it's positioning, and it's talking points. And somehow the process of people becoming involved and determining their own destiny— that got lost.*
>
> *And what I saw with both the staff and the volunteers was this almost organic process of people organizing themselves. And I was the front man, but they were the band . . . when you saw folks like this work, you just didn't want to screw up. You wanted to make sure that you were worthy of these efforts. And I really wanted to win, for the staff and volunteers, as badly as I wanted to win for myself.*

This is the story of his team on the ground—from Iowa to the inauguration—as told by those who lived it.

The 2004 Campaign: The Illinois Primary;
From Crowded Field, Democrats Choose State
Legislator to Seek Senate Seat
—New York Times, March 17, 2004

**As Quickly as Overnight,
a Democratic Star Is Born**
—New York Times, March 18, 2004

Barack Obama Named Keynote Speaker at 2004
National Convention
—NBC Today Show, July 15, 2004

**"Skinny Kid with a Funny Name" Makes Good**
—CNN, July 30, 2004

Bush Wins Second Term
—Guardian, November 3, 2004

**Convention Star Obama Wins Illinois
Senate Seat**
—New York Times, November 3, 2004

Republicans Enlarge Senate Majority: GOP
Majority Now Includes 55 Senators
—Sabato's Crystal Ball, November 4, 2004

# 1

## SWEPT UP

*Fall 2004–Spring 2007*

*I*n my sophomore year of college, my roommate Sean ordered us match-ing dark-blue "Barack Obama for Senate" T-shirts. Sean and I were students at the University of Iowa, and because Iowa was a swing state with presidential candidates visiting all the time, it felt like we were at the center of the political world. It was fall 2004, eighteen months after George W. Bush invaded Iraq, and the stakes of that year's presidential campaign felt life-and-death.

President Bush launching a "preemptive" war in Iraq when I was seventeen is what made me care about politics. As I realized that President Bush's election had led to people my age being sent to war, I started to follow campaigns in the same obsessive way I tracked baseball box scores as a kid. This was before Twitter, so Sean and I would spend hours refreshing realclearpolitics.com, trying to dissect the latest polls—most of which we did not understand—and speculating about what soon-to-be president John Kerry's Democratic Senate majority could accomplish.

Even though we watched dozens of races across the country that fall, I didn't care for most politicians. Obama, who was running for the US Senate in Illinois, was the only one we deemed T-shirt worthy. Every-thing about him felt different. His Democratic National Convention speech included aspirational language that sounded revolutionary compared to his peers. Obama had spent his twenties as a community organizer, written a memoir that examined his biracial identity and detailed youthful drug use, and been elected the first African American president of the Harvard Law Review. He was young, he was smart, he seemed honest, and unlike nearly every other prominent Democrat, he had been right about the most *important policy question in my lifetime: he had opposed the Iraq War before it began. He was also on the verge of becoming only the third Black person elected to the US Senate since Reconstruction.*

*On election night 2004, Obama's win was the only bright spot. President Bush won reelection and carried with him into office half a dozen new Republican senators. Even Tom Daschle, the Democratic Senate leader, went down. Against that backdrop, Obama arrived in Washington, where he was greeted as a rising star in a political party desperate for new heroes.*

*While I was excited about Obama's ascent, Bush's reelection left me despondent. I could not understand how a majority of voters thought a man who had entered the White House after losing the popular vote and had started a war based on false pretenses deserved a second term. Further, I couldn't understand how nearly every Democrat in Congress with presidential ambitions had voted for a congressional war resolution prior to the invasion.*

*Not knowing where to turn, desperate to do . . . something . . . in the aftermath of Kerry's loss, I dove deeper into political blogs and read every book I could find on presidential elections. Looking at the history of past campaigns, I realized I was in a perfect position to get involved in the next one. I had grown up and gone to college in Iowa City, the most liberal town in Iowa's most liberal county. Potential 2008 candidates started to visit the home of the first-in-the-nation Iowa caucuses as early as March 2005, quietly exploring presidential runs.*

*By fall of 2006, my senior year of college, I was attending lots of small local political events, hoping to be inspired. At a Saturday-morning Hawkeye football tailgate, I watched John Kerry politely decline a beer bong ("It was her 21st birthday," the* New York Times *reported under the headline "Bong Girl"). At a backyard fundraiser in Waterloo, Joe Biden pulled me close to share a story about working out with Strom Thurmond in the Senate gym. Mark Warner, former governor of Virginia, spent an afternoon shooting hoops with me and a dozen other Iowa college students.*

*None of them excited me.*

*The politician I most liked, Obama, was the one who never visited. And so, I assumed, he wouldn't run for president. At least not in 2008.*

**Pete Rouse, Obama Senate Chief of Staff:** We had a strategic plan for getting established in the Senate. None of it had anything to do with running for president.

By 2004, I'd been Senator Tom Daschle's chief of staff for nineteen years, ten of those spent with him as Senate Democratic leader. Tom lost his reelection race the same year Obama was elected to the Senate. After the election, Senator Obama asked me to be his chief of staff.

He told me, "I can give a good speech. I know retail politics. I am also aware that I'm coming to the Senate with some notoriety—the only African American, the Boston convention speech. I know that some of my colleagues, including Democrats, are going to be wary of me and concerned about whether I'm going to be a serious senator or a headline grabber. I want to move forward in the Senate, but I want to follow a strategic approach so I can be an effective senator as quickly as possible without ruffling feathers unnecessarily."

That wasn't enough for me, though. I had been in the Senate a long time. I was in my midfifties, and I was thinking about moving on to a new phase of my career. So I said, "That's great. I'm happy to give you advice, but I'm not available to do this."

Senator-elect Obama countered as follows: "One other thing. You may have heard that I'm thinking about running for president in 2008. That is categorically untrue. Maybe at some point I would consider this down the road—2012, 2016, later if I ever have an opportunity. But now my daughters are too young. My wife would never allow me to do it in 2008. I'm focused on getting established in the Senate."

So I thought, "Here's a very smart guy, a very decent guy. He is extraordinarily talented and very important to the future of the Democratic Party. If he's just looking for somebody to help him get established in the Senate, how hard could this be? I'll do it for a year and a half, get him going, and then find somebody else to take it from there."

Nine years later, I left the White House. You just get swept up in it.

**Lauren Kidwell, Staff Assistant, US Senate:** He was not your typical freshman senator. When I was still a staff assistant working the phones, you would see people come by just to take pictures of the nameplate outside his door.

That first year he turned down a lot of national invitations. Scheduling requests came from people who were not from Illinois. I remember picking up the phone one day, and the woman on the other end said, "Can I talk to the scheduler? I want to invite the senator to something."

So I went into our normal spiel about how to send the request in writing and cautioned that we don't accept a lot of invitations.

She was like, "Uh-huh. This is Ethel Kennedy. I'd like to talk to your scheduler please."

So I put her right through.

I was very junior, so I certainly wasn't in any inner circle conversations, but from day one, I was opening letters from people around the country saying, "You need to run for president."

**Stephanie Speirs, Senior, Yale University:** I wrote a letter to Obama's senate office when I was in college. Like a lot of people, I first heard of Barack Obama in 2004, from the DNC speech that he gave. I was so struck by the way he talked about government as a force for good and a unifying force, because that wasn't the era that we were living in under George W. Bush. He talked about how there was more that was common between us than divided us.

In the letter, I talked about how I was really struck by that vision. I was also struck by the fact that he was raised by a single mom who struggled to make ends meet. My own single mom raised three kids on a salary below the poverty line. I, too, was born and raised in Hawaii, where I felt like my story was improbable in any other country than America. Being the child of immigrants, I had a very particular definition of the American dream from my parents—one that Obama also articulated. So for all those reasons, I thought, "One day I want to work for this person in some capacity."

**Alyssa Mastromonaco, Director of Scheduling, US Senate:** There was an accessibility to him in the Senate. It was a much more formal place than it is now, and he was someone that everybody felt like they could talk to. Everything you could ever want to do, he got invited to do, so we had to be calculating. He got invited to a bunch of Ivy League and private schools for commencement season, but the big one we did was UMass Boston. UMass Boston had one of the highest percentages of first-time nontraditional students of any school on the East Coast.

**Carrianna Suiter, UMass Boston Commencement Audience Member:** Senator Obama was my brother's commencement speaker at UMass Boston. It was such a diverse audience. You had kids who were the first in their families to go to college. You had grandparents and mothers from working families who were graduating. The commencement was outside, in the middle of a storm. Despite the weather, everyone paid attention, everyone listened. Looking around and seeing how enamored of this man people were was incredible. Like he understood what people were striving for.

**Jon Favreau, Speechwriter, US Senate:** When Hurricane Katrina happened in August of 2005 and Obama started going around the country speaking about it—not just as a failure of ideology but a failure of government standing up for people in the most basic way possible—that cut across party lines. That's when he started to feel that maybe it was his time to be on the national stage.

All through '05 and '06, as he campaigned for other people and at state party conventions around the country, we were crafting a stump speech. It set him up to be seen as a different kind of Democrat—not ideologically but in that he felt that *people needed to get involved in politics again.* We needed to be honest again. We needed something different. Something outside of Washington. That became his message.

**Tommy Vietor, Press Secretary, US Senate:** He wrote *The Audacity of Hope* and did this long book tour. In the '06 midterms, along with all the travel he was doing, I think he saw the reaction he was getting from other politicians, from candidates and activists. He could tell he was reaching people.

*The first sign Obama might be changing his mind about running for president was the announcement that he would travel to Iowa for the Harkin Steak Fry, an annual fundraiser hosted by Iowa Democratic senator Tom Harkin in September 2006.*

**Alyssa Mastromonaco:** Tom Harkin approached Obama on the Senate floor and said, "Every year I host the Harkin Steak Fry. It would really mean a lot to me and the Iowa Democratic Party would raise so much money if you would be our keynote speaker."

**Pete Rouse:** Senator Harkin didn't want to have to choose among his colleagues who were running: Joe Biden, Chris Dodd, John Edwards, Hillary Clinton. Obama was invited as headliner for the Steak Fry because he was the one option who *wasn't* a candidate for president in 2008. He initially declined Harkin's invitation—he didn't want to generate speculation that he was thinking about running, because at that point he wasn't. But Senator Harkin continued to argue that he ought to reconsider the invitation, saying, "You're not running; you'd be perfect."

**Steve Hildebrand, Political Consultant:** Pete Rouse called me and said, "Senator Harkin has invited Obama to come to Iowa. Barack's going to do the steak fry, and we want you to staff him."

**Pete Rouse:** Steve Hildebrand was known as the "Iowa guy" from the Gore days. Steve knows all the political people in Iowa.

**Steve Hildebrand:** I'd been in politics at that point for a good twenty years. I was getting tired of politicians and decided that if I could get inspired by one of the presidential candidates, I would do one more presidential campaign and then look for a way out.

So I went. I met up with Senator Harkin and his wife, and we went to the airport to pick up Barack. It was such a different time. He got off the airplane by himself, carrying his own bags.

*My friend Sean and I had driven two hours to see Obama at the steak fry. We wore our "Obama for Senate 2004" T-shirts, the political equivalent of merch from your favorite band's first headliner tour. In the parking lot, there were guys circulating petitions calling for Obama to run for president. They claimed to have shown up on their own, unaffiliated with any group.*

*Sean and I entered the Warren County Fairgrounds to scope out the scene. There was a stage covered in hay bales and framed by a barn-sized American flag. At the podium, a half dozen local Democratic politicians wearing blue button-up shirts took turns slamming Iowa Republican Jim Nussle, who was running for governor, each using the same bad pun ("Watch out for the Nussle Hustle!").*

*The display was everything I hated about politics. Empty rhetoric, agrarian props, and partisan grandstanding, all accompanied by a John Mellencamp soundtrack. But what made this different from every other political event I'd gone to was the audience. Three thousand people had turned out for an annual fundraiser that usually attracted fewer than one thousand. There were high school and college-aged kids mixed in among the older people who came every year. This seemed new.*

**Lindsay Ayling, Grinnell College Freshman:** I went to see Senator Obama at the 2006 Harkin Steak Fry. I was really excited because I had loved his 2004 DNC speech so much. I liked the way that he talked about America. He talked about the ability of government to make a positive impact in people's lives. He made the arguments that a lot of

Democrats weren't willing to make because they were afraid of being labeled as "too liberal." I wanted him to run for president. I wasn't sure whether he would, but the fact that he came to Iowa was a good sign.

**Steve Hildebrand:** Lots of things shocked me that day. First and foremost was how anxious that crowd was to touch him. It was unbelievable. Everyone had to shake his hand. Everyone. And to his credit, he shook every hand. He was mobbed the minute he got there, and he was never really able to catch his breath. I saw that this guy knew how to do it, and do it well. He connected with people. He shook hands for—I don't know—an hour after his speech. He was very willing to be there and be a part of that moment.

**Dean Fluker, University of Iowa Senior:** I had never felt this way before about politics. Here was somebody I had no problem getting behind—his values were already generally in line with mine. I could really identify with him because he's biracial like I am. And not only did I believe in this guy, I thought he was electable, mostly because he didn't have all of the baggage of other politicians. I'll never forget saying to him, "If you ever run for president, I would put my life on hold and dedicate it to helping you."

**Steve Hildebrand:** I drove home that night the four hours from Des Moines to South Dakota. I usually like quiet time or listening to the radio loud, but I spent that entire drive on the phone calling everybody I could think of to say, "This is the real deal."

**Alyssa Mastromonaco:** He was really a natural. And in a place like Iowa—a place that's really white—it was interesting to see. His appeal wasn't just on the coasts or among young people.

**Tommy Vietor:** On paper, people might think for a senator from the South Side of Chicago, an African American, something like the Iowa steak fry is not in his wheelhouse. But once you get an hour south of Chicago, it's completely rural. Obama was in farm communities all the time and understood the issues they were talking about. He understood the people. He knew how to reach them.

I don't know whether that was the moment he decided to run, but I think it was certainly a moment where everyone realized that he had the potential to do really well in Iowa.

*I don't remember much of Obama's speech from the steak fry. Like Hildebrand, what struck me most was the crowd. Camera operators, journalists, and Iowans surrounded Obama as he walked from the food tent to the stage; students thrust books in his face for an autograph; seasoned activists jostled for photos; stoic midwestern farmers strained to reach through the scrum and touch him. As Obama shook hands along a rope line after his speech, every few yards someone would bring up 2008—"I hope you run," "You're bringing us hope," "I hope we see you next year."*

*I had watched so many politicians pitch Iowans on the idea of them running for president. This seemed like the opposite—Iowans trying to sell him on taking the plunge. This was the thing I'd been hoping to find. I wasn't sure exactly what campaign workers did. I didn't know how they were hired or, at that point, if Obama would even run. But I decided that if he did, I would find some way to be a part of it.*

*As it turned out, I didn't have to wait long.*

**Barack Obama, US Senator:** I'd gone to the steak fry in 2006. I think at that point, I was still skeptical of the prospect of running for president so soon after I'd been elected to the Senate. The response, frankly, was really positive among the crowd, and along with some encouragement around the country, I started looking at it fairly seriously. Part of the reason I did was because, given how well I had done in downstate Illinois, my Midwest background, my familiarity with agricultural issues, my familiarity with small towns in the region, I thought it was possible that might allow me to compete and build a strong network in Iowa.

**Lauren Kidwell:** I left the Senate office in June of 2006 to go work in Minnesota on Amy Klobuchar's Senate race, in part because I knew that if Obama ran for president, I wanted to have more experience to position myself for a better role on his campaign.

In December 2006 I was back in DC and dropped by the office to say hi. Senator Obama asked me what I wanted to do next. And I said something along the lines of, "Well, if there's a presidential campaign, I'd love to work on it. But I'm exploring all my options."

He responded with something like, "Why don't you keep your powder dry for a little while."

*By January 2007, Obama had announced an exploratory committee to run for president and hired a national campaign staff, joining a field that would include eight other candidates for the Democratic nomination:*

- *Hillary Clinton, two-term senator from New York and former first lady of the United States, consistently voted "most likely to win" in every poll of national political insiders*
- *John Edwards, former senator from North Carolina and John Kerry's running mate in 2004, the economic populist whose 2005 apology for supporting the Iraq War Resolution sometimes was enough to make up for that vote with antiwar activists*
- *Bill Richardson, governor of New Mexico, former ambassador to the United Nations, who would later run ads suggesting he was "too qualified" to be president*
- *Joe Biden, a senator from Delaware since 1973 so confident that he once spent half an hour trying to convince five Obama interns from my office they should join his campaign and make Obama their second choice (they did not)*
- *Chris Dodd, longtime senator from Connecticut who would move his entire family to West Des Moines and enroll his daughter in kindergarten two months before caucus night ("This shows his commitment to the state and the people and the caucus process," a spokesman said.)*
- *Dennis Kucinich, a congressman from Ohio, whose then-far-left platform received even less attention than when he first ran for president in 2004*
- *Mike Gravel, who had been a senator from Alaska in the 1970s and was allowed into most debates despite being widely dismissed by the media*
- *Tom Vilsack, the former governor of Iowa, who dropped out of the race three months after his announcement*

*Their path to the White House began in my home state.*

**David Plouffe, Obama for America Campaign Manager:** From the very moment Barack Obama started talking about running for president to the moment he announced, what crystalized was a belief that we needed to win Iowa. That was really our only chance.

Very early, David Axelrod and I laid out the blueprint—our theory of the case—and it all flowed through Iowa. Obama didn't know Iowa. He had been there for the steak fry, but he hadn't spent a lot of time there. Think about that. Most of the people who run for president have spent a lot of time in these states. He didn't know New Hampshire, and he didn't know South Carolina. He started that campaign with zippo. Nothing.

**Steve Hildebrand, Obama for America Deputy Campaign Manager:** I remember a late-night phone call very early on, where Obama said, "I don't know how to win Iowa. I hope you do."

**David Plouffe:** He had to understand what a caucus was. How do the rules work and what's our view of the state of play? How do we put this together? And how do we compete against the establishment? Were all those questions answered satisfactorily? No. A lot of it was just guesswork.

**Valerie Jarrett, Senior Advisor:** The thought was if we could convince the people in Iowa to support him, then that would pave the way, because at that point Hillary Clinton was the clear front-runner. People in Iowa are very discerning, and they spend a lot of time getting to know the candidates, so there's a level of credibility that you gain if you win the Iowa caucuses.

**Dan Pfeiffer, Obama for America Traveling Press Secretary:** Our strategy was win Iowa, win New Hampshire off of Iowa, survive Nevada, win South Carolina, jump into Super Tuesday. After step one those things could rearrange themselves, but if we didn't win Iowa, we couldn't win anything else.

**Barack Obama:** When I got into the race, I knew that Iowa was going to be important. That as somebody who was a clear underdog, the only way to win the nomination generally would be to win Iowa. And we knew that that was going to be a heavy investment and I was going to have to spend a lot of time there.

**Dan Pfeiffer:** To Plouffe's eternal credit, every decision was about, "How does this help us win Iowa?" If the answer was that it didn't, then we didn't do it.

**David Plouffe:** Where did I put the odds of us winning Iowa at that point? Twenty to twenty-five percent. Where did I put the odds of us winning the whole thing? Probably under 10 percent. You know, we were running against the Clintons. That's like taking on an undefeated heavyweight champion.

None of us signed up thinking that this was going to be even a two-year project necessarily, much less a ten-year project. I remember talking to my wife and it was like, "OK, we'll move to Chicago for basically a year and we'll see." In a way, that was healthy. Nobody that came to that campaign was trying to measure the drapes of their office in the White House—everyone was there because they believed in him. Some wanted the experience of a presidential campaign. For some, this was the next step on the career ladder. But I think the common element was people were excited by him.

**David Axelrod, Chief Strategist:** I almost quit politics in the early 2000s because I felt it had become such a cynical game. I got into it because I believed that through this process, you can steer the course of history in some small way and make a real difference. And it was really my partnership with Barack Obama that kept me in. He was a third-tier prospective candidate when he started running for the Senate. But that Senate campaign in Illinois was so inspiring. The Obama 2008 campaign was really an extension of that.

**Dan Pfeiffer:** You've got a guy whose name is Barack Hussein Obama. It rhymes with Osama bin Laden; he's got Saddam Hussein's name in the middle. He's got a bizarre background, but people are attracted to it.

It is weird in hindsight, because I'm probably a pretty jaded, cynical, political operative type—I think I may have fashioned that identity for myself—who looks at numbers and sees what the percentages are. And as I was considering joining the Obama campaign, that kind of calculus didn't even occur to me. I had the chance to get on the ground floor of something that could be incredibly special. I had the sense either that it was going to be amazing or that it would be over in six weeks. But either way, it was worth the risk.

*While Obama's national headquarters was based in Chicago, campaign manager David Plouffe and deputy campaign manager Steve Hildebrand quickly built out an Iowa leadership team, starting with Paul Tewes.*

**David Plouffe:** I tasked Steve Hildebrand, who ended up being our deputy manager and was part of these discussions in the fall of '06 about whether to run, with finding leaders for these first four states: Iowa, New Hampshire, Nevada, and South Carolina. And he recommended Paul.

**Paul Tewes, Iowa State Director:** I told Steve, "The only job I want is to go run Iowa." I liked Obama. I didn't know a difference between him and Hillary in the policy sense, but there was an idealism about him. What appealed to me was that he had something that struck the imagination, and you can do interesting things with that.

Iowa intrigued me. I knew how important it was going to be. And I knew that when you coupled an organizing retail state with a candidate that struck people's imagination, the upside of what you could do as an organizer was a dream. Anything you'd ever thought of before but couldn't pull off because you didn't have the candidate or the message to do it, you could try with him. It was a laboratory, because of who he was and what he represented and what he invoked in people. And because it was Iowa. I wanted to do *that*.

In January I had a meeting with David, and we talked for hours.

**David Plouffe:** That was an important discussion, not just about Paul's qualifications but what kind of campaign we were going to put together. It wouldn't be a traditional campaign. We both couldn't run a traditional campaign and Obama didn't want to. We had to build it all from scratch.

**Paul Tewes:** David said, "Send me a little plan, a timeline, and a budget of the first month or two." So I did that, and I sent him some names: I wanted Marygrace, because I'd known her for years. And I wanted Mitch Stewart. And I wanted Emily Parcell, because she knew Iowa well. Those were the first three people that I talked to.

*Tewes's first three hires, Marygrace Galston, Mitch Stewart, and Emily Parcell, came into the job as veterans of the Iowa caucus process. All were in their late twenties or early thirties and had spent the 2004 election working on Iowa campaigns. These four staffers would form the nucleus of Obama's Iowa leadership team as it expanded over the next year.*

**Mitch Stewart, Iowa Caucus Director:** I met then-Senator Obama in Minnesota. I was a coordinator campaign director in 2006, and we had a Humphrey Day dinner. He came in and spoke, and I got to staff him. Hildebrand called me before the fundraiser and asked me to gauge the crowd's interest in Obama.

We were at the Hyatt in Minneapolis. He gave his speech to three thousand people, a room that was probably 95 percent white. It was overwhelming. The audience was so moved—I saw people crying.

He'd had a very long day and was very tired. He looked at me, and he asked, "Do I have to go through three thousand people to get out of here?" All he wanted to do was go home. I didn't have another way for him to get out. A security guard came up from the hotel, an African immigrant, and said, "Senator, I can get you out through the kitchen."

He looked at me, and I shrugged. Then he looked at the three thousand people waiting for him to sign everything and said, "Yep, let's go." So we went through the bowels of this very nice hotel in Minneapolis. And as we left, the people who prepared the food, the people who washed the dishes, the people that served the food, the custodial staff, they lined up in the hallway of this huge hotel and clapped for him as he walked out.

I thought, "I can't imagine any other person right now who could have the type of impact he had with these affluent white political activists and then get a similar response from folks that for the most part had been ignored by American society." And I thought, "If this guy wants to run for president, I am there."

**Paul Tewes:** Mitch had a great reputation—he was a natural choice. I wanted Emily, because she had done caucuses before in Iowa and just come off working for the state senate. She knew the state, she knew the people, and she knew the process.

**Emily Parcell, Iowa Political Director:** Even a year in advance of the caucus, it felt like the stakes were much higher than in 2003–2004, because John Kerry had won the Iowa caucus in 2004 and became the nominee. So every campaign was like, "The guy who won last time got the nomination, so we have to go in to Iowa." It was the first time in a while that there was really a true open seat for the presidency— everybody was trying to get in on the ground floor and outdo each other, even in 2006.

Here's the big thing for me: Democrats are better than Republicans. The Obama decision wasn't based on emotion. During the course of the campaign, seeing him and spending time with him on the road, I became a true believer. But I wasn't there when I took the job. I just wanted who I thought could win. I didn't know that he would; I thought he could. So I went back to Tewes and committed to working on the campaign.

**Paul Tewes:** Marygrace had done Iowa for Kerry, but I also knew her going back to 2002, and I wanted someone that I could trust implicitly. There are also things I'm not good at that she was very good at.

**Marygrace Galston, Obama Iowa Deputy State Director:** The second Paul was talking to me about it on the phone I knew I was going to go. I never thought Obama was going to win. But it wasn't about his ability to win so much as his ability to excite people and run a hopeful campaign. I thought that'd be different and something that Iowa had not really had before.

I thought this could be an amazing experience and I owed it to myself to go do it. I told all my friends in Seattle, "I'm doing one year, and then I'm coming back."

I flew to Iowa. Paul picked me up at the airport. We lived in the Embassy Suites for a couple of weeks before Paul, Mitch, and I rented apartments in the same building.

**Paul Tewes:** It was January 23 when I got there. The four of us got together and developed the plan for what we wanted to do over the course of the next year. I'll never forget that meeting. I look back and everything we talked about doing, we did.

This may sound trite, but it was just a couple of core ideas. One was that proximity matters. We wanted to be everywhere, and we wanted to be there longer. Like, I'd rather hire 80 people for two hundred days than 150 people for thirty days, because it's all about building relationships. We talked a lot about how to build relationships.

**Marygrace Galston:** We had to give Iowans multiple points of entry to this campaign. Whether they were hearing about us from kids' teammates, soccer moms, through church, at school, or their book club.

**Paul Tewes:** We wanted to just spend time listening and getting to know people as opposed to engage in a robotic exercise of asking, "Who do you support?"

We wanted offices everywhere, we wanted organizers on the ground earlier, we wanted to embed them in the community, and we wanted to give them time to go do things other than just organizing.

When you produce a plan that way, it's really hard, because it takes intuition, and most campaign plans are very numbers driven. But we discussed getting people on the ground early, leasing lots of real estate so you don't have to drive two hours to find us, and we needed to show up in the community and plant the flag—that says something. That's a sign of respect.

We had a map up on the wall and had a little highlighter. Emily would read off a town, and we'd say, "OK, put an office there."

**Emily Parcell:** Tewes would've had an office in every town in Iowa if he could have. I can hear him saying it now: "If you put up brick and mortar, they will come."

**Marygrace Galston:** Paul said, "We have to go out to these communities and just be there—give people an opportunity to join us."

**Emily Parcell:** This came from the top down. Plouffe was the one saying, "This is going to be a block-by-block campaign." From the first day I started, that's all I heard. The other thing I heard was, "We're not doing politics as usual." Which, when you're the political director, is not what you want to hear.

The intent was there at the beginning: "We're not going to stroke anybody's egos; this is going to be a grassroots campaign, and we're doing this different." And they stuck to that spirit. I had to change my perception of who a valuable endorser was. I had learned to run a caucus campaign in a specific way, focused on a narrow list with a handful of people who seemed "important." Obama's campaign used a completely different model than I'd used before.

**Paul Tewes:** We knew we had to approach things differently. We had to instill imagination in organizers and in the organization. When people walk in, ask them their opinion. Ask them what they want to do, realize it might not even be something that's in your program, and let them do it. Treat them how you'd want to be treated. We put our principles up on the wall at campaign headquarters: "Respect, Empower, Include."

Iowa is the best example of this: how you campaign is a direct reflection of how you're gonna govern. And if people feel good about it, if people feel included and empowered, if people feel respected in that campaign, then they're gonna think—and rightly so—that they know that's how you're gonna govern. And that is refreshing to them. That is exciting to them, that they're gonna be part of this.

**Mitch Stewart:** We started thinking through how many caucus goers we would need to identify as Obama supporters before caucus night. We came up with a couple different turnout scenarios. We thought if

we could identify a hundred thousand supporters, that would probably equate to between fifty and seventy thousand actual people showing up.

As a point of comparison, when I worked for Edwards in 2004,
we were at seven thousand supporters a week before caucus day.
So putting a hundred thousand Obama supporters as our goal on
a piece of paper I thought was just insane. I didn't articulate that to
Paul, but I just remember thinking what a quixotic adventure this was
going to be.

*Dozens of offices, lots of time listening, answering every caucus goer's
question—the Iowa plan was ambitious and time-consuming. It required
a major investment of money that had yet to be raised.*

*Hanging over all the planning was the memory of the 2004 caucus
campaign. In 2004, 124,000 Democrats had caucused, a record number,
and Kerry had won with 38 percent of the delegates. Since the party stalwarts who attended caucuses every four years were largely expected to
support Clinton or Edwards, in order for Obama to win more than 35
percent of the delegates, he would need to dramatically increase the turnout—hence the one-hundred-thousand-supporter goal. To do that, the
campaign would hire a wave of field organizers, whose mission would
include bringing new voters in to the caucus process. These organizers,
mostly twenty-two- to twenty-five-year-olds whose salaries would be
$2,000 a month, would embed themselves in Iowa communities over the
coming year and build a network of local volunteers.*

**Paul Tewes:** I think when we sent our first budget in, they went,
"Oh my God."

**Steve Hildebrand:** There were lots and lots and lots and lots of
discussions about how big our operation in Iowa should get. Paul's
dream was huge. And in the end he got pretty much what he wanted.

**David Plouffe:** We spent an enormous amount of money in Iowa. It
was the only route we saw.

*When Obama announced he was refusing money from federal lobbyists
and political action committees, I donated fifty dollars, broken up into
five-dollar increments so his average contribution would appear lower.
The day my.barackobama.com went live, I signed up to volunteer. After*

*no one contacted me, I sent long, overly formal emails to everyone I could think of in Iowa politics, trying to find a way in. Eventually, my thin résumé found its way to Mitch Stewart.*

**Mitch Stewart:** We had a flood of résumés. All these kids from Harvard and Yale and Princeton who under any circumstance would likely be successful people professionally. But organizing—it's an interesting profession. You don't necessarily have to have an Ivy League pedigree to be a successful organizer. In fact, my experience was quite the opposite.

Organizing is about perseverance and being humble, and going back and being rejected over and over and over again and still getting up and going and asking that fifth person, that sixth person, that seventh person until you finally get that yes. It's a unique personality that can absorb that sort of rejection.

In a perfect world, what you want to do—because ultimately caucus building is about relationships—is try to hire staff that already have relationships in their communities. So we would prioritize Iowans first based off of that.

*I met Mitch for an interview at Hamburg Inn, a local diner, where he laid out the campaign's immediate plans—Obama would announce his campaign for president on February 10 at a massive rally in Springfield, Illinois, followed by stops in Iowa, Chicago, New Hampshire, and South Carolina. Mitch was hiring a small team of people to handle those first Iowa events while they built a larger staff that would eventually include nine regional directors overseeing more than one hundred field organizers across Iowa's ninety-nine counties.*

*Mitch didn't ask much about my qualifications. He seemed most interested in figuring out whether I could carry a conversation and would commit to working one-hundred-hour weeks in the lead-up to the caucus. Not knowing what exactly a field organizer did, I enthusiastically said yes. Graduation was May 12, and I pledged to go anywhere he wanted starting May 13.*

*Near the cash register, I ran into Simeon Talley, en route to his own interview with Mitch. I knew Simeon from around town. He was a year older than me and had moved from Ohio for an entry-level job on the 2006 Iowa midterm campaign. Given his work experience (three whole months as a field organizer in Iowa City), he already had an offer from John Edwards but was holding out for Obama.*

**Simeon Talley:** We had an interview at the Hamburg Inn. I was super nervous. I thought I had to sell all my experience and relationships in Iowa and Iowa City. But Mitch was pretty laid back and wasn't necessarily looking for the hard sell. I guess he wanted to see if I was a competent person. He hired me shortly thereafter.

I had no expectations. It was just a really fucking cool thing at that point. Like, look at the way people respond to this guy! Michael Jordan is a uniquely gifted basketball player. He elevated the sport and the game to a new level. In my mind, Barack Obama held that place. That there was something about this guy that uniquely separated him from every other politician.

I didn't think he'd win the Iowa caucus, and I didn't think he'd win the nomination. It was about being a part of it. Working on the campaign gave me the sense that I was doing something special with my life. I was really caught up in the idea of the first African American candidate who could win a national election. That meant a tremendous amount to me.

As an African American man, I felt it was important for other African Americans or even any nonwhite person to look at Barack Obama and see his success. To see that representation.

*On February 10, hours after Obama's morning announcement in Springfield, Illinois, I drove forty minutes to Cedar Rapids to volunteer at his next campaign event. It was a packed house—a high school gym filled with 2,200 people for what was billed as a "conversation" that quickly morphed into a Q&A with the audience. The temperature dropped below ten degrees as a line formed outside, but the crowd was enthusiastic, young, and—at least for my state, where the population was more than 90 percent white—racially diverse. As was often the case nearly a year out from the caucus, most remained undecided as they left. But there were a few core people clearly ready to start volunteering for Obama, and I walked out knowing this was all I wanted to do.*

*I went back home and started a Students for Obama volunteer group at the university. Through that, I met Megan Simpson, a junior who had spent most of 2004 working for the Kerry campaign in Dubuque and planned to drop out at the end of the semester to move home and organize for Obama. Her certainty felt like proof that I was chasing the right thing.*

**Megan Simpson, University of Iowa Junior:** I was sitting in the library studying for a test, and I got a call from Mitch Stewart. He said, "I got your name from a bunch of folks in Dubuque. Would you be interested in talking about being an organizer on the campaign?" Without thinking—and forgetting that I had promised my dad that I would finish school and that I wouldn't go back on another campaign—I said yes. And I didn't ever second-guess that decision.

My family were pretty undecided on who they were going to support and thought I was kind of crazy going to work for a guy with a funny name. But I never heard from my parents, "You're making a mistake. You shouldn't do this. You have to finish school." They were very supportive.

I had a good friend who was going on his second deployment to Iraq. I was putting myself through college. I'm the oldest of six kids. My parents had me when they were very young, and so they wanted to see me succeed in life, but on my terms.

At that point in our country, with Bush as our president, me not being able to afford college without working two jobs, and friends who were being deployed to Iraq for the second time, it wasn't a hard decision. I felt very strongly that this was a moment in which I could make a difference.

My parents were organizers when I was little. I grew up in field offices and labor halls, and so I felt that my way to give back was to elect people that I believed would do the most good for the country. School would always be there, but there would never be another moment like this.

*In the three months leading up to graduation, I spent all my free time volunteering in the new Iowa City Obama office. When a spot opened up, I was offered a job as a field organizer, starting June 1, at a salary of $2,000 a month. I felt like I had won the lottery.*

## Obama: I'm Running for President
—Chicago Tribune, February 10, 2007

## Obama Says He Opposed Iraq War from the Start
—Reuters, February 11, 2007

## Is Black America Ready to Embrace Obama?
—CNN, March 2, 2007

## Excitement Surrounds Obama's Visit to Oakland: Candidate Calls for Ending War, Solving Problems at Home
—San Francisco Chronicle, March 18, 2007

## Dems Favor Hillary Clinton for 2008, Polls Show
—CNN, March 19, 2007

## Rookie Mistakes Plague Obama
—Politico, March 26, 2007

## The Politics of Money: With Obama Rivaling Clinton in Fundraising for 2007's First 3 Months, No Democrat Is Likely to Achieve Early Dominance in Presidential Race
—Baltimore Sun, April 5, 2007

# 2

# CAMP OBAMA

*May–June 2007*

**May 2007**

*National Poll:* Hillary Clinton 38, Barack Obama 23,
   Al Gore 14, John Edwards 12 (Gallup)
*Iowa Poll:* Edwards 27, Clinton 23, Obama 19
   (American Research Group)

*T*hat summer, more and more out-of-staters began moving to Iowa City and working in the office as interns, a reflection of Obama's message that he could only succeed by bringing new people into the political process. For me, that had been easy—my home state was the center of the action, and I got swept up in it. But to build an organization that could compete for the nomination, Obama's campaign couldn't rely on just early-state volunteers. They needed a training program, a sort of camp, that allowed new people—no matter where they started out—to become organizers themselves.

**David Plouffe, Campaign Manager:** We didn't have an infrastructure, didn't have a political support network—we had to build it all from scratch. Which meant speed.

**Dan Pfeiffer, Deputy Communications Director:** In this period we did big rallies in New York, Oakland, Austin. When we traveled the country, either in the early states or when we went to other places and did these rallies, there was tremendous interest.

**David Plouffe:** We had all these kids from all over the country who wanted to work for Barack Obama. And again, not because they thought he was a sure bet for the White House but because they liked him and the kind of campaign he was going to put together.

*When I would ask new people how they ended up in Iowa, they kept saying the same name: Jon Carson. Carson was the campaign's Illinois state director, whose job was to channel online supporters toward efforts in the early states. Dozens of Obama volunteers and organizers would later credit Carson with convincing them that the only rational next step in their lives was to move to a place they had never visited, where they would work for free on behalf of a presidential candidate who was widely expected to lose.*

**Jon Carson, Illinois State Director:** When I joined the campaign, I had a list of six programs I wanted to run. Camp Obama was at the top.

I was already getting emails, seeing signs, and people were saying the words, "Can I move to Iowa? I just wanna quit my job and go do this." I thought if we made it a formal program, we could funnel that energy a lot more efficiently.

*That spring, Twitter had just debuted at SXSW, no one owned an iPhone, and online organizing was in its nascent stages. Obama supporters could visit Facebook or my.barackobama.com to find like-minded allies in their community, but no app or preexisting volunteer network allowed them to plug into the first four presidential primary states: Iowa, New Hampshire, Nevada, and South Carolina. Sensing that Obama's unique appeal had created an opportunity, Carson started a program to introduce political neophytes to full-time campaign work. This was the genesis of Camp Obama.*

**Jon Carson:** I had this idea that we could run a training program and see if we could convince people to uproot their lives. We developed the concept of Camp Obama and put a link up on the front page of the website of barackobama.com. We had ten thousand applicants in spring of 2007.

We started putting about eighty to a hundred people a week through this training.

*Greg Degen was one of those applicants. Greg had never been involved in politics before—never even voted. A native of Buffalo, New York, and a freshman at Ohio State, Greg considered himself informed but unengaged. After watching Obama's announcement for president on TV in February, Greg started closely tracking his rallies across the country.*

**Greg Degen, Ohio State University Freshman:** I saw these rallies taking place, and it continued to reinforce my sense that this was going to be something big. I didn't know what that meant, because I had never been this interested in any campaign.

One of my earliest memories is of watching Richard Nixon's funeral with my mother. My parents were both Republicans; my father's pretty conservative, and so is my extended family. I was always very interested in presidential history and politics, but I never really took a side. Even when we had a political volunteer requirement in our high school curriculum, I wrote letters to Amnesty International instead.

So I went back and googled him and saw the speech at the 2004 Democratic Convention. I remember watching that and thinking it was incredible. His whole speech was about bridging divides—whether they're political, racial, generational—and coming together as one American family. That was incredibly motivating for me. I thought of him as someone who would genuinely approach politics differently—that he would be a coalition builder in a way that other people couldn't. I sent the speech to other people, friends of mine, when I was still a freshman.

I remember watching his announcement speech in February 2007 from my parents' basement in Buffalo and feeling like this was going to be something huge. He talked about a different type of politics, in the sense that special interests would not continue to rule the day, in a way that was more credible than other candidates because he wasn't very entrenched in it all. He hadn't been there very long, and he promised not to take any money from PACs and lobbyists—all these symbolic ways of showing that he could speak on behalf of the American people unpolluted by special interests.

For me it wasn't as much about the issues. It wasn't a policy on climate change or health care that I particularly liked. It wasn't about the war either—though I know it was for a lot of people. It was about his approach and philosophy of governing.

My freshman year was coming to an end, and I was figuring out what I was going to do over the summer. I got a campaign email. It was an invitation to apply to Camp Obama, the campaign's intern training in Chicago. I didn't have a political background, and I didn't think I could really bring anything to the table—my previous work experience was at Subway, a bulk goods store, and my dad's printing press. But I remember the message being very inviting, asking me to "Join this movement." So I applied and was accepted.

**Kristin Avery, Camp Obama Attendee:** Camp Obama was two days of "how to organize." I'd never done any canvassing or phone banking, really, and was petrified of it.

**Aletheia Henry, Camp Obama Attendee:** I was a social worker for a couple years between undergrad and grad school. I worked in child protective services in Franklin County, Ohio, and I got really frustrated with the work. I felt like we weren't offering people pathways out of poverty, and it was really poverty that was leading to the circumstances where children were being abused. So I kind of dropped out by dropping in, and I went to grad school for journalism and communications. I had just finished my degree when I heard about Camp Obama on NPR one day.

I was like, "I remember that guy—he was against the war." I applied online, and they called and interviewed me. They invited me to come to Chicago. On the way out, I realized, "If there's some test on Barack Obama, I'm going to fail." So I downloaded his book *Dreams from My Father*, and I listened to it on the ride out. I was sold by the time I got there. I thought, "This guy has worked in the same communities I've worked in; he's seen the same struggles that I've seen."

**Anna Humphrey, Camp Obama Attendee:** I applied for Camp Obama online. I assumed it was a really selective process, but I think they were taking anyone with a remote interest. I went with the understanding that I would be gone for the summer. That it would be a training workshop in Chicago and then I would be sent to one of the four early states.

**Shannon Valley, Camp Obama Attendee:** I thought it was going to be this really organized, suited outfit. Then when I got in, we were in downtown Chicago, and there were signs everywhere with handwritten notes and lots of people moving all over, the place in chaos. Everything was informal. I felt like they were making it up as it went along.

*At Camp Obama, attendees sat through a curriculum inspired by Obama's own history as a community organizer—how to knock on doors, train volunteers, and explain the candidate's biography. At a basic level, when organizers meet a voter or potential volunteer, they want to build a relationship and end the conversation knowing how likely they are to support their candidate, how likely they are to participate in the election, and what about the election is important to them. The first step to getting a stranger to open up was forming a connection around your own personal story.*

**James Schuelke, Camp Obama Attendee:** We had some interesting speakers at Camp Obama, including the community organizer who Obama had worked for in the South Side of Chicago. He wanted us to learn how to share our personal stories, and he was particularly adamant that they be compelling. So he went down the row, and the two people just ahead of me had these incredible life stories.

The first was a young woman who was originally from Saudi Arabia but had moved to the United States just before 9/11. Following the terrorist attacks, neighbors had treated her family poorly and hurled racial slurs at them. So this young woman wanted to join the Obama campaign in order to prove that her family was American too. I thought, "Wow, that's an amazing story."

And then the young man sitting next to me shared that he was recovering from brain cancer. He showed us all where he still had a scar running across his head. He shared that he hoped to help Obama build support for health care reform. So, once again, just a very moving personal story of overcoming tremendous adversity.

Then the moderator got to me and said, "What's your story?"

I shrugged and mumbled, "I don't know."

He kept pressing me, insisting that I had to have an equally compelling story. I pushed back and asked, "Isn't it possible that I'm a young guy from a middle-class family who enjoys politics and history and is interested in giving back to my community?"

He said, "No. There's got to be something else that made you do this."

Over the next few minutes, in front of all my peers, he helped me articulate my life story: I'd grown up in a military family with neighbors from immigrant, military, and working-class families. These people were my community, so for me, politics was about leveling the playing field for my old neighbors and friends. That's what I would tell people at the doors.

**Jamal Pope, Camp Obama Attendee:** I could list a lot of different reasons why I was supporting the senator. But it really came down to the fact that I was twenty-four years old and had never even thought it was possible for an African American to be president. Part of it was also thinking, "Maybe I can help this cause, and some five-year-old kid will know it's possible."

**Kristin Avery:** I was really excited when I got to Camp Obama, because there were a lot of other people who also wanted to be involved in the campaign, from all over the country. And I thought that was amazing. There was a computer programmer from California and a woman from Missouri who was older. There was a pastor from Georgia, and there were a couple of people who were college kids like me, just from all over the country. I loved Obama. But nobody cared back in Oregon. Nobody knew who he was.

No one at Camp Obama had any idea what they were getting themselves into. Very few people had actually worked on a presidential campaign, or any campaign.

**Meghan Goldenstein, Camp Obama Attendee:** All these people were there from other states, and I remember being super impressed at their dedication this early on, coming from places where I'm sure the vast majority of people there had never even heard his name, let alone thought about organizing for a primary a year and a half from then.

*While many attendees went back home and started to organize their own communities for later primary contests, Jon Carson's goal was to channel as much energy as possible toward the four early states: Iowa, New Hampshire, Nevada, and South Carolina.*

**Jon Carson:** At the end of the training, I would say, "Now it's time to talk about where you want to go next." Some of them wanted to go back home and organize on my.barackobama.com, but a good chunk of them said, "Yep. I'm ready to go out to an early state." And I would personally interview each one of them on that final night of Camp Obama and convince as many of them as I could that they should go to Iowa.

**Anna Humphrey:** I went hoping that I would be allowed to stay in Chicago at headquarters and do something besides field, because the concept of "voter contact" made me very nervous. But they said there were no internship opportunities outside of field and there were none available in Chicago. So when they asked where I wanted to go, I said, "I don't care." Whoever had said they didn't care were automatically sent to Iowa.

**Jon Carson:** I would get a lot of people who would say, "I wanna do a month in Iowa and a month in New Hampshire and a month in . . ." and a big thing we pushed people on was, "Figure out how much time you've got, and stay in the same place for as long as you can." At this point, today, the idea of organizing is a pretty well-understood concept and a national thing. Like, what do you do when the election comes? We all go knock doors. Back then that was not a thing that most people knew that you did.

We still got a lot of, "I want to write policy" or "I want to help write his speeches." So convincing those people to go be field organiz-ers in Iowa, much less do it for free, took some explaining. We had far more conversations about why we *didn't* need volunteer speechwriters and why we *didn't* need another intern on the policy team. Convincing people who'd come to Chicago for this training that staying in head-quarters was a bad idea was the other thing I had to do a ton of.

**Thomas Zimmerman, Camp Obama Attendee:** I was desperately try-ing to petition for a posting in New Hampshire. My boyfriend was still in Massachusetts, but I was told over and over again that they needed people in Iowa.

**James Schuelke:** Jon Carson cornered me and really drilled it into my mind: "You've got to go to Iowa."

**Greg Degen:** New Hampshire and South Carolina are on the East Coast, and that felt somehow more familiar and not too far away. Nevada has a major city, so there'd be more of us there. When I talked to Jon Carson, I told him I was weighing these different options. He shook his head and said, "Just go to Iowa. There's no question here what you should do—just go to Iowa."

So I ended up listing Iowa as my first choice.

**Meghan Goldenstein:** I didn't have any huge desire to go to Iowa. And then everybody did one-on-one meetings with Jon Carson. I said something about New Hampshire, and he said, "Well, if you're a grad student in Madison, come fall, we'll need out-of-state students to come to Iowa. You can help organize in Wisconsin to send students to Iowa."

**Kristin Avery:** When Jon Carson came in to talk about how important the early states were, he had us chant the dates of the early states out loud to get them in our brains.

**Lauren Kelly, Iowa Deputy Field Organizer:** I have several friends who had random run-ins with Jon Carson at Camp Obama. Each one thought that Jon Carson was telling them and them alone that they needed to go to Iowa. So they did it.

**Jon Carson:** We must've sent well over a hundred people to Iowa who ended up volunteering two, three months or more, many of whom ultimately got jobs.

**James Schuelke:** I told my parents I was going to drop out of college and head to Iowa. You had to accept that Obama probably wasn't going to win because you're uprooting your life and that's not a very reasonable thing to do. But I thought, "Even if he does lose, he's going to be this dynamic and historic candidate. It's important. His candidacy will help shift the national discourse on issues impacting millions of lives. This will be an exciting campaign to have worked on, and it'll go down in history books."

**Anna Humphrey:** I went with the expectation that I would only be there for the summer. My family thought that the Clintons would crush us and that we would be done by Labor Day.

**Jamal Pope:** My grandfather played a major role in my decision. He had taken me to the Million Man March when I was twelve years old. And he said, "I'm doing this because I didn't march with Dr. King, and I felt like I should have." Part of me was like, I don't want to be sixty years old and regret I didn't take part in this.

**Jon Carson:** Most of them had not done a lot of campaigns before. They had that sort of millennial generation assumption that service was a good thing. I've always said the Barack Obama candidacy in 2000 wouldn't have gone off any better than Bill Bradley. It was the moment. People were just so sick of the Bush years, and they wanted something different. And Obama gave them this inspiration. Then from there, I think there's a certain amount of peer pressure: *other people are doing this, and I want to get swept up.*

**Shannon Valley:** I just remember from *The West Wing*, there was an episode where Josh and a couple other folks were out in Iowa. These guys with their suits and their shirtsleeves pulled up, out in the cornfields. That was my only image at the time of grassroots politics, of where the road to the presidency began. I wanted to do that. I didn't know what that meant, but I just wanted to be out there. So I packed my bags and got on a Greyhound to Waterloo.

I guess I was thinking of myself as an explorer at this point. I had the whole junior year abroad experience and was chasing that next big adventure. Getting out there and doing something crazy, and that's what it felt like. I didn't have any other plans lined up after college. I just knew I didn't want to go home, and there was this amazing opportunity to try and make a difference.

**Greg Degen:** I was still nineteen. It was the first time I had left home in such an unstructured way. Most people I was friends with were not sure what I was doing or why I was going to Iowa. And I didn't understand why they wouldn't understand this was such an important thing. I don't know what made me decide to do it. At the time I was just looking for something that would get me outside my comfort zone. And I wanted to be a part of Barack Obama's campaign, if I could.

I mean, there's personal stuff too. I'm gay, and at the time I was in the closet. I've talked to a lot of people who have gone through a similar thing when they were in the closet, where there's this big void in your life and you grow up taught to believe that you need to have a family with a woman and raise kids. *That's* what you're supposed to do when you graduate from college—you get a job, you get married, you have a family.

And I still had not come to terms with it, but there's always that nagging in the back of your head. You always have this sense that the future expected of you is not possible for you. Out of that comes this desire to add meaning to your life. Because if you can't have it in the way that you're supposed to, you really want to pour your energy into something that can both distract you from that and fill that void you naturally have by not being honest with yourself.

I wasn't that comfortable in my skin. I constantly had this desire to get away from where I grew up. So I think that, combined with the fact that I genuinely believed in this candidate and believed he had the capacity to change the country for the better—those two things made me decide to pack up and move.

*A first wave of roughly fifty organizers had deployed across Iowa earlier that spring. Having opened the campaign's first local offices, these were the people responsible for welcoming new Camp Obama graduates like Thomas Zimmerman, a former American aid worker in Afghanistan, assigned to intern in Sioux City.*

**Thomas Zimmerman:** I had sold my car before I moved to Afghanistan, so I hopped on a Greyhound bus and took it from Chicago to Sioux City, Iowa.

I remember I just wanted to be in Des Moines. The only thing I really knew going in was that Sioux City was famous for being the site where the only member of the Lewis and Clark Expedition died.

So I got off the bus, and this guy came bounding up in this fantastic *Star Wars* T-shirt, asked if I was Thomas, and then threw me into the car and drove up to the office. I didn't have any income and hadn't saved up a lot of money. But my new colleagues Adam and Nate very kindly informed me they had space in their basement. They rolled out some sheet carpeting, put these super psychedelic tapestries in the corner to build out the other two walls, and then put down an air mattress, a plastic lawn chair, some filing cabinets as a dresser, and a lamp.

For the first two months of the campaign, that was my home.

**Anna Humphrey:** I don't want to say that my parents thought I was brainwashed after I went to Camp Obama and spent some time in Iowa, but it was all I could talk about or think about or have feelings and emotions about for such a long time. They probably thought I loved Obama to an unhealthy degree.

I was expecting, I think, to find the set of *The West Wing*. I didn't really understand what "field" was, so when I showed up to this dingy building with homemade decorations and thrown together donated supplies and furniture—I don't think I was totally prepared for that.

**Kristin Avery:** It's a huge life decision. You're giving up everything, moving to a new state for no money. I had no car. I had no idea where I was gonna be living.

I really had no idea what I was getting into.

## Oprah Endorses Obama
—New York Times, May 3, 2007

## Secret Service Guards Obama, Taking Unusually Early Step
—New York Times, May 4, 2007

## Coulter: Obama's Poll Lead Good for Al-Qaida
— Dubuque Telegraph Herald, May 9, 2007

## City Nobamathon: Disappointing Crowd for Rally in Hil Territory
—New York Daily News, May 13, 2007

## Obama's Surge of Iowa Offices Boost Visibility; But Huge Crowds at His Rallies May Leave Voters Feeling Cut Off
—Chicago Sun-Times, May 24, 2007

## Obama Calls for Wider and Less Costly Health Insurance Coverage
—New York Times, May 30, 2007

# 3

# "THE SUPER BOWL OF POLITICS"

*June–July 2007*

### June 2007

*Iowa Polling Average:* Edwards 26, Clinton 24,
   Obama 20 (RealClearPolitics.com)
*National Poll:* Clinton 37, Obama 36, Edwards 13
   (*USA Today*/Gallup)

*A*round the time Camp Obama was getting off the ground, I started on staff as one of five field organizers based in Iowa City. The campaign had already lasted four months, but few voters were paying close attention. In addition to big rallies, the key metric that made Obama a credible candidate was that he'd raised more money than the Clinton campaign in the first quarter of 2007. This was shocking, since the Clintons had been the dominant figures in the Democratic Party for fifteen years. No state would vote until January 2008, so these quarterly finance metrics became national news and were closely watched by political observers as a sign of candidate viability.

Like many of the new people arriving in Iowa, I didn't have a great sense of what my new job would look like day to day. But I was one of the few who came into the role already familiar with Iowa's caucus process.

The most important thing to understand about the Iowa caucuses was that they're not a statewide election—they're 1,781 simultaneous neighborhood meetings attended by no more than 10 percent of the total population. That process influenced how you organized. To get to know a community, you would start by trying to meet community leaders, *because those are the people their neighbors would look to on caucus night. The rules of a caucus allow one voice to change a room—if you can convince your neighbors to back your candidate, no matter what the results are statewide, you can win your neighborhood.*

*I saw this play out at an early age. When I was fourteen, my dad signed up to be a precinct captain on Bill Bradley's long shot campaign for president against Al Gore. My dad worshipped Bill Bradley—growing up in New Jersey, he watched Bradley captain the Princeton Tigers to the 1965 Final Four. Finding himself living in Iowa thirty-five years later, he jumped at the chance to help his childhood hero. Despite having never volunteered for a candidate, every Sunday he would cold-call a list of his neighbors on our landline, asking them to support Bradley at the caucus. Few Iowans shared his hometown connection to the candidate, but on caucus night, as Gore dominated statewide, my dad led Bradley's supporters to a 4–3 delegate victory in Iowa City Precinct Sixteen.*

*This was the biggest difference between me and the out-of-state newcomers—I didn't know how to organize, but I knew the community where I was stationed. Our campaign office was across the street from the community rec center where I learned to swim, one block east of the library where I learned to read, and around the corner from the hookah bar where I celebrated my twenty-first birthday. Aside from being at work most of the day, my life continued as it had before. I still lived with friends from high school, sort-of dated my college girlfriend from senior year, and ate dinner with my parents on Sundays. I was aware that most of the other kids left behind relationships, jobs, or school for the chance to move to a state they had never visited and work in a new community. It took a unique personality to make that leap.*

*As organizers deployed to their assigned turf, first impressions of the state varied. In some rural areas, you could go days without seeing another Obama staffer. In cities like Cedar Rapids, Davenport, or Sioux City, a half dozen could be clustered in the same office.*

**Marygrace Galston, Iowa Deputy State Director:** You always hear about the Iowa caucuses when you're studying politics. The importance of Iowa and the first in the nation. People called it "the Super Bowl of politics."

**Victoria McCullough, Winneshiek County Field Organizer:** I can't overstate how little I knew about campaigns and what field organizers did. I just had no clue.

**Francis Iacobucci, Des Moines, IA, Field Organizer:** I didn't realize the campaign would continue after summer was over. Everyone kept telling me, "Obama's not gonna make it past July or August." I arrived in June, which was when the second full wave of organizers hired in Iowa arrived.

I had no idea where I was living. I had no idea how much I was getting paid. I mean, they told me this information, but I was barely twenty-one years old—I wasn't paying attention. So I stayed in a hotel the first night, which my parents were kind enough to spot for me. I was so nervous that I ordered one of everything on the Embassy Suites menu.

This was my first real job. I had bought new slacks and new brown dress shoes, and the next morning I put them on with my button-up shirt and jacket. I walked into the office and saw kids my age running around in flip-flops, torn shorts, torn jeans, and T-shirts. There were pizza boxes scattered everywhere, paper everywhere, wires hanging down from the ceiling attached to nothing.

No one talked to me at first. They probably thought I was a reporter or something the way I was dressed. Finally someone introduced herself and put me on the phones. I made phone calls all day, until someone had the time to explain what was going on.

By the end of that first day, I was exhausted. I had been talking to people who were more familiar with the process than I was, trying to convince them to support a candidate I knew very little about. It was a really terrifying time but also invigorating. And it was nice to know I could wear flip-flops to work.

**Yohannes Abraham, Des Moines, IA, Field Organizer:** The team had been around for a few months at that point, and I started the exact same time as a guy named Francis Iacobucci, who would end up being my roommate. We were the two youngest. It was just that very classic new-kid-in-school feeling.

**Francis Iacobucci:** I was introduced to Yohannes Abraham, who was kind enough to offer me a room in his apartment. He needed someone to live there because he couldn't afford the rent. We were making $2,000 a month before taxes. He showed me to my room, which was a closet. I smoked at that time, and we would sit and smoke three or four cigarettes on the balcony and just talk about what this all meant.

*After starting on staff, most us would gather in Des Moines for an orientation, where Paul Tewes and the state leadership defined what it meant*

*to be part of the Iowa team. You would meet the leaders of each depart-*
*ment, who would set expectations for the coming year and frame how*
*our work fit into the campaign's plan.*

**Josh Earnest, Iowa Communications Director:** Paul invited all of the
field staff to come to Des Moines to undergo a staff training. I thought
I'd be making a presentation to a group sitting around a table. There
was a room full of people who'd already been hired by the campaign,
seventy-five or eighty, who were all there to hear from me about exactly
what our message was.

**Francis Iacobucci:** They went around and introduced everybody:
Emily Parcell, Anne Filipic, Josh Earnest, Tommy Vietor.

**Yohannes Abraham:** Part of the training was they set expectations.
Things like, "Look, we're going to be down in the national polls. Those
don't matter. Iowa is the key to everything."

**Victoria McCullough:** There was no real training on "Here's what
Barack Obama thinks. Here are his views." The training was more
about, "Here's the structure of a day. Here's what an organizer does."

**Yohannes Abraham:** The biggest thing that sticks out to me from the
training is Mitch Stewart being incredibly intense talking about the
importance of the work we were doing. How each of us had the ability
to impact the outcome of the election on caucus night. They had us all
100 percent convinced that was the case.
    The other thing that stuck with me was . . .

**Francis Iacobucci:** "No star fucking."

**Yohannes Abraham:** "No star fucking." He said that explicitly. Every
minute you're spending with the candidate or surrogate is a minute
they're not spending with a caucus goer.

**Megan Simpson, Dubuque County, IA, Field Organizer:** That training in Des Moines had such an impact. Paul Tewes said, "The most
important thing you need to know about organizing is that it's all about
stories and why people are doing what they do. So I want everyone to

go around the room, introduce themselves, and tell your soon-to-be friends and coworkers why you're here."

**Dean Fluker, Johnson County, IA, Field Organizer:** Tewes kept saying to us, "Why are you here? Why are you here?" That was a fundamental question—*what drives you to be here?*

**Megan Simpson:** I felt so personally invested in everyone's reasons why. And *that*—telling stories and connecting with people—had a really big impact on how I viewed organizing.

**Paul Tewes, Iowa State Director:** I firmly believe this—people have their own belief system, their own values, and that's what they act upon. A political campaign or a cause is your own way of acting upon your own belief system and values. So by tapping into that, you're tapping into something internal as opposed to external.

I would tell this to the organizers: "You're not here because of Barack Obama; you don't know him. You're here because of something you believe."

Most of these kids had no idea who Barack Obama was—they didn't know him, they didn't talk to him. I wanted people to work from an internal place and understand that those values were important and what they were doing was acting upon those. That's what I was trying to convey. We were all there for different reasons, and those reasons are very internal to each of us. That's much more powerful than an external factor.

**Greg Degen, Johnson County Intern:** I had never volunteered for a campaign before. Besides my Camp Obama training, I had never had to articulate why I supported Barack Obama.

I vividly remember the first time that I ever knocked on doors being intensely anxious and afraid of talking to a stranger. It was the summer, one of my first days in Iowa, and all the other campaign staff seemed much more senior to me, even though it was a bunch of kids out of college who had just been hired. There was a lot of emphasis on having a well-thought-out conversation with a voter, because Iowa caucus goers expect a lot out of presidential campaigns.

But more than that, I had a lot of social anxiety. I wasn't supposed to come back with any missing doors. And after being dropped off,

I just paced back and forth for a while because I was trying to summon the courage to go do the task that I'd been asked to do. I had that same feeling at the first couple hundred doors I knocked on. For the first couple months of the campaign generally, I had this feeling that I sucked at this. But I really wanted Barack Obama to be the president, so I forced myself to keep doing it.

**Carrianna Suiter, Muscatine, IA, Field Organizer:** I thought I was gonna be working in Davenport. We were at the first statewide training in Des Moines. Mitch came over and said, "I know you're about to sign a lease in Davenport. Don't sign it. You're moving to Muscatine." He gave me no room to argue, no room to say anything. I wanted to be in a city.

I was really angry when I got sent to Muscatine. I was isolated. I was by myself. I had four counties in southern Iowa. GPS didn't work in many of the places I would go. They would tell me, "Turn left at the corn silo, and when you get to Jeff's old place, turn right." If I tried using GPS, it would take me to bridges that hadn't been there in years. Organizers in other regions and cities had other organizers to lean on, to hang out with, to grab a beer with. We worked such long hours, and it was hard not to have that built-in social outlet in the early days. It was lonely.

**Michael Halle, Linn County, IA, Field Organizer:** The first day I was in Cedar Rapids, there was this smell in the air that was indescribable. It smelled the way that mash smells when you're making beer.

The second day, there was a different smell that was kind of cinnamony, and I was just like, "What the fuck is going on?" Turns out there's a General Mills factory there. When they'd make different cereals, the town smelled different. I remember people there would look forward to the Cap'n Crunch days.

*As transplants fanned out across Iowa, they introduced themselves to "tier one" activists—local leaders historically active in their local caucus. These Iowans formed the backbone of past candidates' organizations, and some had participated in half a dozen campaign cycles. They were used to getting attention from future presidents.*

**Grant Lahmann, Tama County, IA, Field Organizer:** When I landed on the ground, my objective was to make myself known in the local

Democratic Party establishment, make cold calls, try to find people to meet with.

It's crazy, but the folks who are involved in Democratic politics in Iowa are totally used to it. "Oh, the Obama guy's in town. Gotta meet with him." You know? "Oh, the Clinton person's in town, gotta have coffee with them, tell them what I know." That sort of thing. It's a ritual that many of those folks are very accustomed to, and I realized this was not an out of the ordinary request.

**Ally Coll, Council Bluffs, IA, Field Organizer:** I was sent to Council Bluffs, a suburb of Omaha. I had no idea what to expect. I was worried that I wouldn't know anybody in Iowa and wouldn't have any friends. I didn't really understand that the campaign would become my whole life.

My turf was the four counties in the southwest corner of the state. They bordered Nebraska and Missouri. There was one central town in each county, the county seat, and those towns were more like five or ten thousand people. I could count on one hand the number of people of color. The first thing I did was I went around and I met with all the county chairs. Most of them had not made up their mind, or else they were leaning toward supporting Clinton or Edwards. There was nobody ready to help me get going for Obama. At the end of the meeting, I would ask them for ten more names of people I should talk to, and then I would reach out to those ten people.

**Carrianna Suiter:** One of the first stories I heard from the cochair of the county Democrats was that he had gotten pizza delivered to his house by a presidential candidate. I believe it was Howard Dean. He said, "Dean brought pizza to my house. Is Barack Obama gonna bring pizza to my house?"

**Greg Degen:** When you work on a campaign in Iowa, you have to be incredibly deferential and respectful of their traditions and customs— no matter how strange they may seem.

I remember talking to one person—I asked her if she had decided whom she was supporting in the caucus, and she told me that she hadn't met all of the candidates yet. This was not a donor, this was not a party member, this wasn't any kind of influential figure. This was an ordinary citizen who expected to actually meet presidential candidates in person and probably ask them a question.

**Linda Langston, Linn County, IA, Supervisor:** Iowans take their politics very seriously. I've seen candidates come in over and over again, making an assumption that it's like politics they've seen elsewhere—they come in and they get brutally questioned by people here who are very well informed, which I think makes them better candidates. That, to me, is the gift that Iowans give the rest of the country. And I suspect it's very much the same in New Hampshire.

**Tommy Vietor, Obama Iowa Press Secretary:** The caucuses are imperfect to say the least—if you're disabled or if you're working nights, you can't give that kind of time. But I think those flaws are also balanced out by the importance of a process where you have to take hard questions from real people every day.

The first time I heard about section 215 of the Patriot Act was in some farmer's backyard in Iowa. Because there was just some really smart guy who was worried about the Patriot Act. That candidate accessibility, transparency, and respect for the press in a political process that ultimately is about an interaction between two individuals—and then believing that they'll do what they say they're gonna do—is the key to the whole thing.

It can be a dumb, weird, imperfect way to choose a president, but there's something incredibly valuable that comes from retail campaigning. It creates a lot of hardship for these candidates, and they have to show they can manage it in real time.

**Libby Slappey, Cedar Rapids, IA, Democratic Activist:** When you're an Iowan, you have an obligation to do your homework. I have friends in San Francisco who are political junkies and who are so envious of us in Iowa because we get to vet everybody.

**Linda Langston:** People in New York pay thousands of dollars to go to fundraisers and if they're lucky will see a candidate across a room of 250 people. But in Iowa you'll have a room with 30 people in it. You get to ask really tough questions, and you get to watch what their response is.

**Mark Smith, Iowa State Representative:** My wife and I have friends that simply cannot believe that I have sat down and had dinner with Senator Christopher Dodd, that I had the opportunity to introduce Hillary Clinton. It is unfathomable that these three million people that call Iowa their home have so much opportunity to spend time with the presidential candidates.

**Jan Bauer, Story County Democratic Chair:** The first time you get called by one of them, it's very shocking. You think, "Whoa. This is who?"

**Cathy Bolkcom, Quad Cities Democratic Activist:** I was here one morning, the phone rang, and I answered it.

"Cathy?"

"Yes."

"This is Barack Obama."

"Hi, Senator. How are you?"

"Oh, I'm very well. How are you? I'm running for president, and I'd really like to have your support."

And I said, "You know, I appreciate that. It's early. I haven't really made up my mind yet."

**Steve Dunwoody, Cedar County, IA, Field Organizer:** My regional director gave me the names of a few people to get in touch with and to talk to in Cedar County to get the lay of the land. So one of the first people I met with was Clara Oleson. Clara was, at that time, around sixty-five years old, a retired white civil rights lawyer.

**Clara Oleson, Cedar County, IA, Democratic Activist:** Steve Dunwoody showed up and said, "How about coming on board for Obama?"

I said, "Are you insane? It's too far out. I would be doing nothing except this man's campaign for the year until the caucus. I can't do it. It's too early. I love him, but no, it's too early."

It took quite a few meetings in my living room for Steve to convince me. I had been very active in every campaign. The first presidential campaign that I became involved with was in Iowa, and it was the Shirley Chisholm campaign in 1972. Black congresswoman, feminist, strong. I went to Brooklyn and heard her announce it in the Bedford-Stuyvesant grade school that she had gone to. Before that, I had been involved in the antiwar movement and with feminist activities.

I've seen every presidential candidate. I was with Jesse Jackson twice, in '84 and '88. Motivation for being with these candidates varies—it's based on a belief in what America is and could be.

I didn't think I would live long enough to work on a campaign with a Black person who had a chance for the presidency. You wouldn't have Obama without Jackson or Shirley Chisholm, because change in America is not instantaneous—it takes decades. Democracy is like a garden. A tree does not grow in a year.

**Steve Dunwoody:** Despite having lived in Iowa for many years, Clara was still in a sense locally viewed as an outsider because she was from New York. When I met with her, she gave me a lot of advice. She said, "Well, one of the things you're going to want to do in every conversation you have with people is tell them you're a veteran right away. That will establish trust. That will give you an entrée."

And it's funny, because the way that she was speaking to me is kind of like the way a lot of Black youth get spoken to by their parents at a young age. It's called "the talk." You get "the talk" when you're old enough to go to stores on your own or old enough to walk around on the street. My parents told me, "Always get a receipt whenever you purchase something. Never walk around in a store with your hands in your pocket. Always say please and thank you. Smile as much as you can." The way that she was speaking to me was reminiscent of that. I could tell it was coming from one part curiosity, but it was also concern for how I might be treated in the county.

**Clara Oleson:** I said, "OK, I've been down this road for thirty years. I'm gonna give you 'the talk.'" Which is, "You don't run up your credit cards. You don't run up long-distance calls on other people's phones. You don't hit anybody." Because these are all things that staffers had done in the past.

And I said, "Can we talk about race? Did anyone in Des Moines mention that you were coming to a county with, according to the census, sixteen Black people?"

**Steve Dunwoody:** She asked if the campaign sending me, a Black man, to Cedar County was a way to test feelings and attitudes toward race. She was truly trying to understand why this twenty-five-year-old kid was being sent from Detroit, Michigan, to Cedar County. And I told her I didn't know.

**Clara Oleson:** I said, "For the first month, you will not go to a bar after eight o'clock at night. When you go to a small town, the first stop you will make will be at the cop shop, and you will introduce yourself as follows: 'Hello, I'm Steve Dunwoody, I'm an Iraq War veteran, and I'm on staff for Senator Barack Obama,' in that order. And then you will shake their hands. You will be shaking hands with people who have never touched a Black person before. The reason you're going to the cop shop is because otherwise when you knock on doors, they're gonna call the cops, and you're gonna meet them for the first time in the middle of the street."

Steve Dunwoody had the Blackest face of anybody I'd ever met. He was the first one in Cedar County—there weren't any Clinton people at that point. And I said, "This place will be swarming before the caucus with young white people, and your face will stand out. They'll remember you—it's gonna be an advantage—just hang in there."

**Steve Dunwoody:** I didn't take that the wrong way. It felt more like the way a mother would advise her child on being careful. In fact, I came to call Clara my "surrogate mom" in Cedar County. To me, Clara was Cedar County, in the sense that she was my first contact. There were very few people there who were openly for President Obama at that time. And she prepared me for what would come later on.

The most difficult time I had there was when I would canvass in these communities and get stopped by the police. I was always used to being looked at extra hard at parades. Like, "What's this Black kid doing here?" I ignored that. But being stopped by the police was probably the toughest experience in Iowa.

Later, when I started having coffee in the local community with my blazer and jeans on, I got asked by several women if *I* was Barack Obama. I had to disappoint them and tell them that I wasn't. There just was not a lot of exposure to Black people there. I took Clara's advice. In subsequent meetings, I said, "I'm Steve Dunwoody, and I'm a veteran."

\*      \*      \*

*Despite huge turnout at Obama's first rallies, early interest had failed to translate into momentum in the polls—he ran second nationally and third in Iowa, behind Senator Clinton and Senator Edwards. Reports of Obama's performance in front of Iowa crowds throughout the early spring had left his staff seriously concerned.*

**Emily Parcell, Iowa Political Director:** Obama's first Iowa event was the most boring event I've ever been to in politics. It was successful because we had twenty-two hundred people. But it was so boring. It was like, "I thought this guy was supposed to set rooms on fire. What is going on?" He didn't have his campaign legs under him at all. It was like being in one of the world's most boring college lectures.

**David Plouffe, Campaign Manager:** Our first trips to Iowa during our announcement tour were great successes. And some of our initial forays after that had big crowds, core people signing up. But it's Iowa—people need to be convinced to support you. So then we went into a period of drudgery. Crowds got smaller. There were fewer people signing up, since they were all getting courted by different candidates.

**Emily Parcell:** When we started, we did have giant crowds from day one, but we didn't start with *support*.

**Alyssa Mastromonaco, Director of Scheduling and Advance:** The crowds were never about support. They were about curiosity. Part of why people were so hot to come out and see Obama was because they were like, "Who is this guy?" Curiosity really drove the first couple of months.

**Dan Pfeiffer, Deputy Communications Director:** By the early part of the summer of 2007, we had come down to earth pretty quickly. Because what happened was we got through that first excitement—all of this campaigning, a bunch of early endorsements, we outraised the Clintons in the first fundraising quarter—and then we hit a wall.

The first debate didn't go great; the second debate went worse. In the world of political prognosticators, they started arguing that maybe this Obama thing wasn't all it was cracked up to be, that maybe Hillary really was unbeatable—she had a huge lead in the national polls.

Then-Senator Obama was struggling a little bit with the rigors of campaigning. Doing the same event four, five times a day wasn't interesting for him, and that became palpable.

**David Axelrod, Chief Strategist:** He didn't get a chance to work in semiobscurity to refine his material and get used to the pace of a presidential race. We opened on Broadway, and the critics were right in the front row. That put a lot on the organization and on him in particular. And he wasn't flawless to begin with.

There was a health care debate in Nevada early, and he just disappointed. He hadn't done the intellectual work on health care yet. The briefings were inadequate. And this was something that Senator Clinton knew cold, having worked on the issue for so long. Senator Edwards had been a candidate longer and had been a candidate in 2004, so he was prepared, and the basic story out of Vegas was, "Obama's not ready."

The same was true of his first debate in South Carolina. He just wasn't very sharp. And he was very honest about it. He did say, "I'm not a good candidate now, but I will be. Give me the time to learn how to be a good candidate and I will become a good candidate."

**Alyssa Mastromonaco:** I don't think anyone looked at Senator Obama and thought, "He's having the time of his life." One of the things that people love about him is his authenticity. Running for president you had to do a bunch of events that were like a goat and pony show. And I think part of him was like, "Is this really what it's about? I really just want to be talking to people." The reality of how this was really going to be was kind of setting in.

**David Plouffe:** After the initiation of getting in, Barack Obama experienced what most people experience, which is, "This is really hard—I'm basically asking people for money, and when I'm not doing that, I'm asking people in states like Iowa and New Hampshire to support me. And no one is saying yes because they want to wait and see."

**Paul Tewes:** The problem he always had was that the first impression people ever got from him was the convention speech in 2004. So the second impression was never gonna be as good as that. Especially when it's on TV and he's this "mythical figure" and all that. They see him up close, and maybe he's a little tired or something. You just can't measure up to that constantly. So by the nature of that, people would walk away and think, "Man, he wasn't as good as he was at the convention."

**Tommy Vietor:** Campaigning is like anything you do—you get better with reps, and he needed a lot of reps.

**Marygrace Galston:** At one point, we were going through the schedule with him so he could see what the next couple of days looked like in Iowa. He said, "Wow. We're running a schedule like it's October or November, and it's only June."

I remember thinking, "He has no idea what's ahead. This is going to get much busier." I'm not the first person to say this, but he did not get it at the beginning. Iowans could tell that he didn't understand why he was having to call a central committee member of the Iowa Democratic Party, "Joe Blow" in Cedar Falls, as opposed to a state senator or regional union leader. That that person is going to talk to all the candidates, spend time with all of them, and not make a decision until a month before the caucus.

So in the spring, Tewes told Plouffe we might as well not have him meet with Iowans until he got better. It was doing more harm than good.

**David Plouffe:** He wasn't performing as well as he knew he could. It took a while to find his footing, and I think he struggled with the pace of the campaign, bouncing between Iowa and New Hampshire, Washington, and Chicago. The early part of the Iowa campaign is talking to a lot of people, and none of them sign up for you because it's "too early." That can be dispiriting, so I think Paul's message was, "If we're not going to make the kind of progress we need to make, and you're not performing as well as you can, time's valuable. Spend it with your family. Go to New Hampshire. Work on your speeches. You've got to get better."

The conversations I would have with Barack Obama in the beginning were largely centered around, "At some point you have to own this." Like, "Iowa can't be something you're scheduled to do. You're the one who has to say, 'Why aren't we going back in two days?' and, 'Hey, we haven't been to Sioux City in a while. Why aren't we going there?' You need to really recognize everybody when you go there. Know their names. Ask them how it's going. You've got to become essentially the CEO of this." Own it. Live it. Breathe it. And he didn't do that for a long time.

**Barack Obama:** Whenever you start a campaign and you haven't been campaigning for a while, it takes a while for you to get back into game shape. It feels like a grind. You're away from home; you're waking up early; you're going to bed late; your meals are irregular; you're traveling—at that time—in vans and in cars and making phone calls in between, trying to raise money. You're making mistakes and, generally speaking, you're frustrated that you're not sharper.

**David Plouffe:** In a caucus state like Iowa, it's about the candidate building relationships with people at the grassroots level. As we got into the summer, it clicked. He just got comfortable in Iowa. He started to know what he wanted to say with a little bit more clarity and confidence, and the organizer in him kicked in. It became something he enjoyed because it was so familiar to him.

**Barack Obama:** The experience of talking to people directly—that was always fun. The town hall meetings themselves were always encouraging. And probably the thing that really kicked us into gear was just seeing this incredible young staff that slowly developed.

I've always said that it was really the team on the ground—and I would include the volunteers with that—those staff and volunteers that carried us in those early months at a time when we were still honing our message and I was still finding my way as a candidate.

**Bess Evans, Spencer, IA, Field Organizer:** I was in the middle of nowhere with one other staffer. We were really alone out there. The people in Des Moines—it felt like they were in a different world.

Spencer is a town of about ten thousand. It has a main drag of Grand Avenue—that was a really big deal, to have our campaign office in Spencer on Grand Avenue. We opened it at the end of June. They did all of these events in Spencer hosted by the Spencer Chamber of Commerce. All the stores on Grand Avenue would give out hot dogs. It was called Thanks with Franks. We participated, and the local radio station said we had the best hot dogs, because we had Chicago-style hot dogs to honor our candidate. I remember scouring every shelf in Hy-Vee looking for the kind of relish I wanted and the kind of peppers I needed to make a real Chicago-style hot dog. It felt very important.

**Carrianna Suiter:** You really turn to the community. You know so much about these people's lives. You become a part of it. They become your family. Your volunteers really are the ones that get you through all of it.

You weren't just having one conversation and trying to persuade these people. I had a lease. I lived there for eight, nine months. You knew their grandkids. You saw them at the grocery store. I joined a knitting circle.

Mitch Stewart wanted us to get more involved in our communities, to get out of the offices more. He wanted us to connect with people on a personal level and not just on a political level. There was a yarn store across the street from my office, and there were these wonderful ladies who taught me to knit. You didn't talk about politics when you were doing those things. We had no free time, so having permission to do something and have two hours every week to just be part of something was awesome. I entered a bag into a competition. Ultimately one of the women from that knitting circle became a precinct captain.

**Thomas Zimmerman, Sioux City, IA, Field Organizer:** Early on in the caucus, you had all of these twentysomething politicos dumped into town, so we all kind of hung out together. We would have the Edwards folks and the Clinton folks and the Dodd folks and the Richardson folks, and we'd go out drinking.

For some reason, the Edwards folks were really into flip cup. That was their thing to burn off stress. They set it up so that the flip cup would be "tier one" candidates versus "tier two" candidates. At one point the Clinton people demanded the Edwards people move to the tier two side of the table for balance. That didn't go over well.

**Yohannes Abraham:** I talked to my buddies who were in more rural parts of the state, where it was very clear there was one Obama, one Clinton, and one Edwards organizer. They woke up every morning and knew who their competition was.

**Tyler Lechtenberg, Marshalltown, IA, Field Organizer:** I would leave the office at night and drive by the other offices, like the Edwards office and the Clinton office and the Richardson office, just to make sure that all their lights were off by the time I left.

You run into these other organizers at events. I realized that these people were essentially like me, people who cared about making the country better and had a passion for politics and wanted to make a difference. But I also had this clear competition with them. Under any other circumstances, we might have been friends. But I just couldn't stand them.

**Joe Cupka, Story County, IA, Field Organizer:** When the Hillary people were still leading us in the polls, I remember they wanted to be friends with everybody. As far as I was concerned, they were trying to stop me from doing my part to change the world. I didn't have time for that.

**Bess Evans:** The Clinton campaign had an office in Spencer. It was right off Grand Avenue, just around the corner from us. We could see their office from our office. At one point I actually went on a few dates with one of their organizers from another town. He told me several of their campaign targets. He was fired not long after.

*There is a stereotype that all Iowans are deeply engaged in the caucus process, but in reality it's a very small subset of the population. The 2004 election had set turnout records when less than 5 percent of the state (124,000 people) showed up, so the only way to identify 100,000 Obama supporters would be reaching Iowans who were less politically engaged, partly through hours of cold-calling and canvassing every day.*

**Yohannes Abraham:** It was very common to be sitting in the campaign office during call time and have to explain who Barack Obama was. If you were calling a hundred people and you connected with twenty of them, you were going to have a few of them asking, "Who is Barack Obama?"

**Greg Degen, Johnson County, IA, Field Organizer:** You would explain to them, "Well, he's the candidate from Illinois—he's a senator, and he was a state senator before that." You would say, "You may have seen that he had this very prominent speech at the Democratic National Convention in 2004. He's the candidate that was against the Iraq War from the start." But then you would basically have to tell people, "Yes, he's the Black candidate running for president."

After that, people generally knew who he was.

**Lauren Kidwell, Regional Field Director:** The universe of caucus goers was so small relative to the number of staff we had, so we were organizing at such a direct level. Each field organizer could name the people on their persuasion list. They knew them because they called them so many times.

**Bess Evans:** The hard part about working for any candidate that you care about is when people don't match your passion with their passion. I remember making my first phone calls and thinking, "Have I made a terrible mistake?" People would hang up on you. I took everything very personally, because it felt personal to me.

**Shannon Valley, Decorah, IA, Intern:** A struggle for me was trying to build relationships with a lot of people very quickly. It was an experience that I would not trade for anything. I made some amazing friendships within the community, some that are still ongoing. Anybody who's doing political work should go through the field. But I'm an introvert at heart. Dealing with a mass of people as often as I had to on a day-to-day basis was so exhausting.

**Annick Febrey, Floyd County, IA, Field Organizer:** I had in my head that this campaign experience was going to be me and a whole bunch of other folks my age doing politics, working really hard, but also having this sort of shared experience together.

I went to Charles City, which was this small town of eight thousand people up north in a very rural area, and it was all cornfields for hours. It was this really sleepy little town that was about two blocks long. I rented an apartment that was in the low-income housing section, because most people lived on farms.

I vividly remember doing anything to entertain myself for four hours of call time. One of them was focusing on the stranger-sounding names. That was actually why I called Carl Vogelhuber. He preferred to talk in person, so he came by the office a couple of times to chat. And then he started coming in every day, and he'd volunteer all morning. There was one restaurant in town, so we'd walk there and get lunch, and then I'd walk him home because he lived a block from there.

He essentially became my best friend. He was eighty-four at the time, a retired rocket scientist. I had no friends in the area. I was living by myself in this really sad apartment. Carl came in every morning, and he knew so much about the town and knew so much about who the influential people were outside of the elected officials.

He made a ton of phone calls. He did weekly letters to the editor. He and his wife had a number of house parties. And he was an elder in one of the local churches, which I think had nine members. They ran an interfaith group on Saturday mornings that I started going to. I found that once I gave up being sad and lonely and really became a part of the town, it got a lot easier. It took a little while for me to let go of what I thought it was going to be versus what it actually was.

**Ally Coll:** At one point, I got a school board member to agree to go canvassing with me. I remember being so struck by the effectiveness of that. The difference that it made to the people in her neighborhood to see her. It changed the way people responded to me at the door and their receptiveness to the message that I was trying to share.

The job pushed me completely out of my comfort zone and forced me to become comfortable talking not only to strangers but to strangers whose background I had very little in common with and whom I immediately was asking to do things for me. That was so unfamiliar, but I was really struck by—sounds like a cliché—the friendliness of the people who I met. The way that they welcomed me into their communities was very tangible and very immediate. I didn't have teams of volunteers all meeting up together, but I had individuals who accompanied me on most canvassing shifts one-on-one.

More than 10,000 Obama Supporters Take Part in More Than 1,000 "Walk for Change" Events Across the Country
—Targeted News Service, June 9, 2007

Obama Apologizes for "Hillary Clinton (D-Punjab)" Memo
—New York Times, June 19, 2007

"Cheap" Jab Blurs Obama's Clean Run
—Des Moines Register, June 19, 2007

Obama Tops His Rivals, Raising $32.5 Million in Quarter
—New York Times, July 1, 2007

Obama's Camp Cultivates Crop in Small Donors
—New York Times, July 17, 2007

Obama Gives Tough Talk on Pakistan, Terrorists; He Says He'd Reserve the Right to Invade and End Aid if the U.S. Ally Didn't Fight Terror. His Liberal Base May Take Issue
—Los Angeles Times, August 2, 2007

Obama's Foreign Vision Is Exciting—and Also Naive
—Roll Call, August 2, 2007

Clinton Demurs on Obama's Nuclear Stance; She Says It Is Unwise to Rule Out Using the Arms Against Terrorists
—Washington Post, August 3, 2007

# 4

# ONE HUNDRED THOUSAND 1S AND 2S

*July–August 2007*

### August 13, 2007

*Iowa Polling Average:* Clinton 26, Obama 24, Edwards 20
*National Polling Average:* Clinton 42, Obama 21, Edwards 12

*O*ne of my first community events as an organizer was Iowa City's
Friday Night Concert Series, a weekly summer gathering on the
town Pedestrian Mall, around the corner from our office. Thousands of
locals gathered there every Friday, setting out lawn chairs and listening to
cover bands. My colleagues and I set up a face-painting table on the perimeter staffed with high school volunteers—one of us would paint kids'
faces while the other pitched their parents on Obama. Skeptical adults
would ask, "How much does this cost?"

"Nothing," I'd reply. "Have you heard about Senator Obama?"

Responses included the following:

"Yes, I've been following him."

"No, who is that?"

"9/11 was an inside job. Have you seen the documentary Loose
Change?"

No matter the response, I would try to draw them out on something,
anything, in those two minutes and bring it back to Barack (I always
called him Barack).

Upset about the war? "That's why I'm supporting Barack, the only serious candidate who had the courage and judgment to oppose the Iraq War before it began."

Fed up with Washington? "That's why I'm so excited Barack is the only candidate not accepting money from federal lobbyists and political action committees."

Want weed legalized? "Have you read Dreams from My Father? What's your email?"

Most of all, I would listen, collect their contact information, and send an earnest follow-up note. To my amazement and endless frustration, people often remained undecided or, worse, unengaged. One Friday I showed up and found the Clinton campaign already spread out in the spot I used each week. Their setup included a man handing out American flags and making balloon animals with a helium machine. I unfolded my table next to them and tried to act like this was no big deal. That night I stayed in the office until 11:00 p.m. composing a nine-hundred-word email decrying the move as a "perfect metaphor" for Clinton's campaign and comparing Obama to Abraham Lincoln. I'd been on staff for six weeks.

In talking about Obama with voters, I would often be asked about the difference between him and other candidates. Partly because it was so early, and partly because negativity would backfire, I rarely talked about Edwards or Clinton directly while pointing out Obama had been the only major candidate to oppose the war in Iraq before it began. There were very few substantive policy differences, so the conversation was more about Obama's approach to governing. I'd highlight his work in the Illinois State Senate to pass bipartisan legislation that advanced progressive goals like expanding health care or reforming the criminal justice system while stressing what I thought made his approach to campaigning unique—a commitment to grassroots organizing and refusal of PAC and federal lobbyist money.

By the end of July, one of the first tangible policy differences did emerge, when Obama said during a debate that, as president, he would meet with hostile foreign leaders without preconditions. "I thought that was very irresponsible and frankly naive to say you would commit to meeting with Chavez and Castro or others within the first year," Senator Clinton said.

"If there is anything irresponsible and naive, it was to authorize George Bush to send 160,000 young American men and women into Iraq apparently without knowing how they were going to get out," Obama replied later.

Shortly after, Obama gave a major foreign policy speech, one designed to reassure voters that a senator with barely two years of experience could handle being commander in chief. There were two major pledges in the speech: (1) As president, if there was "actionable intelligence" Osama bin Laden was in Pakistan and the Pakistani military wouldn't take action, he would send American troops over the border to do so. (2) If elected, he would deploy an additional "two brigades" (six thousand troops) to the Afghanistan theater.

Other candidates attacked him over the Pakistan pledge. "You shouldn't always say everything you think if you're running for president, because it has consequences around the world," Senator Clinton said in a debate.

Senator Biden said he stood by his statement that Obama "can be ready to be president, but right now, I don't believe he is. The presidency is not something that lends itself to on-the-job training."

This was a pattern both in Iowa and nationally. Despite the criticism, Obama stuck by these pledges, arguing they reinforced what "change" meant as a new way to approach America's role in the world. Nearly every Democratic voter I spoke with agreed that invading Iraq had been a mistake, but some were also concerned about the possibility that an "anti-war" nominee might prove unelectable.

All these interactions with Iowans—on the Pedestrian Mall, at an Obama rally, over the phone, at someone's door—were logged in the Voter Activation Network ("the VAN"), a database containing the name, address, and vote history of all registered voters. Each contact was assigned a ranking from 1 to 5 indicating their level of support for Obama and likelihood of showing up at the caucus. Like all organizers, my last nightly task was to submit my numbers to my regional field director, totaling that day's conversations. These reports would flow from the nine regional field directors up to Mitch Stewart and Anne Filipic in Des Moines. Each day, Mitch and Anne reviewed the results and assessed our progress to one hundred thousand "1s" and "2s"—those most likely to caucus for us. As we rolled into August, careful attention was paid to the caucus history of every new supporter.

**Anne Filipic, Iowa Field Director:** August was a really dark month for us. A few things happened. First, the polling wasn't great. And there had been a series of debates that just didn't go great for Barack Obama early on. But the biggest thing was our field program.

**Marygrace Galston, Iowa Deputy State Director:** Field is a numbers game. You have to figure out, "What's your winning number of supporters, what's your deficit, and how are you going to get to the winning number?"

**Anne Filipic:** The field strategy for past successful caucus campaigns was that you would go to people who had previously caucused and convince them to go caucus for your candidate. So we felt like it was a smart investment of our time and our staff's time to really focus on those former caucus goers that August. We set a program for the field organizers where they would go to a former caucus goer's house and actually have a long conversation with them. It was a real quality-over-quantity approach.

And when we did that, we got destroyed.

**Mitch Stewart, Iowa Caucus Director:** It was the worst month of the campaign. People were demoralized; our volunteers were demoralized.

**Anne Filipic:** Every night after the field staff went out and did their work, they would enter the data from their conversations. It was really striking. The number of "4s" that were coming back versus "1s" and "2s." Fundamentally the number of supporters for other candidates— and not for Barack Obama—was so strikingly lopsided that it was really hard to see a path to victory.

It didn't take much convincing the field staff that the August program didn't work. They hated it. We were looking at the numbers. But they were living it every single day.

**Yohannes Abraham, Des Moines, IA, Field Organizer:** August was terrible. First of all, I can't overemphasize the extent to which there's a physical element to the job of being a field organizer. When it's really hot, you're really hot, because not only were you knocking on doors somewhere between eight and twelve hours every weekend, but also you were basically living in your car.

At that point most folks on the campaign had been there for months, so we were really feeling it mentally and emotionally.

**Lauren Kidwell, Regional Field Director:** The fact that we were working end-of-campaign pace from July onward was really stressful.

Summers are so hard on campaigns because voters are tuned out and volunteers are busy with other things. You don't have the same support, and we were never up in the polls that summer, so we were fighting just to be considered a legitimate candidate.

**Simeon Talley, Iowa City, IA, Field Organizer:** It's a grind, man. As magical or inspiring as attending an event with the candidate is, there comes a point where you start to settle in. The monotony and the smallness of what you're doing can be challenging. It's not glorious work.

**Lauren Kidwell:** You're tired. You're barely halfway through the caucus. You're beating your head against the wall to break through to people and get the volunteer recruitment numbers up.

**Yohannes Abraham:** You had access to the internet, and we were getting pummeled in the national press for the fact that we were not only not gaining ground on Senator Clinton but losing ground nationally. That was when questions would creep in.

**Anne Filipic:** Our field staff probably knew even before we did that this was not the path to victory. So people were eager to try something new. Ultimately, we realized we didn't have a chance if the only people who caucused for us were people who had previously caucused.

It made us really take a step back and leave behind what had worked for other campaigns and say, "This is a different candidate, and we have to approach this differently." We needed to expand the electorate and get people that had never previously caucused to go caucus for Barack Obama.

**Mitch Stewart:** That was the big shift we had in late summer. That was our only path to victory, because Edwards and Clinton had the previous caucus goers wrapped up. It was liberating and terrifying at the same time.

We came up with this program called Caucus Education. The idea was that we would have either the precinct captain or this fresh wave of field organizers sit down with these folks who hadn't caucused before, or who weren't registered to vote, or who were independents, and demystify the caucus process. Then we started tracking that as a metric.

*The Caucus Education program required an infusion of new staff. Dozens of Camp Obama attendees, many of whom had spent the summer as unpaid interns, were brought on the payroll and told to report to their regional director. C'Reda Weedon was one of the new hires. A recent law school graduate from University of California–Berkeley, she started driving west from Chicago, unsure of her destination, when she heard from Chris Lewis, her new boss.*

**C'Reda Weedon, Fort Dodge, IA, Field Organizer:** In the Chicago office, everybody who came in was a supporter. It was not hard. You just had to walk outside, and you could find a bunch of people. Everybody loved him.

I'm Black in America, and he's Black in America, so it occurred to me that somebody wouldn't like him, but we happened to be around all these people who just loved him. So I was like, "This will be so great."

As I was driving on I-80, on the way from Chicago to Iowa, they told me I was going to Fort Dodge and gave me some lady's address. I found out, once I got there, one of the reasons they sent me to Fort Dodge was because . . .

**Chris Lewis, North Central Iowa Regional Field Director:** Fort Dodge is one of the few places where you have a significant African American population.

**C'Reda Weedon:** It's not a big percentage, less than 10 percent, but they were concentrated in a couple of precincts. A really interesting part of history: through the Great Migration, there was a company that went down to Mississippi and recruited a ton of Black people. Almost whole towns left Mississippi and went to Fort Dodge, which was great because they had a community to themselves, but then once it closed, all these people had basically uprooted their families and had been there for at least one generation.

**Chris Lewis:** The tradition for whatever reason in the African American community in Fort Dodge had always been strong absentee voter drive for the general election, but very, very, very low—almost nonexistent—Black turnout at caucuses.

**C'Reda Weedon:** I was told part of my job was to get folks who hadn't really been involved in the caucus. If we could rock out on these two or three districts, we could really change the game.

To start doing that, I was told I had to talk to Charles Clayton. Everybody was like, "You gotta know him. He knows everybody."

**Chris Lewis:** The Clayton family is huge in Fort Dodge.

**Charles Clayton, Fort Dodge, IA, Volunteer:** I'd never been to a caucus before 2008. I was someone that always voted, not really a party-line voter, but I've got three sons, and I want to instill civic duty in my sons and the youth that we work with. That was about the length of what I did: making sure that I voted but not going to any Democratic rallies or meetings or caucuses.

I didn't know Iowa was the first state to vote. Not at all. I didn't plan on doing any caucusing. I thought he had a shot, but did I 100 percent believe he would win? No. Not that he wasn't qualified, but this was an African American trying to win president of the United States of America.

**Chris Lewis:** Charles was probably, what, around forty at the time? I don't know how old he was, but he was young in a town where industry had left, and with it the jobs, and with the jobs the young people.

Charles was African American, worked with young people, mentored them. So Charles said, "Well, I'm hosting a get-together for Obama supporters."

**Charles Clayton:** We started doing political awareness meetings. We started very small by holding pizza parties and explaining to people why it was important to vote.

After we did that, we started doing voter registration events, going to African American churches and getting people organized in the African American community. The people we were drawing were minorities—low-income first-time voters who had never been involved in a political campaign.

**C'Reda Weedon:** So I met Charles, then I met another volunteer, and she told me everybody I needed to know.

You'd go to a lot of church meetings. It was great once I figured out the system—there were maybe six or seven big families, and everybody was in one of these families or affiliated somehow. So what I had to do was figure out who the grandmas were in those families, and once I did, it was like the keys to the kingdom.

*Under the umbrella of the political department, all of these constituency organizing groups were created to offer new caucus goers entry points to the campaign. "African Americans for Obama," "Women for Obama," "Latinos for Obama," "Republicans for Obama," "Veterans for Obama." These did not exist in every county—your focus depended on the demographics of your turf (it made little sense to prioritize "Republicans for Obama" in a small liberal college town or "Latinos for Obama" in a 99 percent white county).*

*What was universal for every organizer was a program called Barack Stars, targeted at high school students. Obama had a unique connection with high schoolers. He was the youngest candidate running, he had opposed the war, and for a politician, he was, well, cool. And because the rules of the caucus allowed anyone who would be eighteen by Election Day in November 2008 to participate, every high school senior in the state became a target.*

**Rachel Haltom-Irwin, Iowa Youth Vote Director:** Every high school senior can caucus because they're going to be eighteen by the general election. Every high school senior in Iowa has to take US history. So there were all these history teachers who were thrilled it was Iowa caucus season and they had this great teaching tool. Paul Tewes mandated that every organizer give a talk at local US history classes.

**Bess Evans, Spencer, IA, Field Organizer:** We knew if we could convince these kids to show up at the caucuses, then they would overwhelmingly support Barack Obama. Justin McCormick was my favorite. He was fifteen years old, and I saw him every day.

**Justin McCormick, Spencer, IA, High School Student:** Walking into the office and meeting Bess for the first time, I had no clue what I would be doing or what volunteering would entail. I had no idea what the caucus was. I had no idea that it was the first in the nation and the significance that we'd play in the political process.

I was very opposed to the Iraq War. I think most people of my generation were. After researching the other candidates, I became an Obama supporter. When I first got involved, it was summer. I would come in for eight-, ten-, twelve-hour days, doing what the staff would do: knocking on doors, phone banking, helping making signs, everything. Later, when school started, other students would ask me, "Who's this guy Barack Obama?" Even teachers would ask me. It was new to me, having a teacher ask my opinion and actually engage on issues. Being fifteen, I still didn't have a car, so late nights after dark, Bess would give me rides home; she'd pick me up from school to go canvassing in other towns.

**Bess Evans:** Justin was really our entryway into the high school. He would take stacks of lit to pass out at lunch and convince other students to come to our office, despite the fact that he wasn't even old enough to caucus. I think it was the first time Justin had been so passionate about something.

**Megan Simpson, Dubuque, IA, Field Organizer:** I spent a day at each high school registering students to vote, giving them all my contact information, doing mock caucuses with cookies showing them how to caucus and making them give speeches on why their cookie was the best cookie. I did trainings on how to be a volunteer leader and got them involved in a way I never was when I was a high school student.

**Rachel Haltom-Irwin:** I would phone bank all the high schools' US history teachers and say, "We're inviting you to this event, and you can bring all your seniors. If you bring your seniors, we'll make sure that they meet Senator Obama after."

So after every event, the senator would take a few questions from them, and it wasn't in a larger crowd where they'd feel intimidated by all the people who had been part of the caucus many times before. It was just with him.

*The list of new supporters slowly continued to grow. Even so, we never stopped trying to persuade longtime caucus goers that other campaigns were also targeting. Because the number of people that attended each precinct caucus was so low, every Iowan was worth an inordinate amount of attention. As an Iowan who had caucused in 2004, I would*

*get calls from Dodd, Edwards, and Clinton organizers asking if I knew
who I was supporting in 2008. I would always claim to be undecided and
keep them on the phone as long as possible, trying to decode their talking
points.*

*The caucus process provides a level of access to candidates where no
matter what station you occupy, you can afford to deliberate before making a choice. Each day I would call or visit undecided voters in my turf,
cycling back through my list every few weeks in hopes of bringing them to
our side. Afterward, I sent personal letters with enclosed issue fact sheets,
making clear I'd like to continue talking. During these conversations, I'd
be asked about Obama's experience: "Do you really think he's experienced enough to be president?" But just as often I would be asked about
"electability": "Do you really think he can win?"*

**Josh Earnest, Iowa Communications Director:** Most of the reporters
who were covering us had covered the Howard Dean campaign four
years earlier. And the story of the Dean campaign was a similar trajectory to the early days of the Obama campaign, which is that there was
obvious energy—Governor Dean was drawing much larger crowds
than the other candidates, and he had this message that resonated not
just with Democrats in Iowa but with Democrats across the country.
He was somebody who didn't have a long track record in Washington.
People didn't know a whole lot about him, but he was saying some
really interesting things that were energizing people.

But of course he was not able to successfully translate that into a
winning political organization in Iowa. And so there was a lot of well-
placed skepticism among both Iowa reporters and national reporters
covering our Iowa race about whether or not Barack Obama would be
able to successfully translate the energy in the field, his own charisma
and message, into a well-organized, coherent political organization
that could turn out people on caucus night. My sense was that was the
fundamental question of the entire race.

**Dan Pfeiffer, Deputy Communications Director:** There were two
things we were dealing with. One was, are we just gonna flame out
like other "grassroots wonders," like Howard Dean? There was also this
question surrounding the whole thing, which was, will white people
vote for a Black presidential candidate? And Iowa was obviously the
ultimate test of this.

Race was a huge part of the first year. Endless stories were written about the Bradley effect, the idea that white people say they're "for" a Black candidate but don't actually vote for him. I mean this is an *insane* thing to think about now—but there were also questions about whether Barack Obama was "Black enough" for African Americans to support him, because he didn't come out of the civil rights movement.

Up until the Iowa caucuses, this was all theoretical. We knew we had a great operation in Iowa. We knew we had supporters, and we felt good about that, but you just didn't know—this was an untested proposition.

**Michael Blake, Iowa Deputy Political Director:** People would say, "This country is not going to elect someone named Barack Obama; it's not going to happen. *They* won't let that happen." You had people who were watching national polls the entire time, which are not a reflection of what's going on locally.

*The population in Iowa was 94 percent white—despite pockets of heavily African American neighborhoods in some cities (Des Moines, Davenport, Waterloo), many small Iowa towns have no more than one or two Black residents, if any. Rather than white voters bringing up race directly to me, it would often come up in the context of questions about the candidate's background. Chain emails circulated false rumors that Obama had been schooled in an Indonesian madrassa or that he was born in Kenya and sworn into the Senate on a Quran.*

**Carrianna Suiter, Muscatine, IA, Field Organizer:** In some of the more rural areas that I covered when I first got there, there was pretty blatant hostility. There was a house I drove by every time I went to Henry County that had a "Barack is the Antichrist" sign outside of it.

What made me really sad was we'd be making calls and hear, "Barack Obama went to a madrassa. I hear he's a Muslim." We were telling them the correct information, that he was a member of a Christian church, but it deeply saddened me. That the idea that "he followed Islam" was a reason that people just crossed him off their list. When we would hear people say that, we would correct the record, but I struggled with that. I sometimes felt that by correcting the record, it was in some way validating that it was justified to use religion to disqualify a candidate.

**Graham Wilson, Jefferson County, IA, Field Organizer:** In my first conversation with a former county party chair, he said Barack Obama was not electable because he was "a Muslim." This wasn't some random person on the street. This was the head of the Democratic Party organization for this part of the state.

**Grant Lahmann, Tama County, IA, Field Organizer:** When I came on, one of my first conversations was with a city councilman. He said, "I'm all for Obama, but the guys at my plant—they still use the N-word." He wanted to make sure I understood this was going to be a tough sell in the community.

**Dennis Stewart, Marshalltown, IA, Obama Supporter:** We discussed it matter-of-factly, not as a negative but as choosing a candidate that was electable. We had already decided to support him, so it wasn't racially motivated, but our concern was whether the rest of the country would feel like we did.

**C'Reda Weedon:** I didn't know if race was going to be an issue or not. Sometimes when I would do call time in Iowa, I would say I was Miss Weedon. People think I'm white on the phone if they don't know my name.

People would say, "You know, because those Blacks . . ." Shocking. So strong, but not necessarily vehement. Just matter-of-fact.

My very first door, it was this elderly white guy. It didn't seem like he was able to get out a lot. He invited me in, we were talking, and I was asking what he thought. He was like, "Oh, I haven't made up my mind, but maybe I would vote for him, because it would be good for the colored people to have something for once."

He said those words. I was like, "The *what? What?*" But then . . . he was leaning Obama, so I marked that down. I got back to the office. "Am I on *Punk'd*? For real? That's the very first thing that happens to me in Iowa?"

**Josh Earnest:** We were cognizant that there was some built-in resistance because of the senator's race. I don't think there was ever any reluctance to discuss it. And I think it would have been foolish to try to deny it in some way.

One of the things that we went to great lengths to do is to tell the then-senator's story in a way that helped people understand how generally consistent his story is with the story of so many other Americans. There are some things that, on the surface, are not the same: I don't think there are that many Iowans who spent part of their childhood in Indonesia, for example. Not too many Iowans named Barack Obama. But there are other elements of this story: raised by a single mother who worked really hard to make sure that he got every opportunity that she could provide for him, raised by grandparents who loved him. He worked hard to put himself through college and, with the support of his family, was able to do that. To go and start a career as a community organizer because he's really invested in the community.

So many of the things about his background and what animated him were things that voters could relate to. And so we did go to great lengths to make sure that people could understand that that was the case. Even if his race and his name might be different than yours, the story of his life and the values that drive him are entirely consistent with the kinds of values that you, as a progressive Democrat, share.

**David Axelrod, Chief Strategist:** We never ran on the idea that this was a historic candidacy. As Obama used to say, "I am proudly of the Black community, but I'm not limited to it, and I'm not running to be the first Black president—I'm running to be president, and I happen to be Black." We were all aware of what that would mean.

In one of the early meetings where we were discussing the campaign, Michelle was a skeptic at first, and she said to Barack, "What do you think you can contribute that no one else can contribute?"

And he said, "What I know for sure is that the day I lift my hand and take that oath of office, the world will look at us differently. And there are millions of kids across this country that will look at themselves differently, and their prospects differently, and their potential differently."

So we were all aware, but we made a very conscious effort not to make that a centerpiece of the campaign because we didn't want to get pigeonholed in that way.

**Simeon Talley:** This was my pitch to a lot of people: "Imagine your son seeing Barack Obama as president, seeing someone who looks like him, and what that would mean for what he thinks his life can be."

**Yohannes Abraham:** I was asked when I was a kid what I wanted to be when I grew up. At that particular moment I said I wanted to be a congressman, and the question back was, "Don't you want to be president?" I remember thinking, "I can't be president because I'm Black."

I didn't spend a lot of time thinking about, "Oh man, we're going to make history." I spent a lot of time thinking, "I cannot be the weak link that keeps history from happening."

There was an older African American woman who volunteered who became like an aunt or grandmother figure for a couple of us. She would regularly remind me that the fact that Obama was a relevant candidate was inconceivable to her. And there was an event in Des Moines where Senator Clinton showed up and I saw that volunteer there. At one point I turned around and saw her giving Senator Clinton this huge bear hug, and she came over to me and winked and said, "I'm still for our guy, but it's history either way, baby," and walked away.

*In courting Iowans, you were never alone. No matter if a person was a seasoned activist or a new caucus goer, if there was someone on the fence you might be able to convince to become a precinct captain, you could ask state and national leadership for a personal call or meeting.*

**Lauren Kidwell:** I remember David Plouffe doing some meetings in Marshalltown. That was the cool thing about Iowa. You had people who were senior campaign leaders going into meetings with three or four or five people, because it was worth it if you got those people to caucus, if you got them to bring two or three people with them.

**Tyler Lechtenberg, Marshalltown, IA, Field Organizer:** I took David Plouffe up to the Veterans Home in Marshalltown in my Dodge Neon. He talked to just four or five people that day.

**David Plouffe, Campaign Manager:** I was the national campaign manager for a presidential race, but that was the most important thing I could be doing at that point. I remember hitting all these counties in a two-day period, just making the case. Some of these were political leaders; others were just average caucus attenders and potential precinct captains.

Most people say, "Tell me how you're going to win, not just Iowa but the nomination and the presidency." They talked a lot about "electability." Because you have to understand, when the Iowa caucuses were over, people still lived there. You still meet people today of a certain age who refer to themselves as "Carter" people or "Kennedy" people from the 1980 caucuses. So choosing their candidate is a big step. You have to live with this decision. And going against the Clintons was not something people took lightly. Most of these conversations in the spring and summer and fall, she looked like she was going to win the presidency, certainly the nomination.

Being out in a small county and getting five people was hard, because that's not how politics works in a lot of places. But for me those were always the best moments of the campaign.

There are no home runs in this thing. It's just hard work each and every day.

Candidates Duel over Georgia's Black Votes: Democratic Frontrunners Look for Breakthrough as National Polls Show African Americans Almost Evenly Split
—Atlanta-Journal Constitution, August 5, 2007

**Obama Seeks to Make the Sale to Hispanics; Despite Ability to Draw Crowds and Donations, Senator Is Still Largely Unknown to Crucial Group**
—Wall Street Journal, August 8, 2007

Clinton firmly positioned as Democratic front-runner
—CNN, August 9, 2007

**Rep. Patrick Murphy Endorses Obama, Becoming First Congressman from State to Do So: Move Also Gives Illinois Democrat Support of Only Iraq War Veteran Serving in Congress**
—Morning Call, August 22, 2007

Barack Obama Rocks Santa Barbara
—Santa Barbara Independent, September 10, 2007

**John Edwards Throws Himself on the Mercy of Generation MySpace**
—Wired, September 27, 2007

14,000 Rally in Oakland to Hear Hillary Clinton Speak
—San Francisco Chronicle, September 30, 2007

# 5

# THE WEIGHT OF THE WORLD

*August–September 2007*

### September 23, 2007

*Iowa Polling Average:* Clinton 26, Edwards 24, Obama 21
*National Polling Average:* Clinton 42, Obama 23, Edwards 14

Given all the attention on Iowa, it was easy to forget that there was a national campaign. I knew very little about our operations outside of Iowa. My understanding of the race nationally was heavily influenced by cherry-picked poll results we promoted to our supporters and the cascade of headlines in my daily news clips. The campaign in Iowa was a cocoon, designed to isolate you from the national media narrative as much as possible. My world shrunk to my seventeen precincts, my regional director, and her bosses in Des Moines.

When I had started on staff in June, I was given a staff contact list that included four hundred people. The Iowa team only made up 25 percent of the operation. There were dozens of finance staff raising money; political, advance, operations, and communications staff in Chicago; and nearly one hundred people in other early states. My window in to everyone else's work came through the morning news clips—headlines about endorsements in New Hampshire, a new office in Nevada, an Obama event in South Carolina.

Outside the early states and Illinois, there were not enough resources to build a traditional campaign infrastructure. Supporters would find each other by starting groups on my.barackobama.com and hosting house parties, debate-watching parties, and canvasses with very little direction from headquarters. Sometimes busloads of these volunteers would *appear in early states for a weekend and canvass with us, but by and large, they existed on their own, organizing in a vacuum.*

*By late summer I began to notice headlines from what would become known as February 5 states, indicating they were becoming a priority . . . if the campaign could last that long.*

**Jon Carson, February 5 Director:** There were three other early states, which each had their own very distinct character: New Hampshire, Nevada, and South Carolina. Iowa was first and most important—and I'm sure it felt like that if you were in Iowa—but we were watching all of these states. And then, around July of 2007, I was asked to start focusing on February 5, because there were twenty-two states scheduled to vote on the same day. I was given a budget of about $2 million and a couple dozen staff and shipped them out to all these states.

At the time everyone just thought we were going to be the next Howard Dean campaign. The idea of my.barackobama.com was kind of new for a campaign. Volunteers could create any kind of group they wanted, keep themselves busy, start to get themselves organized.

We got the first taste of what that meant as we started sending staff out to February 5 states. The best example was Idaho. By the time we sent our first organizer out to Idaho, Idahoans for Obama had created this online community and had an office-opening celebration for him the day he showed up. They had already gotten themselves an office! They had gotten phone lines installed. They'd written a manual on how the Idaho caucuses worked.

By late summer, early fall of 2007, we had staff in a whole bunch of these February 5 states. But it all depended on winning Iowa first.

**Marygrace Galston, Iowa Deputy State Director:** They had New Hampshire, Nevada, South Carolina; they were fundraising and getting ready for the other states. But they knew Iowa was going to take a massive amount of money and attention to do well. So the attitude at national headquarters was "What does Iowa need?"

**Jon Favreau, Speechwriter:** By the summer and into the fall of 2007, the Chicago office was pretty down, pretty grim, because we were reading the national media coverage and the national polls, even though we shouldn't have been. And as much as Plouffe told us to resist the national media narrative, it was hard to do that. Bill Burton had the *New York Post* headline that said "Clinton Nearly Ready for Her Coronation" hanging on his wall.

**Dan Pfeiffer, Deputy Communications Director:** All the national polls had us down, and some people came to us with an idea: "Why don't you guys try to run national ads to get your national poll numbers up, which will then help with donations and show momentum?" We rejected that idea because it didn't help us win Iowa. Everything went through that filter. Iowa was the central focus.

**David Axelrod, Chief Strategist:** We weren't going anywhere unless we won Iowa. We needed to prove in Iowa that we could win in a venue where there were virtually no minority voters to open up the potential in other places. That was our strategy from the beginning. We felt that it was doable, but it was a strategy that was roundly criticized by the political establishment, who said it was crazy to invest so much time in Iowa. By the fall, we were thirty points behind nationally.

It was so bad that a group of donors gathered in Chicago to complain to Obama about David Plouffe and me in October. They thought that Obama should bring Bob Shrum in to run the campaign, because we didn't know what we were doing.

But to his credit, Obama always scrutinized us about what we were doing. He asked really good questions and expected good answers. And if he didn't get them, he would demand more work. But he forced us to justify the Iowa strategy.

**Jon Favreau:** The plan was that we would win in Iowa if we expanded the universe of people who caucused. The other campaigns and political professionals were very skeptical. People had been saying they were going to expand the universe of caucus goers for years. It never happens. The young people never show up. The people who are not strong Democrats never show up. It's not just taking a ballot and putting it in—it's taking a night and going to caucus.

But there was a confidence in the team that started with Obama, went through Plouffe, went through Paul Tewes. That we had a plan and we were going to stick to this plan. If the plan worked, then we won, and if it didn't, we didn't. But what kills us is if we start veering back and forth and losing confidence in the plan that we have. And that's a tough thing to believe during the campaign's darkest times.

**David Plouffe, Campaign Manager:** My mind-set became that we in Chicago were just there to support these kids in Iowa, not the other way around.

**Mitch Stewart, Iowa Caucus Director:** In August, Plouffe and Ax were in town for a debate, so we asked if they could come address the crew. I felt like the organizers understood that the weight of the world was on their shoulders and that what they needed was a pat on the back and a "great job."

I caught Axelrod to let him know that the staff could use some encouragement, and I tried to catch Plouffe, but I couldn't track him down in time. So Axelrod went out there, and he was perfect. He was like, "You guys are so great. I have never been more impressed. The senator is so thrilled with all that you have done. I know how tired you are, you are working so hard, and I just wanted to say thank you."

And then Plouffe got up and did his normal talk, which was, "Everybody in the world right now is looking at us, and they are looking at you. If we win Iowa, he will be the next president. If we fail here in Iowa, we will have let the world down."

As he was talking, I was looking around at the organizers. With Axelrod, their chests were puffed out. They were feeling pretty good about themselves. Then Plouffe spoke, and you could see organizers physically start to crumble as they started feeling the weight of the world on their shoulders again.

I felt like that every day. I think our organizers felt like that too. I got shingles because I was so stressed out about the campaign—I was like a sixty-year-old man when I was thirty-one.

What was unique about Iowa was from the minute you got there, it was a sprint. And ultimately, if you're doing this right, you *should* go to bed a little sick to your stomach every night. Because that's how important this is to you and how important it is to this country. So you were constantly exhausted and constantly anxious and constantly worried about letting down not only the country and these big lofty things but the people you work with.

**Dan Pfeiffer:** There was something special about what was happening there. You could feel it. It was like a different universe from the national political discussion. In those dark days, it was our beacon of hope. We still thought we could win Iowa, and if you could win Iowa, then everything was possible.

*The first time I saw the entire Iowa team in one place was at the end of August, during our staff retreat. More than a hundred of us drove to Madrid, Iowa, to spend forty-eight hours at a 4-H Camp, talking through the coming year.*

*The main topic of the weekend was demystifying the caucus process. They laid out in more detail how the Iowa caucuses work. At 7:00 p.m. on January 3, Iowans would gather in 1,781 precincts. Each precinct was assigned a certain number of delegates, which would be divided proportionately depending on how many supporters showed up in each room. The rules were complex and, despite guidance from the party, often prone to errors by the local precinct chair, who has wide-ranging authority. Each caucus would be a public event, but direct participation was limited to locally registered voters.*

*Unlike a regular election, the caucuses are not a competition for votes but for delegates. Individual votes were not counted; rather, participants divide into two rounds of "preference groups." In the Democratic precinct caucuses, candidates unable to secure 15 percent of those present in the first round must find a new candidate or combine with a rival group in the second round—a process known as "realignment"—to be eligible for delegates (the 15 percent threshold is higher in precincts with less than four delegates at stake).*

*This reality—that second-choice preference was reported as the final result—was crucial to understanding why precinct captains go to great lengths to avoid antagonizing supporters of lower-tier candidates: they hope to bring them over after realignment. Talking points, cookies, and neighborly horse trading are just a few of the tactics used to win over potential converts.*

*We talked about these rules for hours. It was crucial that everyone understand them. But perhaps the greatest benefit we got from that weekend was being in the same place as other people doing the same work.*

**Marygrace Galston:** There are multiple reasons why you do a full staff retreat, but one of the biggest is to build team morale. You get to see other people. You're sharing all your stories. You're realizing you're not alone in your misery. Everybody goes back out to their regions reenergized. You see the bigger picture again. It's no longer, "Oh my God, I'm alone in my field office and I'm losing my mind."

**Greg Degen, Johnson County, IA, Intern:** There were members of the national team who were at the retreat, including David Axelrod. He sat at a table with me and other organizers for a long conversation and was genuinely interested to hear what voters in Iowa were saying, what we were hearing on the ground.

**David Axelrod:** I remember what that weekend meant to me. We were so beaten up by the pundit class for what we were doing, and it was really a tonic to go and meet with these young organizers in Iowa who didn't give a rat's ass what *Politico* or political tip sheets were writing. They didn't read them; they didn't care. All they cared about was the people who were right in front of them.

They had come from all over to do this. Some of them were volunteers, and their level of commitment and belief was so energizing and inspiring. They were so embedded in their communities, and they were so motivated—not just by Barack Obama. It's important to note that. There was this iconography with Obama's image and all of that, but it was bigger than him. It was about wanting to change the country for the better.

**Bess Evans, Spencer, IA, Field Organizer:** When I was hired, one of the three interview questions that Mitch Stewart asked was, "Do you want to come to Iowa and help us change the world?" He didn't ask me, "Do you want to come to Iowa and help us change the world, which will happen only if Barack Obama wins these caucuses?" Sure, it was implied, and maybe it being disconnected from winning was just something I told myself to get through some of the harder moments. But it felt bigger than that and bigger than anything I had ever done before and maybe ever will.

I think part of it was the staff retreat. It was the all-staff calls that we did regularly. It was the all-staff emails that people would reply-all to when they got a precinct captain. I think I felt that way because there were other people out there working their assess off for the same exact reason that I was, which was that I believed this man could change the world. And it seemed really hokey to say, but I felt that in the fiber of my being. I felt that so deeply.

**Greg Degen:** What was important about the retreat for me was I felt this powerful sense of belonging. I had arrived in Iowa under the impression that this was going to be a summer internship. The retreat came at this time when I wasn't sure if I was going to stay in Iowa or go back to college. And that was really the first time that I felt like I belonged to anything in my life.

I was nineteen. My only other life experiences were public high school and one year of college, where I had been very uneasy in my skin—I was a closeted, scared kid who was trying to be invisible so no one would notice that I was gay. The campaign transformed the way that I saw myself and the way that I engaged with other people, because a campaign is inherently an extroverted enterprise. You *have* to make yourself vulnerable by talking to strangers and telling them your story. For me, that was a revolutionary experience, because it made me break out of my shell.

I remember a conversation with Paul Tewes at the bonfire at the retreat where he asked whether I was going to stay through the caucus or not. He offered—or threatened, depending on how you looked at it—to call my mom about me staying on the campaign.

The feeling I remember most was a sense of community that I had never had before. For the first time, I was around a lot of other young, enthusiastic people who had the same interests that I had. It was the first time I ever really felt like I belonged. It was the first time I ever felt like other people would notice if I wasn't there. And it was the first time that I felt like I really had a group of friends, to be honest.

I had really been struggling to figure out my place in the world, like so many other kids at that age. And the campaign was where I found a home. So I stayed.

**Marygrace Galston:** You've gotta be a different kind of person to want to do this. You're not going to get paid a lot. You've got to be truly passionate and excited about the person you're working for, because you're giving up a lot to do it. I missed a lot of family functions and lost a lot of friendships being on a campaign. But you gain a lot, because you're going to gain family members. You work closely with and spend anywhere from twelve to twenty hours a day with your fellow campaign workers, with your office mates. They become your confidants. They become your drinking buddies. They become your boyfriend or girlfriend or wife or husband. You're going to make all these memories.

**Emily Parcell, Iowa Political Director:** All of my best friends, to this day, are people I met on campaigns. My husband and I were canvassers together in the summer of 2001. When we got married, we had twelve people in our wedding party. Ten of them had either been on that canvass or had worked on campaigns with both of us. I always tell people it's a lifestyle; it's not a career.

*I had always been skeptical of people who worked in politics long-term. I assumed it was impossible to go from campaign to campaign and retain any idealism. But at the retreat, I saw example after example of seasoned political professionals and volunteers becoming emotional talking about this work. I came away convinced the people who ran things believed in what we were doing as passionately as the people I saw in my field office every day.*

**Paul Tewes, Iowa State Director:** There was a guy in Fort Madison. And I went down there for a day, did a bunch of meetings. I got to the office, and out in the parking lot, this old truck pulled up. It was rusty but had Obama colors painted all over it. And the guy got out, and the first thing you noticed was that he had a little wheeled thing with oxygen, and he must have been in his midthirties. That was the other thing you noticed: here was a guy on oxygen, in his midthirties, and he was driving an old truck. The organizer went, "Oh, that's our office manager, Bruce."

Bruce walked in, and I was gregarious with Bruce, thanking him for all his help. I was like, "Bruce, why are you doing this?" You could tell this guy had never been involved in politics. He was diagnosed with something—he probably had a year or two to live.

And that was what he said: "I don't have much time to live, and I have kids." Didn't have a job—and he couldn't, I suppose. And he said, "I really want to make my kids proud of me and leave my kids something better. That's why I'm doing it."

And you walked out of there going, "My God, that's powerful." And you walked out of there feeling like that was how you wanted this to feel for everybody; we had to honor these people. Not honor them by necessarily getting Obama elected but by making them feel like they were part of this. That was the key. You make someone feel like they're part of something, and they'll change the world. It wasn't just about Obama—it was about *them*. How do *they* feel about doing this? What are *they* bringing to it? That's emotional. That's spiritual, in a way. You were constantly reminded by interactions like that.

*The first real test of our organization was the Harkin Steak Fry in September 2007. Unlike my trip to the steak fry the year before, all six major candidates would be in attendance, and each was asking their supporters to appear. Since the event was nearly four months before the caucus, it attracted little national media attention but was watched closely by Iowa activists for signals about the campaigns' organizations.*

*We rented buses to drive our supporters from across the state to Indianola, where the steak fry was held in a giant balloon field. I was nervous because a* Wall Street Journal *reporter was riding along on my bus, working on a story about whether high school students were actually volunteering for us. It was a subtle sign the world outside Iowa had started to pay attention to our work.*

**Paul Tewes:** This was the first moment where all the campaigns were gonna be together on the same playing field. We wanted to prove to ourselves that we could bring a lot of people together and have them organized. And we wanted to prove to the outside world that we were a legitimate organization. Not just to the press, but to other activists who would see that and either want to be part of it or fear us.

Nobody likes to feel alone when they're doing this kind of work. It's the most dangerous, demoralizing feeling there is. That's why we built these offices everywhere. That's why we wanted senior staff to go everywhere. That's why we brought everybody in for big events. You wanted this idea that we were all in this together. And we were going to make change together.

**Bess Evans:** We brought volunteers, precinct captains, our entire staff. I had to get myself to Sioux City, the hub of our region, and then we went on school buses to Indianola.

**Leah White, Voter, Davenport, IA:** My mom and I took a school bus to the steak fry. My mom, Beth, was one of the first people in the Davenport area to walk into the local office and say, "How can I help?" I was intrigued by Obama, but I hadn't really decided yet whether to support anyone.

I think I wondered if it was too good to be true and wondered, "Does Obama have the experience?" He was a very eloquent speaker, and I liked what he had to say, but I just didn't really know how he stacked up. Joe Biden was running; Hillary Clinton was running. There were a lot of people who had pretty good experience in areas that he didn't have. So I wasn't sure.

**Peter Gage, Advance Staffer:** The steak fry is out in a big field where they fly hot-air balloons—it's a stage and a big field, no trees, and a big parking lot across the street.

We decided we could show how strong we were by doing a separate pre-rally over a hill down the road. We found this chunk of grass and farmland a third of a mile from the gates, with a great dirt road that ran right from that spot to the steak fry entrance.

**Jan Bauer, Story County, IA, Democratic Party Chair:** It was a beautiful fall day. We all went to the pre-rally, and Senator Obama was there. We had our little placards, which were just the logo in a circle. He was up on the catwalk, pacing around.

**Bonnie Adkins, Muscatine, IA, Volunteer:** That pre-rally was when Obama told the story about the woman in South Carolina who invented the "fired up, ready to go" chant.

*Obama had started ending his speeches with a story that built up to a refrain about the power of one voice. It was set during one of his first visits to South Carolina on the campaign that spring. The story began with Obama waking up and being reminded he had to make good on a promise to travel to a small town, Greenwood, if he wanted to earn the endorsement of a local state representative.*

> *BARACK OBAMA [Speech Excerpt]: I wake up and I feel terrible, and I think I am coming down with a cold. I go outside my room and get the* New York Times, *and there is a bad story about me in the* New York Times. *I go downstairs after I pack, and my umbrella blows open and I get soaked, so by the time I get in the car I am mad, I am wet, and I am sleepy.*
>
> *We drive, and we drive, and we drive. Finally we get to Greenwood. We pull off to a small building—a little field house in a park—and we go inside, and lo and behold, after an hour-and-a-half drive, it turns out there are twenty people there. Twenty people. They look all kind of damp and sleepy—maybe they aren't really excited to be there either.*
>
> *But I'm going around, I'm shaking hands, saying, "How are you doing?"*
>
> *As I go around the room, suddenly I hear this voice cry out behind me, "Fired up?!" I jumped up. I don't know what's going*

*on. But everyone else acts as though this were normal, and they say, "Fired up!"*

*And then we hear this voice say, "Ready to go?!" And every-body says, "Ready to go!" And I don't know what's going on. So I turn back, there's this little lady standing there, she's got a big church hat and a gold tooth, and she's smiling at me. She says, "Fired up?! Ready to go?!"*

*And it turns out that this lady's name is Edith Childs and she's a councilwoman from Greenwood who also moonlights as a private detective. And she is famous for her chants. They call her "the chant lady." She says, "Fired up?!" And the people say, "Fired up!" And she says, "Ready to go?!" And they say, "Ready to go!"*

*And for the next, it seemed like five minutes, she just kept on chanting, "Fired up?! Ready to go! Fired up?! Ready to go!" Everybody's joining in. And I don't really know what to do. I'm looking at my staff, and they're shrugging.*

*But here's the thing. After about a minute of this . . . I'm starting to feel kind of fired up. I'm starting to feel like I'm ready to go. And I was just energized for the rest of the day. And all my staff, everywhere we went, we kept on saying, "Fired up? Are you fired up?" "Yeah, I'm fired up. Are you fired up?" "Yeah, are you ready to go?" "Yeah, I'm ready to go."*

*And it shows you the power of one voice to change the mood of a room. Because when you change the mood of a room, sud-denly you change the mood of a city. And when you change the mood of a city, you change the mood of a state. You change the mood of a state, you change the mood of a country. You change the mood of a country, you change the mood of the world. So I want to know right now, from all of you . . . are you fired up?!*

*Crowd: FIRED UP!*
*Obama: Are you ready to go?!*
*Crowd: READY TO GO!*

*As Obama finished, the Isiserettes, a Des Moines youth drumline, fell in to position along the perimeter of the pre-rally. The crowd, all wearing the same navy Obama '08 T-shirt, lined up behind the drums. The Isiser-ettes began a cadence, and we slowly made our way down a long, narrow dirt road toward the steak fry entrance.*

**Joe Paulsen, Scheduling and Advance Staffer:** We had three or four organizers up at the front entrance of the steak fry in Obama shirts, and there were Clinton people everywhere, Edwards people everywhere, Dodd people everywhere.

**Annick Febrey, Floyd County, IA, Field Organizer:** No one knew we were doing this big pre-event rally that was hidden over the hill.

**Emily Parcell:** I was standing inside the grounds of the steak fry, right next to the Edwards table, eavesdropping on the Edwards staffers. They were underestimating Obama. "They think they have such a good organization. They don't have anybody here."

**Peter Gage:** We intentionally had almost no presence within the gates, and then this din began to come up over the hill.

**Mitch Stewart:** All of a sudden you could hear that *thump* from the Isiserettes, and it was like rolling thunder. Everybody stopped and looked at this massive show of force.

**Jan Bauer:** Those Isiserettes, man, they are powerful. They're loud. They get your attention.

**Bonnie Adkins, Muscatine, IA, Precinct Captain:** We came down the road, a solid line of blue T-shirts, hollering, "Fired up! Ready to go!"

**Emily Parcell:** Over the hill comes this massive sea of people with Barack Obama at the fore.

**Megan Simpson, Dubuque, IA, Field Organizer:** All of a sudden, there were hundreds of Obama supporters walking into the steak fry with the Isiserettes, holding Obama "O" placards.

**Nancy Bobo, Des Moines, IA, Precinct Captain:** It was a parade like you'd never seen before. People chanting and cheering and coming together.

**Carolyn Kriss, Fort Dodge, IA, Intern:** The crowd was a lot of middle-aged white people, but for Iowa, it was a very diverse group—doing call-and-response, waving around signs. It felt amazing.

**Jeff Phillips, Indianola, IA, Field Organizer:** It was one of those moments that gives you chills.

**Jaime Mulligan, Online Organizer:** To this day, the sound of the Isiserettes gets me choked up.

**Annick Febrey:** It was like out of a movie.

**Chris Lewis, North Central Iowa Regional Field Director:** I'll never forget this—one of the organizers I knew from the Edwards campaign tapped me on the shoulder and went, "I can't believe you guys did this." And to me, that was the best part of the steak fry.

**Jaime Mulligan:** Everyone who was on Team Obama was so happy that day. It felt so full of possibility. It was joyful.

**Peter Gage:** There's a picture of Obama during that march with his arms out like he's flying. He's got this great grin on his face. What he's actually doing is imitating Johanna Maska, our person in charge of press for that event, who is squatting down facing him, backing up with her arms out trying to push the press back and clear a path to the door.

**Thomas Zimmerman, Sioux City, IA, Field Organizer:** The Harkin Steak Fry was the moment when I was like, "We *can* win this thing."

**Chelsea Kammerer, Eastern Central Iowa Regional Field Director:** It was the first time everyone reaped the rewards of their work. I remember we said this over and over again: "If they're willing to get on a bus and go two hours to Indianola, they will show up in January when it's freezing."

**Derek Eadon, Cedar Rapids, IA, Field Organizer:** There was so much excitement out there. You had to show people that, in order for them to feel comfortable getting on board with this. A lot of supporters who had been knocking doors in August when it was really shitty and seeing bad polls were able to see, "Oh my God, there are thousands of people just like me across the state."

**Leah White:** I was pregnant and had morning sickness, but the bus ride back was a ton of fun. The atmosphere, the chatter, and the excitement that this might actually happen. It was really incredible to be a part of that. I think it was a shared purpose that really resonated for me.

After listening to all the candidates that day, it confirmed that I really did believe Obama had what it took to be the next president. My mom was super involved, and that was very exciting, but I'd never been involved in a campaign or volunteered in any way before that. I always voted, but I'd never caucused.

**Tripp Wellde, Davenport, IA, Field Organizer:** After the steak fry, Leah came on board to be a precinct captain. What I remember in particular is her saying that the feeling of comradery and connectedness on the bus rides was almost like being back in school. It was like a sense of community that she hadn't experienced.

**Leah White:** I was twenty-eight years old. I felt like my parents' generation and older generations owned the political space. It never felt accessible to me. And when you got on that bus and you saw all different ages of people, but especially younger people, it felt different. It felt more like a movement than even about a person. It was about a collection of people who were in this shared cause.

It seemed like Obama had tapped into something to say, "We need you, and this country needs you." For the first time since I had started voting, I felt like my voice mattered and that it was time to step up and help.

Clinton Widens Lead in Poll; Senator Also Tops Obama in Latest
Fundraising Data

—Washington Post, October 3, 2007

Obama Knocks Dems: Presidential Hopeful Barack Obama Said
Wednesday that U.S. Troops Aren't in Iraq Just Because of President Bush

—Daily Iowan, October 4, 2007

Maybe Obama "Gets" Iowa: Campaign Is Organized, Relentless

—Des Moines Register, October 5, 2007

It's Now or Never for Bam. Iowa or Bust for Barack and the Rest as
Moneybags Hil Continues Charge

—New York Daily News, October 8, 2007

Clinton Winning Over the Skeptics; The Demonized Image Fades When
Voters Are Reintroduced to Her. Women, Seniors Form a Solid Base of
Support

—Los Angeles Times, October 8, 2007

Too Young to Vote, but Old Enough to Caucus in Iowa; Obama Campaign
Targets Turnout for 17-Year-Olds; The "BarackStar" Vibe

—Wall Street Journal, October 10, 2007

Rivals Pounce on Clinton's Iran Vote; Obama and Edwards Compare Her
Support of a Senate Resolution Last Month to Her 2002 Vote Backing
Force in Iraq

—Los Angeles Times, October 12, 2007

Civil Rights Icon Lewis Endorses Clinton

—Cox News Service, October 12, 2007

Trying Times for the Obama Faithful

—Washington Post, October 25, 2007

Obama, Edwards Attack; Clinton Bombs Debate

—Politico, October 31, 2007

# 6

## HOLDING LIGHTNING

*October–November 2007*

### November 10, 2007

*Iowa Polling Average:* Clinton 30, Obama 24, Edwards 20
*National Polling Average:* Clinton 46, Obama 23, Edwards 13

*W*ith the caucus three months away, my focus narrowed almost entirely to finding captains for my seventeen precincts. Since each caucus site was a distinct entity and the rules were complex, we needed trained Iowans to both reach out to voters in the months before the caucus and lead our group inside the room on caucus night. These volunteers captains would form the core of our organization on January 3.

Occasionally I would hear precinct captains speculate on who Obama should pick as his running mate. I never knew how to answer when this question was posed to me, partly because it was impossible for me to visualize him being the nominee. The scenario seemed so far removed from our current situation that discussing it felt like a waste of time. Eventually, I stumbled upon the perfect stock response: "I don't know, but I sure hope he picks Michelle."

Michelle Obama was the campaign's best surrogate. She would eventually earn the nickname "the Closer" in Iowa. She had this stump speech where she would talk about going with Obama to a community meeting and listening to him talk about "the world as it is" versus "the world as it should be." The takeaway was that organizing is the method by which you narrow that gap.

*After seeing her in person, a local lawyer I'd been trying to win over for months, Mel, signed on the dotted line. Mel would go on to be my ninth precinct captain, which left me with eight slots to fill. It was impossible to spin these relationships up overnight—given the commitment and training, you needed time for them to stick.*

*There was a sense as we approached November that despite continuing to trail nationally, the organization in Iowa was starting to fill out. Most of my colleagues had more than half of their precinct captains locked down, and we invited all of them to come to Des Moines for the Jefferson-Jackson Dinner.*

*The dinner was the biggest political event of the year in Iowa. Nine thousand spectators packed together in Des Moines's Veterans Memorial Auditorium to cheer on their pick for president. Six candidates were expected to appear, with Speaker of the House Nancy Pelosi as MC. Scheduled two months out from caucus day, the dinner was viewed by activists and the press as the best opportunity to gauge a campaign's organization strength. There is no declared winner—many attendees were bussed in as supporters for the rival campaigns—but the event, officially a party fundraiser, served as a competition to impress future caucus goers, debut a stump speech for the home stretch, and dazzle reporters. Since it was held less than two months before the caucuses, it was viewed as the unofficial kickoff to the final sprint in Iowa.*

**Jon Favreau, Speechwriter:** There was no better or bigger chance to get our message out in a succinct way, in a powerful way, than the Jefferson-Jackson dinner. We also felt like we had tried and failed so often in the prior couple months to do something like this. By the time we got to the JJ, we knew this was it.

**Linda Langston, Linn County, IA, Supervisor:** There was a lot of trepidation going into the JJ dinner, a lot of concern. There was a lot riding on it. I've seen it happen in multiple caucus years—campaigns can really turn on that event. Candidates can either blow it or knock it out of the park.

**Jon Favreau:** What we were most excited about with the JJ was that it gave each candidate only ten minutes to make a case, and he or she had to memorize it. So we knew that Barack Obama would need a speech that said everything we wanted to say, since this was basically his last shot.

**Peter Gage, Advance Staffer:** This was the one event where the candidates were on the stage together going into the homestretch. People read into these events as concrete examples of the organizing ability of the campaigns. It's a reflection of how they're actually doing at a grassroots level compared to what you get from polls.

**Mitch Stewart, Iowa Caucus Director:** We shipped in people from all over Iowa for JJ. Each county had a certain number of tickets that they could allocate through their precinct-based operations.

**Rick Siger, Iowa Advance Director:** Instead of just filling the JJ up with people, we booked Hy-Vee Hall, which is immediately adjacent to the auditorium where the JJ was, and threw a massive rally with John Legend. We had every single person who had a ticket to the JJ in the Obama section go to this rally—three thousand people. At the end of the rally, we led them out the front door of the hall, shut down all the streets, and had a parade led by the Isiserettes.

**Karen Osbourne, New London, IA, Precinct Captain:** Barack and Michelle led us that evening from Hy-Vee Hall to the Vets Auditorium, chanting. There were tons of us behind them walking along, dancing— we were a huge group.

**Tommy Vietor, Iowa Press Secretary:** We marched up the street, this massive army of people. My dad and my stepmom saw the Obamas walking with this enormous crowd, and they just thought it was the wildest thing they'd ever seen. The energy—you could feel it. It was palpable.

**Thomas Zimmerman, Sioux City, IA, Field Organizer:** When we did that march, I shouted so much that I couldn't do call time for the next two days. I couldn't speak.

**Tommy Vietor:** I kept walking by these reporters, who were giving me "holy shit" looks. The whole idea was you wanted to show your organizational prowess and give a great speech that night. We'd spent months planning.

**Joe Paulsen, Scheduling and Advance Staff:** Everyone was nervous, because we had set a high bar at the steak fry. The day of was like judgment day.

**Mitch Stewart:** I think I threw up three times that day from the stress.

*Speaking order that night was determined by random lot: John Edwards kicked off the evening, followed by Richardson, Biden, Dodd. Then Clinton and Obama. Each speaker stood on a stage in the middle of the coliseum, surrounded by tables, while thousands of spectators looked down from bleachers above. When we walked into the room, it felt like the most high-stakes pep rally of all time. But as the program dragged on, nearly every Iowa statewide elected official was given the chance to speak. At one point, a seventy-three-year-old congressman auctioned off a scarf. Finally, after nearly four hours, Hillary Clinton took the stage.*

**Jon Favreau:** The order of the speeches ended up being perfect for us. As the JJ started and progressed, those first speeches were really boring. Joe Biden gave this speech where he asked the audience to imagine what the world would have been like if Joe Biden had been president on 9/11. And I love Joe Biden.

I'm thinking, "Shit, I thought this was going to be a great order, but people are milling about. No one's paying attention." I was convinced at that point the whole thing was over.

**Tommy Vietor:** It went so late. For some reason they did an auction in the middle. People were falling asleep in the fucking stadium.

**Linda Langston:** No political candidate—certainly at the presidential level—is known for their brevity.

**Jon Favreau:** Then Hillary got up, and we were very lucky, because it was Hillary Clinton, and the crowd totally quieted down. Everyone paid attention again. And their campaign did what we originally wanted to do, which was focus on a slogan.

**Francis Iacobucci, Field Organizer:** "Turn up the heat."

**Jon Favreau:** "Turn up the heat. Turn America around."

**Jan Bauer, Story County, IA, Democratic Party Chair:** I can't remember what the lines were, but she had people chanting, and it was exciting.

*HILLARY CLINTON [Speech Excerpt]: There are some who will say they don't know where I stand. I think you know better than that. I stand where I have stood for thirty-five years. I stand with you. And with your children. And with every American who needs a fighter in their corner for a better life.*

*Change is just a word if you don't have the strength and experience to make it happen. We must nominate a nominee who has been tested and elect a president who is ready to lead on day one. I know what it's going to take to win . . . So when the Republicans engage in fear-mongering and saber-rattling and talk about World War III, what do we do to them?*

*CROWD: Turn up the heat!*

**Rose Vasquez, Des Moines, IA, Obama Volunteer:** "Turn up the heat." I thought, "Oh, that's going to be tough to top."

**Francis Iacobucci:** We were the fucking last speech in the whole thing. We were all ready. We were all anxious to do this.

**Jon Favreau:** "Why does Barack Obama believe he should be president? Why should he be president instead of her? And why should he be president at this moment in time?" Those questions had to be answered for everyone—for us and the campaign, for the people who were going out and trying to evangelize about Barack Obama, for the people who were going to caucus, and for all the very cynical people in the press corps.

**Yohannes Abraham, Polk County, IA, Field Organizer:** Unfortunately the stress of the caucus turned me into a regular smoker. At some point before then-Senator Obama's speech, I snuck out to have a cigarette at the exact same time that Marvin Nicholson, who was the senator's trip director, was out having a smoke. I didn't really know Marvin. We're just shooting the breeze, and I don't know what compelled me. I asked him, "How are we going to do today? Do you have a sense?" And Marvin looked at me with utter supreme confidence and said, "The senator's got this."

**Joe Paulsen:** Because you can record your own entrance music, the JJ speeches turn into something like a WWE professional wrestling match. David Axelrod, who is a big Chicago Bulls fan, somehow got in touch with the Bulls announcer and convinced him to record Obama's introduction over the Chicago Bulls entrance music, made famous by Michael Jordan.

**Mike Owen, Cedar County, IA, Obama Volunteer:** All of a sudden, these spotlights with the Obama logo started rippling through the crowd, all over the arena.

**Danielle Crutchfield, Deputy Director of Scheduling and Advance:** The JJ is the most insane political thing I've ever seen. When he came out there, it gave you chills.

**Rose Vasquez:** Like *Rocky*. They announced him like he was coming into the ring.

> ANNOUNCER: *Aaaaaaaaaaaaaaaannnnnnnnd now, from our neighboring state of Illinois . . . a six-foot-two force for change: Senator Barack O-BAMA!*
>
> BARACK OBAMA *[Speech Excerpt]: Thank you, Iowa!*
>
> *We have a chance to bring the country together in a new majority—to finally tackle problems that George Bush made far worse but that had festered long before George Bush ever took office—problems that we've talked about year after year after year after year.*
>
> *And that is why the same old Washington textbook campaigns just won't do in this election. That's why not answering questions because we are afraid our answers won't be popular just won't do. When I am this party's nominee, my opponent will not be able to say that I voted for the war in Iraq, or that I gave George Bush the benefit of the doubt on Iran, or that I supported Bush-Cheney policies of not talking to leaders that we don't like.*
>
> *I am running in this race because of what Dr. King called "the fierce urgency of now." Because I believe that there's such a thing as being too late. And that hour is almost upon us.*
>
> *I will never forget that the only reason that I'm standing here today is because somebody, somewhere, stood up for me when it was risky. Stood up when it was hard. Stood up when it wasn't popular. And because that somebody stood up, a few more stood up. And then a few thousand stood up. And then a*

*few million stood up. And standing up, with courage and clear purpose, they somehow managed to change the world. That's why I'm asking you to stand with me, that's why I'm asking you to caucus for me, that's why I am asking you to stop settling for what the cynics say we have to accept.*

*In this election—in this moment—let us reach for what we know is possible. A nation healed. A world repaired. An America that believes again.*

**Francis Iacobucci:** We knew right away we'd won.

**Jon Favreau:** The whole speech was built around *why we need something new in this country at this moment in time.* To raise the stakes and raise the urgency of why you need to take a risk and why the bigger risk is to go with what we already know.

**Norm Sterzenbach, Iowa Democratic Party Caucus Director:** It was one of those moments when Barack Obama reminded people about the commanding presence that he has on stage. Not only did he prepare so well for the speech itself and what he said, but how he said it, how he worked the room, how he worked the stage—it just came off brilliantly. And so that message then reverberated out to the national press. It reverberated out to people around the country.

**Linda Langston:** That was the moment a number of people walked away saying, "I think Obama's going to be able to win the caucus." It's not to say that Clinton didn't do a really good job, because she did. It's just that Obama did better.

**Jan Bauer:** He'd found his voice. Before that JJ dinner, he had seemed sort of professorial, but at that speech, all of a sudden, he found his voice.

**Bess Evans, Clay County, IA, Field Organizer:** The night of the Jefferson-Jackson dinner, I felt like I was holding lightning. It was so electric, and you didn't want to let go of that, because you were afraid that you'd lose it and it'd never come back.

**Yohannes Abraham:** There was a difference pre- and post-JJ. Post-JJ was when you started to notice the text messages and emails: "How is it looking? How is it feeling? What's going on there? Are we winning?" Friends and relatives outside of Iowa who hadn't really expressed an interest before.

**Thomas Zimmerman:** You got the sense that everyone else saw us as the primary threat, which hadn't really been the case before.

**Mitch Stewart:** Up to that point, it was still like, "We are these scrappy underdogs, and if we pull off this miracle, it will be something else." After the JJ was over, I remember Paul Tewes came up to me and said, "It's ours to lose now."

**Jon Favreau:** The JJ became the stump speech. Everywhere he went from the JJ on—the energy and the urgency of the moment was there, and that had been missing before.

**Rick Siger:** The next morning, we invited every field organizer in the state and their parents—if they could make it—to a cafeteria at a high school in Des Moines. Closed press. The senator had no voice left—he had been traveling for five days. It turned out to be one of the most meaningful events in the whole campaign.

**Bess Evans:** My parents had come for the Jefferson-Jackson dinner. The next morning, the senator and Mrs. Obama made remarks to our parents, thanking them. Then they worked the rope line and took photos with every single family. My mom cried. Both of my parents were incredibly nervous, and it was probably the first time that I realized how invested they were in what I was doing.

**Tommy Vietor:** This is a classic Paul thing and a reminder that Obama is a good person. They knew that our team was like a hundred twenty-two- to twenty-seven-year-olds. There were a whole lot of parents who had gotten a call earlier that year from their kid, saying, "I'm gonna go work as a field organizer for Barack Obama."

This is not a job that pays a ton of money. It's not law school. It's not safe sounding. It's like, "What are you doing, kid?"

**Jaci Urness, Polk County, IA, Field Organizer:** Barack and Michelle were speaking to the parents and basically saying, "Thank you so much for giving us your kids." And during the receiving line, my mom was just frozen, crying. She didn't even meet him, because she was completely overwhelmed. I think that threw her, being that emotional.

To her, in northern Minnesota, the Iowa caucuses seemed so far away. So I went off to Iowa to work on this campaign, and she didn't fully understand what it all meant. And then to come down and see my passion and that of the other staff throughout that weekend, she was so touched by it.

**Valerie Jarrett, Senior Advisor:** That same energy that Senator Obama brought to community organizing on the South Side of Chicago he saw through the eyes of the organizers in Iowa. They reminded him of himself. And so he knew how hard he worked for what he cared about, and the thought that they were working that hard for him—that was about the nicest compliment he could receive. But it was also an incredible responsibility, not wanting to disappoint them. Wanting to be good enough to be worthy of them was really important to him. Because if he wasn't worthy of them, then he couldn't possibly be worthy of the people in Iowa.

**David Plouffe, Campaign Manager:** When you ask him about his 2008 campaign, he talks about two things: the volunteers and his organizers.

The staff and volunteers thought that Barack Obama thought they were the most important people on the campaign. And he thought they were. You can't manufacture that. Why did so many people spend time helping him in '08? There's a lot of talk about good technology and a lot of money. No—none of that matters if there's not that bond.

Obviously every presidential candidate has his or her core supporters and is grateful for them. But the bond between Barack Obama and his organizers and key precinct captains in Iowa was really—I've never seen anything like it. Part of it is that he understands there's a lot of BS in presidential campaigns. All the media coverage and the sound bites and the polls. What's real is the work that's happening on the ground.

**Barack Obama:** Part of what made Iowa so important to me was that it was a test of my most fundamental beliefs about democracy. When I was their age, I had become a community organizer—not even really knowing exactly what that meant and not necessarily being as good at it as any of them were. But it was based on a premise that drew from my reading of the civil rights movement and my reading about the union movement and the women's suffrage movement. This vision of a politics from the bottom up. And so often electoral politics was something completely removed from that. It's money and it's TV ads and it's positioning and it's talking points. And somehow the process of people becoming involved and determining their own destiny—that got lost.

And what I saw with both the staff and the volunteers was this almost organic process of people organizing themselves; I was the front man, but they were the band. And the spirit of what they were doing wasn't just carrying us in Iowa; it was really carrying us nationally—because at that time our poll numbers nationally were still bad. But Axelrod used to say that whenever he got down and tired and worn-out, he just needed a couple of days in Iowa to goose him back up. And it was true that everybody around the country was modeling what they were doing on what we were doing in a much more concentrated fashion in Iowa.

**Paulette Aniskoff, Iowa Get Out the Caucus Director:** On every campaign I'd worked on, field was the bottom, and they were treated like shit. People go into field organizing a lot because it's like the salt-of-the-earth job. Paul Tewes built a culture, and it ended up having a name—"Respect, Empower, Include"—that was genuinely lived by everyone.

**Tommy Vietor:** Paul was this quirky, grizzled, part football coach, part hilarious, part explosive leader who everyone respected. There was no job he asked you to do that he didn't do himself. One time he told the senior staff that that Saturday they were going canvassing, and we had to draw out of a hat to see what county to go to. We soon realized that the only counties he had chosen were the ring counties at the edge of the state—so as far from Des Moines as possible.

I got a county north of Mason City, on the border of Minnesota. It took me two hours to drive there to go canvass for four or five hours and then two hours to drive back. So it's like no one was above any job. He would fucking smack you down hard if you acted that way. And I was someone who could be too big for my britches sometimes, so Paul and I definitely clashed a few times.

**Paul Tewes, Iowa State Director:** I just wanted them to feel like I wasn't above them and that nothing was beneath anybody in this organization. That was important.

**Tommy Vietor:** He inspired a lot of passion, and the staff loved him. The guy had a huge heart, and he loved Barack Obama, and you just felt like he was in there for the right reasons. I think he was an incredibly powerful leader. Now, he wouldn't have been able to do what he did and be that person without Marygrace Galston, who was the unsung hero of the whole place. She kept everything together, was kind to everyone, was wildly competent, and could lead. She was amazing.

Same with Mitch. Funny, inspirational, worked his ass off, great job overseeing the team. But then also, there were people like Emily Parcell, who was just the driest, calmest, and most outwardly emotionless but ruthlessly effective political person ever. Barack Obama just loved her because she was relentless. She knew who was full of shit and which endorsements mattered because they'd actually do work for us.

It was just an incredible team of true believers. There were no mercenaries there.

**Jon Carson, February 5 Director:** Leadership matters. If the leadership in a state on a campaign is spending all their time in a closed-door office with the message guys and the media guys and that's where the energy is and the organizers feel like they are sitting out there by themselves making phone calls that no one gives a shit about, that sends a very different message than the message that was established in Iowa. That what mattered—what Paul Tewes was spending his time on, what he was talking to people about—was the organization that we were building.

And not just theories about it, but celebrating building it at scale. So those organizers sitting at their sad little desks in the Iowa headquarters—they were the center of the action. They weren't missing some other cool thing that was happening somewhere else—they were the focus. Them and 150 other organizers.

So many campaigns waste so much time trying to create the bright, shiny object that's going to get attention. The bright, shiny object in Iowa was the organization itself.

**Barack Obama:** Tewes was an old, grizzled vet, but everybody else were kids. They were in their twenties. What was wonderful about all the young people who were fanning out across the state was they were terrific at making relationships. By the time I got there and certainly by the end of the campaign, they were known, they were trusted, they were loved. In some cases, they were treated like the sons or daughters of community leaders there because they had lived there and they'd shown themselves to really care.

**Anne Filipic, Iowa Field Director:** Every time Barack Obama did a rally or an event in Iowa, he'd call the field organizers from that region up to the stage.

**Emily Parcell, Iowa Political Director:** Bringing the field organizers onstage and introducing them—he wanted to do that. God forbid we have an elected official onstage, but we better have every organizer from that county up there. That stayed with me. It was a moment that made me feel like, "God, this guy has to be president. He's not some out-of-touch politician." He had done the hard work as an organizer when he was their age. He had been on the streets. He had gone door to door. He had worked on these problems.

**Greg Degen, Johnson County, IA, Field Organizer:** It was such an incredible gesture. It made you feel like not only were you part of something big but also you were the most essential part of something big. For someone who was poised to be the most powerful person on earth to be elevating me . . . it was really, really empowering.

**Barack Obama:** If we won there the way we were running, given the nature of the caucuses, the feeling was not only that my campaign would be viable but that my faith in this kind of politics was vindicated. And that's why, when you saw folks like this work, you just didn't want to screw up. You wanted to make sure that you were worthy of these efforts.

Obama's Superb Speech Could Catapult His Bid

—Des Moines Register, November 12, 2007

Early Caucuses Put Student Vote in Play; On Jan. 3, Campuses Will Be on Break. This Could Help, or Hurt, Obama, Who Benefits Most from the College Electorate

—Los Angeles Times, November 21, 2007

In Iowa, Clinton Intensifies Attacks; With Race Close, Obama Stresses His Electability

—Washington Post, November 26, 2007

Oprah's Star Power to Hit Campaign Trail; Obama Campaign Announces Dates for Talk Show Queen to Appear at Rallies for Him in Iowa, South Carolina, and New Hampshire

—Chicago Sun-Times, November 27, 2007

Obama the Terrorist: The Vote-Baiting Smear Begins

—Daytona Beach News, December 4, 2007

In S.C., It's Still Anyone's Primary; Polls Show Clinton Leading Democrats; GOP a 5-Way Fight

—Charleston Post and Courier, December 8, 2007

Hill Tops NH Again—Double-Digit Lead over Rival Obama

—New York Post, December 20, 2007

Obama Turns Cheek. Resists Attack on NH Voter Who Said, "It's Very Important He's Not a Muslim"

—New York Daily News, December 24, 2007

# 7

# 1,781 ROOMS

*December 2007–January 2008*

### December 26, 2007

*Iowa Polling Average:* Clinton 29, Obama 27, Edwards 24
*National Polling Average:* Clinton 44, Obama 25, Edwards 14

*I*n the weeks leading up to the caucuses on January 3, Iowa was overrun with out-of-staters. There were twenty-five hundred credentialed journalists at the Democratic Party media center in Des Moines. Campaigns brought in hundreds of volunteers to help with "get out the vote" (GOTV, or in this case, GOTC, "get out the caucus"). Politicians like San Francisco district attorney Kamala Harris and Los Angeles city councilman Eric Garcetti flew in; Magic Johnson (Clinton), Kevin Bacon (Edwards), and Scarlett Johansson (Obama) were some of the dozens of celebrity surrogates touring Iowa towns for the first time.

Each organizer was assigned a half dozen out-of-state volunteers to knock doors in the seven days before the caucus—in Iowa City, our group included a multimillionaire venture capitalist; a community organizer from Oakland, California; union workers from Illinois; a woodworking artist from Pennsylvania; a Manhattan attorney; and two nonprofit executives from Washington, DC. Looking through the list in 2019, I recognize then-little-known names that would become familiar to Americans later as cabinet secretaries (Samantha Power), White House chiefs of staff (Denis McDonough), and presidential candidates (Pete Buttigieg).

*But in the moment, no one's station outside of Iowa mattered—all were evaluated on one criterion: the ability to knock as many doors as possible in cold weather and have a sincere conversation with an Iowa voter.*

**Paulette Aniskoff, Iowa Get Out the Caucus Director:** We were recruiting hundreds of out-of-state volunteers. But you've really got to match people to what's appropriate for them—in some cases all the volunteers want to come to Des Moines because they think that they'll see some kind of action, and we were like, "If you really want to help, go to small-town Iowa and see how this really happens."

**Marygrace Galston, Iowa Deputy State Director:** Almost all of the National Finance Committee came out for the last week of the caucus. People flew their private jets to Iowa to knock on doors.

**Graham Wilson, Fairfield, IA, Field Organizer:** The out-of-state volunteers—the well-selected people who were very respectful and volunteered to have real conversations with Iowans—were really helpful to us.

There were these three NYU sophomores who came out to my turf, stayed in the same house, and did everything together. Iowans were burned-out by the end. There were seven campaigns. Four or five of them had functional voter contact operations, even in rural areas. They had candidates coming through all the time; they had people like me knocking on their door, neighbors knocking on their door. Having these three young women come in full of energy was incredibly helpful, because they were so happy and excited to be there.

**Katherine Onyshko, New York University Sophomore, Out-of-State Volunteer:** They were looking for people to come from right after Christmas until the caucus. I decided to do it, and two of my roommates from NYU came along. It felt like we could really *do something* on the type of campaign that might not come around in the future. Christmas night my friends flew out to Chicago, and the next morning the three of us drove to Fairfield, Iowa. I remember pulling up to this old Victorian house in the middle of winter, and the next day we started going door to door.

**Cody Keenan, Out-of-State Volunteer:** Here's what they had me doing: "Here's your list of names for you to hit today. Here's a map of the neighborhood. Go get to it." Once you're door knocking, you hone your pitch, and you think up new arguments as you're talking to people. There was a Casey's General Store between two of the neighborhoods I was assigned. I would pop back in there every two hours, because it was less than ten degrees out. I had a goatee at the time—my breath would freeze on it, so I had little icicles in my nose and dripping down my beard. It was cold as hell.

**Katherine Onyshko:** I had my parents' car for the week, so my two friends and I would get three routes for each of us to walk. One of the first houses my friend went to, she rang the doorbell, and the voter was like, "I'm in the garage, come around." She went into the garage, and the guy was boiling deer antlers—his garage was bloody. She stood there and had a conversation about why this man should caucus for Barack Obama while he prepped a recently killed deer.

That week very much lived up to what I had imagined. A lot of phone calls and door-to-door. What was new was the culture surrounding caucusing. It was an adventure in the best way.

**Joe Paulsen, Scheduling and Advance Staffer:** The week leading up to the caucus, we had dozens and dozens of surrogates come to the state. It was always a delicate balancing act because you had a lot of people come in that assumed Iowans would want to see them and build events around them. That wasn't the case. It also was not a good use of staff time to be building events when they needed to be planning for caucus day.

I was basically telling surrogates, "Happy to have you in the state. You'll be canvassing."

**Karen Wohlleben, Cedar Rapids, IA, Deputy Field Organizer:** Some people came and felt like we should be grateful that they were in Iowa, and other people showed up and were grateful they got to be in Iowa.

At one point, a busload of volunteers from Illinois arrived, and Mrs. Robinson, Michelle Obama's mother, was on it. Somebody was like, "We're really honored Mrs. Robinson is here today. Mrs. Robinson, would you like to say a few words?"

She had on her coat and her gloves and was so elegant. She just looked around the room and said, "Well, I think we should probably get to work, because we're losing half the day." Everybody grabbed their packets.

**Joe Paulsen:** Iowans have so many people there in the final weeks before the caucuses—candidates, surrogates—they don't care. They're just not fazed by it.

We had rented a separate office where all we did was put caucus packets together. You were doing that with volunteers, field organizers, consultants . . . anyone who had any stake in the campaign, whether they were a supporter or on the payroll.

Kal Penn was the best surrogate because you didn't have to send a staffer with him. His big pull for the campaign was with high school kids, because they had all seen *Harold & Kumar Go to White Castle.*

**Rachel Haltom-Irwin, Obama Iowa Youth Vote Director:** There were two things that were so precious. One was the senator's time and the other was the field organizers' time. The organizers' priority right then was to recruit and train all their precinct captains. They couldn't build events. So I brought Kal to where there was already a preorganized event: college cafeterias. Kal and I drove around the state eating in cafeterias. Slowly but surely, someone would be like, "That's that dude." And people would walk over to Kal and ask, "Why are you here?" Then he would start talking, and they would ask him policy questions.

**Kal Penn, Out-of-State Volunteer:** You watch the cable news narrative about young people: "Young people—are they actually going to vote? They don't really give a shit about this."

But they really did give a shit, in a significant way. When other surrogates and I were in Iowa, we always did a Q&A at these events—very rarely would we ever get a question about the TV shows or movies we were working on. All the questions were about student loans or health care or human rights or national security, which was really inspiring.

There were less controlled environments, like walking through a college campus, that could quickly devolve into a "I just want to get a selfie before I go to class" situation. I love the people who watch and support the movies and TV shows that I do, but I didn't come to Iowa to take selfies with them. So when we were in that environment, I always made sure I had a stack of supporter cards on me to capture everybody's information. That was the whole reason that I was there. Once you had those supporter cards, with people's email addresses and phone numbers, somebody from the campaign would follow up and say, "Would you like to volunteer? Have you decided who you're caucusing for? Can we get you to caucus for Barack Obama?"

**Rachel Haltom-Irwin:** Your worth in Iowa is based on how many supporter cards you can get, and Kal was pulling fifty supporter cards per event. He would get these supporter cards and call through them while I drove, to remind them, "You said you would caucus for Barack Obama. Remember, here's the date. Here's where you need to show up."

*My time that final week of GOTV was devoted to training my last precinct captains, door knocking our supporters, and making one last attempt at undecided voters. By the end, we were visiting "3s" for the fourth or fifth time and following up on handwritten letters in hopes of converting them before caucus night or at least becoming their second choice.*

**Jamal Pope, Sioux City, IA, Field Organizer:** There was a lady who was the president of the local NAACP, Flora. She was pretty forthcoming when I first met her: "Listen, I supported John Edwards in 2004; that's who I'm supporting right now."

**Flora Lee, Sioux City Community Activist:** I didn't think Obama had a prayer—I'll be honest—because he was a Black man, he was young, and he didn't have a great deal of experience.

**Jamal Pope:** I was like, "Cool." I didn't try to push. Eventually, we got her in to meet Senator Obama, and she told him that she wasn't a supporter. I thought, "If she told him that, we don't have a chance."

**Flora Lee:** Senator Edwards was really talking about issues. He was talking about poverty; he was talking about race and inequality. And those were the two things that really got me.

**Jamal Pope:** Her son came to town, and they invited me to Christmas dinner with the family. I made banana pudding. I didn't want to go empty-handed, and that was something my mom would always make. I went to the local Hy-Vee and got some vanilla wafers, bananas, and pudding mix, but I really didn't know how.

**Flora Lee:** I knew he was here in Iowa by himself, no family. And it was a holiday, and I thought, "Gosh, if that were one of my kids, I would hope someone would invite them over." And I liked him . . . he didn't talk politics all the time.

**Jamal Pope:** So I made this banana pudding, ate Christmas dinner with the family, and played cards. She had three kids and a husband, and we were just sitting around the table talking.

**Flora Lee:** I said to my son, "Well, who do you like in all this presidential stuff?"

He says, "I like Obama."

"Well, why do you like him?"

"Well, because he talks about things that are important to me. He was talking about education, he was talking about student loans, he was talking about jobs . . . he's talking about not sending people to war."

And the clincher was this—he said, "You older people have messed up things. Let's give us a try."

**Jamal Pope:** Closer to the caucus, I had to make the hard ask. I was a little nervous.

**Flora Lee:** Jamal was so persistent. He was knowledgeable. But he wasn't persistent in a way that just started to nag at me . . . he was very respectful.

**Jamal Pope:** I called her and said, "Hey, Flora, I haven't really talked to you about supporting Senator Obama yet, but we have a week. You're an influencer in the community, and if you support him, there'll be a lot of other people who will feel comfortable doing the same."

She came back a day later and said, "After talking to you, after talking to my son, I'm going to caucus for Senator Obama."

I was super pumped. I emailed everybody about it. When that happened, I thought, "We're finally moving in the right direction. We've got everything together now."

That's kind of how I saw the whole Iowa thing. There were two hundred people like me. A lot of Iowans said, "I'll do it because Jamal's been here for so many months. He's not from here—I can go caucus for an hour."

*Every night of GOTV, there would be a statewide conference call in which the nine Iowa regional directors shared their daily numbers and a moving anecdote from the doors or from a final event, and we'd all applaud into the phone. Paul Tewes would wrap it up by announcing, "Today, we won!"*

*These calls were my connection to the rest of the state. Our out-of-state volunteers, interns, and friends who came to help would huddle around the phone together, entering data, sharing the experience. There were constant reminders that we could still lose—the* Des Moines Register *endorsed Clinton, a colleague's host family announced they were switching to Edwards, and volunteers would flake for their shifts without warning. By New Year's Eve, three days before the caucus, I was still searching for two precinct captains, hungry for reassurance that things would go our way.*

**Kristin Avery, Sioux City, IA, Field Organizer:** New Year's Eve was the night that the *Des Moines Register* poll came out.

**Lauren Kidwell, Regional Field Director:** The *Des Moines Register* poll had predicted the winner of the past couple of caucuses, so everyone was eagerly awaiting it. I was sitting in Mitch and Anne's office, and everyone was clicking refresh on the *Register* website. I remember Anne seeing it pop up and yelling, "Oh my gosh. We're up. We're winning!"

**Michael Blake, Iowa Deputy Political Director:** It had us up seven points.

**Lauren Kelly, Des Moines, IA, Deputy Field Organizer:** The whole office went nuts. Everyone was screaming, hugging, dancing, and being super excited.

**Lauren Kidwell:** Immediately, there was an email. "Everyone get on an all-staff conference call." We gathered around, and everyone was still really jubilant. Paul got on the call and was like . . .

**Michael Halle, Cedar Rapids, IA, Field Organizer:** "Polls don't mean shit."

**Lauren Kidwell:** "Polls don't mean shit."

**Michael Blake:** "Polls don't mean shit."

**Kal Penn:** I assume everybody has quoted Paul Tewes. If not, I hope they do. "Polls don't mean shit."

**Lauren Kidwell:** The air instantly went out of the room. His fear was that everyone was gonna become overconfident.

**Paul Tewes:** That's true. I mean, there were polls daily at that point. Some had us ahead, some had us in third place, and some had us in second. People had started pouring champagne, and I didn't want them to think it was a done deal. We still had to get all these people to go to caucus.

**Megan Simpson, Dubuque County, IA, Field Organizer:** It was like a brief moment of celebration, a lot of validation, and then everyone went back to putting together walk packets.

*       *       *

*As the "countdown to caucus" clock shifted from days to hours, I could barely sleep. It felt like there was no future after January 3—the organizing principle of my life over the past year had been Barack Obama's campaign to win the Iowa caucuses. Win or lose, that was going away.*

*Two more polls came out showing Clinton with a lead. There were rumors that Edwards was surging in the final week, with momentum too late to appear in poll results. A debate quickly emerged in the press over whether the* Des Moines Register *poll was an outlier for assuming record-setting high turnout. A consensus seemed to emerge around one point: if new people who said they were going to caucus actually turned out for the first time, Obama would likely win. If attendance was closer to past years, we would lose.*

*On January 2, Obama held his final rally in my area—several hundred people in a Marriott ballroom. He called the eleven organizers from my office onstage and thanked us for our work. Referencing skepticism about young people caucusing in the press, he said, "They don't think you're going to show up . . . are you going to prove them wrong?"*

*Looking out at the crowd, I could spot dozens of volunteers and precinct captains. For nearly eleven months, we had dedicated ourselves to finding, training, and empowering these Iowans to lead their neighborhoods. The result would be in their hands when doors to 1,781 rooms opened in twenty-seven hours.*

**Carrianna Suiter, Muscatine Field Organizer:** The day of the caucus was the scariest day of my life. This thing that you've been working for so hard, you've put everything into. The idea that you're gonna finally find out what happens is just terrifying.

**Michael Blake:** In many ways we spent ten months preparing for ninety minutes.

There is nothing in politics like a caucus. You're walking into a room, and everyone—your family, neighbors, colleagues—will see who you're choosing. That's very different. It would be easier to just go vote for him behind a closed curtain. Everyone's watching you. You can't hide your support; you've got to be actively out there.

**David Plouffe, Campaign Manager:** You basically had to believe in a bunch of people who had never caucused before, who weren't political creatures, whom every expert told you you couldn't count on. We were reliant on them.

**Barack Obama:** You know, that's my favorite night of my entire polit-ical career. To me, that was a more powerful night than the night I was elected president.

We went to a school where a caucus was being held. For us, the whole issue was always whether our supporters were going to turn out and whether there would be high turnout, because that meant we were doing well.

I remember pulling up and seeing all these cars in the parking lot. Getting out of the car and watching folks streaming into the school. We got inside, and it was just this sea of people. Every age and different backgrounds; you had farmers in overalls and seed hats, and you had young African American kids and Latina moms. The fact that people had brought their kids and there were a lot of families who had shown up gave it this festive feeling.

**David Plouffe:** We saw there what we'd tried to build. Young people. Old people. African Americans. "I'm a Republican. I've never cau-cused before." "I'm an independent. I've never caucused before." "I'm a Democrat. I've never come to one of these before. I only vote in general elections." And there they were.

**Barack Obama:** I still remember, there was a guy who looked like Gandalf. He was dressed in this white robe, and he had this long white beard. And he had this white staff, and at the top of the staff he had jerry-rigged this little video screen that was playing my JJ speech looped over and over again.

There were my supporters, and there were Hillary supporters, and Edwards supporters, and Biden supporters. So it wasn't just that my folks had turned out; it was this sense that people were really *engaged*, that they were going to figure out who they wanted representing them in this presidential election.

I remember leaving there just feeling as if we had pulled something off. That whatever happened, somehow we had succeeded.

**Valerie Jarrett, Senior Advisor:** He was very quiet in the car. And I looked at him and realized he was tearing up.

**Barack Obama:** I thought about my mom at that point, who was very idealistic and I think was the person who was most responsible for giving me a sense of my values and belief in helping people, and who had passed away over a decade earlier. Thinking about her, I started tearing up. And that was the only time, I think, during the campaign where the full weight of what we were trying to do really affected me that way. There would be other times where I'd be excited or happy, but that night, that moment, I felt as if what I believed about this country and what I believed about politics had been made manifest.

*There was a one-hundred-person line to check in for my caucus when I arrived. The gym was so crowded with people that they started sending individual candidates' preference groups to other rooms. The Obama supporters filed into the hall, and I stood in front of the exit. Periodically attendees would approach the door to leave before the caucus ended, and I would frantically ask anyone wearing an Obama sticker to stay while calling precinct captains for updates on my flip phone.*

**Marie Ortiz, Marshalltown, IA, Precinct Captain:** I had never caucused before, but it was like an adrenaline rush because we were all there. We were at one of the veterans' home, and it was packed full of people. My mom was there. One of my high school teachers, my sisters, even my daughter and her friends were there. We were chanting "O-ba-ma!" on our side. It was wonderful.

**Leah White, Davenport, IA, Precinct Captain:** My precinct was in an elementary school gym right down the street from my house. I had knocked on a lot of doors and stopped all my neighbors and said, "Please come, please come, please come."

When we got there and watched people flow in, it challenged your assumptions and biases. A little old lady would walk in, and I would assume, "Oh, she's going to go to the Hillary camp because she's never seen a woman president in her lifetime." But it wasn't like that. We had people from all walks of life coming up and joining us. It was so cool. My heart is racing, thinking of it now. It was just so inspiring. It was really cool to see that the bulk of the people within our corner were white, because I think everyone had this expectation that Obama wouldn't get the white vote. And that was not true at all.

**Pat Hammerstrom, Sioux City, IA, Precinct Captain:** In my precinct, when we came to do the first count, Hillary had a great deal more people there than Barack did. I thought, "Oh boy, this isn't going good." Edwards had quite a few people—there were a couple Richardson supporters and Biden supporters, but they were in much smaller numbers.

You had to have 15 percent of the total number that were there in the room to be viable and earn delegates. When we got done with the first round, Edwards and Barack and Hillary were the only ones viable. The next thing that happens is an appointed person from the group goes to try to persuade the others to come over to support his or her candidate.

**Tom Harrington, Ames, IA, Precinct Captain:** I went to the Richardson people. A lot of them were interested in his antiwar position. I said, "You know, the best antiwar candidate here outside of Richardson is Barack Obama."

**Leah White:** We were running around trying to convince people to come and join us from other candidates. It's not hard to do when you really believe in it. I was pregnant and standing on a chair, counting people. My precinct blew it away. He took it, and it was amazing.

**Joe Cupka, Story County, IA, Field Organizer:** I had been getting texts periodically from my precinct captains, from other staffers, from friends of mine around the state. Every one of them was incredible news. Our organization was destroying. Like, "Holy shit, this is happening."

**Norm Sterzenbach, Iowa Democratic Party Caucus Chair:** We were predicting 175,000 people; 240,000 showed up.

**Paulette Aniskoff:** We were watching the numbers and figuring out how far ahead we potentially were when someone came rushing in from the other room and said, "They just called it. We won!"

**Yohannes Abraham, Des Moines, IA, Field Organizer:** I checked my phone, and Booch and others were texting me, "We won! Come back to headquarters!" I ran to my car and sped the entire way.

I just remember bursting through the front doors. Folks had already popped champagne and were crying. I run up to Booch, and he gave me a huge hug and picked me up and . . . I can't describe it you.

**Leah White:** Total elation. Total excitement. It was amazing. It was really, really special to be there and just to share it with everyone. It was an amazing moment to watch the kids that were working nonstop— Tripp and all his group. And to realize just how they pulled it off.

**Tripp Wellde, Davenport, IA, Field Organizer:** I'll never forget that as long as I live. Because it wasn't about politics. Sure, I guess it was about winning an election. But the reason why it mattered so much is because it was about believing in the potential of people. And that through concepts like hope and community and togetherness and having one another's back, you could do something that hadn't been done before.

**Meghan Goldenstein, Out-of-State Volunteer:** There were so many older people, so many younger people, people were sharing stories from their different caucus locations. It was really loud. You would have thought he'd won the whole thing at that point. And I think we thought, "OK, if we could win here, then he could win anywhere. We've shown the nation."

**Megan Simpson, Dubuque, IA, Field Organizer:** Getting in my car, I got a call from my dad, and he said, "I'm so proud of you. You did such a great job." And I sat in my car and cried for five minutes.

**C'Reda Weedon, Fort Dodge, IA, Field Organizer:** I'm not a very emotional person, but I was crying. I could not pull myself together I was crying so hard.

**Shannon Valley, Ames, IA, Deputy Field Organizer:** Nothing else in the campaign ever touched that night.

**Francis "Booch" Iacobucci, Field Organizer:** I sat down at my desk and just cried. I cried for two, three minutes. It was tears of joy, it was exhaustion, it was a little bit of sadness because it was over, but then I got up and called my parents.

**Yohannes Abraham:** I immediately wanted to talk to my parents. They were crying as hard as I was. As immigrants, as refugees, as people who literally came here with nothing, this was an important chapter for them. They similarly have Ethiopian names, and I think to them it was like the promise of the country that they chose coming true in one night. For them they didn't need this in order to be prideful Americans, but it was the ultimate validation of that choice, because I think they could in very concrete terms see that there were zero limits on what their children and their grandchildren could achieve.

**Greg Degen, Johnson County, IA, Field Organizer:** I haven't experienced anything like that since. That rush. Part of it was that we were the underdogs, and it was the ultimate validation. But part of it, too, was the bond we all had formed with each other.

**Cody Keenan:** At the county victory party, I stayed to the side a little bit, because you could tell that this was a group of people who had just spent a year of their lives together, and suddenly, even though it had all paid off, it was coming to an end. There was something a little bittersweet about it. It was a magical night, and everybody knew when you woke up the next morning, things were gonna change.

**Nancy Bobo, Polk County, IA, Precinct Captain:** When we got to the rally at Hy-Vee Hall in Des Moines, it was all I could do to stand up. I had just been diagnosed with rheumatoid arthritis, and my legs were gone. There were so many people crying down there that night—high-fiving and hugging and kissing each other and screaming.

Somehow I jumped up in the air. I had been part of the biggest thing I'll ever be a part of in my life. That whole campaign—how it was handled, how people were treated, the leader we were advancing.

It was very emotional for me. I'd given my all to that, but to look around and see I was just one of thousands of people that had given their all to this thing, I felt to my very core, "There is a new day coming." Like we had moved mountains and nobody could take that away from us.

**Bess Evans, Spencer, IA, Field Organizer:** I remember screaming. Screaming in the streets. We all lit sparklers outside of the office on caucus night. I remember feeling like this was the most amazing thing I would ever do.

**R. T. Rybak, Out-of-State Volunteer and Mayor of Minneapolis, MN:** I will never ever forget what that night was like, because to be there with my kids meant a lot to me. They'd been down to Iowa with Howard Dean, and they're very political, but they did not want to get dragged back into another big loss. Obama won, and the place went nuts. They announced, "The next first family of the United States of America," and I just turned to my kids and said, "*This* is what it's like! *This* is why we have done this!"

As they were getting into their mid and late teens, I didn't want them to see this cynical thing. I wanted them to believe that this could happen. And it did. It just—as a dad, it meant a lot for them to see what politics could be.

> *BARACK OBAMA [Speech Excerpt]: They said this day would never come . . . But on this January night, at this defining moment in history, you have done what the cynics said we couldn't do.*
>
> *I'd especially like to thank the organizers and the precinct captains, the volunteers, and the staff who made this all possible . . . I know you didn't do this for me. You did this because you believed so deeply in the most American of ideas—that in the face of impossible odds, people who love this country can change it.*
>
> *The belief that our destiny will not be written for us, but by us, by all those men and women who are not content to settle for the world as it is, who have the courage to remake the world as it should be.*
>
> *That is what we started here in Iowa, and that is the message we can now carry to New Hampshire and beyond. The same message we had when we were up and when we were down; the*

*one that can save this country, brick by brick, block by block, callused hand by callused hand, that together, ordinary people can do extraordinary things.*

**Corey Munson, Sioux City, IA, Precinct Captain:** At that instant I realized how big things had gotten—how they had exploded beyond what I thought was possible. The recognition that this thing could end up beyond our wildest expectations.

**Alba Perez, Des Moines, IA, Volunteer:** It was very emotional for me. I was crying, because I never thought, in all my life here, thirty years as an immigrant, that I would see the day. Where I could say to my children, "You can see yourself up there. Maybe you don't want to be president, but you can see someone that looks like you."

**Carrianna Suiter:** We were all transitioning between crying and laughing and crying and laughing, the volunteers, the organizers, my friends who'd come in from out of state. We got a message that there was gonna be a call at midnight with Obama, so we went down to the office. It was organizers and volunteers, the core group that had been there every day for months. We were listening to the call, and Obama was saying thank you.

About that time, I fell asleep on a pile of walk sheets. Everyone else went back to the watch party. I slept in the office the rest of the night.

**Jamal Pope:** There was a conference call that night where the senator talked to us. I guess I won't get in trouble now, but I gave that call-in number to my grandpa and my mom to listen in. My grandfather was just so pumped up, man. I think deep down there was a part of me that was always doing it for him too.

**David Plouffe:** It wasn't just the margin of victory but also the scale of the turnout. Everything had to go right to do that. Can you really increase turnout by an astronomical margin? Will you get young people not just to commit to caucus, including high school seniors, but will you get independents and Republicans to show up? Will you become the second choice for people during the reallocation? We put all of those eggs in the basket of a bunch of twenty-something-year-olds. And they made it happen.

**David Axelrod, Chief Strategist:** To me, it was politics at its purest. Politics that was motivated by a sense of idealism. Politics that was motivated by a real conviction that through this process, you can leverage change. That night was filled with possibility.

**David Plouffe:** Even when I talk about it, it sounds a little bit too precious. But it was a remarkable achievement. It wasn't just the gateway to the nomination and the presidency. There was something that was really special about it. To me, it's what can be good about politics. What can be good about people believing in something, even if it's a real long shot. What can be good about people banding together in common cause.

Before we flew to New Hampshire, Obama spent some time with the Iowa caucus leadership team, and it was very emotional. A lot of tears. A lot of hugs. I think he realized they had done this for him.

**Michael Blake:** He had no voice. He just kept saying, "Thank you."

**Paul Tewes:** I hugged him. And the first thing I said was, "We made history."

**Paulette Aniskoff:** I think one of the reasons the president still gets weepy every time he talks about Iowa is there were a bunch of young people who didn't want jobs in the White House—they weren't looking to go into politics to get a leg up or add a line to their bio when they ran for office. They just really wanted something to be different, and they thought he was the guy to do it. They worked their hearts out for all the right reasons, and that is a unique and beautiful thing.

**Barack Obama:** I just loved that team. They had given me so much and had such faith in me and carried me over the finish line. I gave them big hugs and told them how much I appreciated them.

That's probably the other time I teared up. Because what had happened in Iowa was really their accomplishment—it wasn't mine. Ultimately, we would go and lose New Hampshire, and we would win South Carolina, and have all the ups and downs of the campaign. And my broader team of Ax and Gibbs and Plouffe and everybody rightly could take credit for the incredible national organization that we built.

And I'll take a little credit for eventually becoming a pretty good candidate. But Iowa really belonged to those kids. It was their achievement. And I was there to witness it. And it was, I think, as good and clean a politics as this country has ever seen.

Obama Takes Iowa in a Big Turnout as Clinton Falters; Huckabee Victor
—New York Times, January 4, 2008

**Bam Slams Hillary in Historic Victory. He's First Black to Win Iowa Caucus as Voters Embrace Message of Change**
—New York Daily News, January 4, 2008

University of Iowa Campus Precinct: Clinton Gains No Delegates at Youth-Heavy Gathering
—Des Moines Register, January 4, 2008

**Focus Turns to the Independent Voters; In New Hampshire, Unaffiliated Are Key for McCain, Obama**
—Wall Street Journal, January 4, 2008

Obama Rockets Past Clinton in New Hampshire
—Reuters, January 7, 2008

**Obama Has 13-Point New Hampshire Lead**
—New York Post, January 7, 2008

Can Clinton's Emotions Get Best of Her?
—ABC News, January 7, 2008

**Clinton Is Victor, Turning Back Obama; McCain Also Triumphs**
—New York Times, January 8, 2008

Polls Were Right About McCain but Missed the Call on Clinton's Primary Win
—Washington Post, January 9, 2008

**For Democrats, Nevada Is a Throw of the Dice; A Win Would Provide a Boost, but Candidates Must Gamble That Voters Know the Caucus Game**
—Wall Street Journal, January 16, 2008

Judge Allows Casino Sites for Nevada Caucuses
—Washington Post, January 18, 2008

**Clinton, Obama Exchange Harsh Words in South Carolina Debate**
—Wall Street Journal, January 22, 2008

In South Carolina, It's Obama vs. Clinton. That's Bill Clinton
—New York Times, January 22, 2008

**S.C. Primary May Come Down to Race Divide**
—Politico, January 22, 2008

# 8

# EARLY STATES

*January 2008*

*T*he final delegate breakdown from the caucuses was Obama, 37.6 percent; Edwards, 29.7 percent; and Clinton, 29.4 percent. Joe Biden and Chris Dodd dropped out of the race that night after failing to break 1 percent. Beyond the fact that we won, the turnout was the top story. The caucuses are traditionally dominated by retirees, but that night the percentage of caucus goers under thirty years old and over sixty-five years old were exactly the same—57 percent of those young people stood in our corner.

On January 4, I woke up to a world in which an Obama presidency suddenly seemed possible for the first time. New Hampshire would vote on January 8, followed by Nevada and South Carolina later that month. As in Iowa, for most of the past year, we had been losing in New Hampshire, but the hope was a repeat of John Kerry's experience in 2004: the caucus victory would give us enough momentum to pull off a win in the subsequent early states. On February 5, twenty-two states would vote, and that was the day we all assumed the nomination would be decided.

I had never thought seriously about what I would do after Iowa, but it quickly became clear there was little time to celebrate. My future and the futures of my fellow Iowa organizers were placed in the hands of Jon Carson, the man in charge of the campaign's nationwide field operations.

**Jon Carson, February 5 Director:** There were three very distinct plans prepared for after Iowa: plan A, plan B, and plan C.

Plan C was, "We got beat so bad, this is all over—God bless you, you can go home now."

Plan B was, "We're still in this fight, but we don't expect we're gonna have any money—here's a map to Idaho if you can get there on your own. Your Barack Obama email account will still work."

Plan A was, "You're gonna get a $600 work stipend, and we have a gas card for you. Here's your plan."

I was driving through Iowa as the caucus results were starting to come in. I emailed Plouffe and said, "Are we a 'go' with plan A?"

And he responded back, "Go."

So the day after the caucuses, we called all the Iowa staff together. We had everyone get on a conference call from the hinterlands of Iowa, while the room was full of Des Moines staff, and walked them through how this was going to work: "Some of you are gonna go to Nevada, some of you are gonna go to South Carolina, but most of you are going to February 5 states."

**Greg Degen, Field Organizer:** At no point had I ever considered what would happen after the Iowa caucuses. In my mind, January 3 was a cliff we went off with no thought of what was beneath us. After this conference call, I realized that I could just continue working on the campaign.

**Lauren Kidwell, Regional Field Director:** My whole team got split up and sent to different states, and I wanted to take more of my people with me to my next state. I felt very emotional. And I also felt pretty entitled following our big win—too much so. I remember Chelsea Waliser and I having a conversation with Jon Carson, the national field director—taking him to task for the way people were assigned—which, in retrospect, is mortifying because (a) he is so nice and (b) he outranked us so greatly. I remember him being so pleasant and tolerating this rant from two Iowa regional field directors, whereas a lesser person would have been like, "Who the fuck are you guys?"

**Yohannes Abraham, Field Organizer:** There wasn't a lot of opportunity for preference voicing. They gave you a date to be there, told you where you were going, and sent you on your way. I got told I was going to South Carolina, another early state.

**Anne Filipic, Iowa Field Director:** There wasn't time for the sentimentality you would expect. It was very operational, because it had to be. None of it mattered if we didn't do the next thing really well too.

**Linda Langston, Linn County, IA, Supervisor:** A lot of people had been here almost a year. It was bittersweet on both sides. People were leaving relationships that they built, people that they'd come to count on.

**Megan Simpson, Field Organizer:** At 7:00 p.m. we had to kick volunteers out so we could finish cleaning the office. No one wanted to leave, because it felt that you would never get that feeling back of, "Holy shit. Can you believe that we actually did it?" Everyone wanted to recap their special moments.

**Francis Iacobucci, Des Moines, IA, Field Organizer:** The last night before we all left I remember saying goodbye to Yohannes. It was so uncertain. It was so odd, because it was like winning a big battle and knowing you had to go continue the fight. You were leaving the people you had been in the trenches with for so many months. Who knows if you're ever gonna see them again? And who knows if you're ever gonna do what you did in Iowa again?

**Lauren Kidwell:** All of us kept in touch as people went to other states. I got a lot of emails from my organizers, ones that had always pushed for more resources or more candidate visits in Iowa who went on to other states that were less resourced than Iowa. Those organizers would say, "Oh my God, we had no idea how good we had it when we were in Iowa."

And I was like, "Yeah. That's what I was trying to tell you the whole time."

*Most of my colleagues were deployed to Nevada for the January 19 caucus. I was assigned to Alabama, a February 5 state. My parents suggested my 1990 rusted Toyota Corolla wouldn't make it on the interstate, so I loaded as many campaign materials as could fit into my mother's car, and we drove two days to Montgomery, spending the night in Evansville, Indiana.*

*When I was growing up, my mom had been the person who introduced the idea of political activism to me. She would share stories about working for a Georgia state senator in college, canvassing for Jesse Jackson in the '80s, and taking me to nuclear freeze rallies as an infant. She was never a lock for Obama and as a feminist had struggled somewhat with whether to support Senator Clinton, but it was partly seeing my enthusiasm for Obama that brought her onboard.*

*That drive to Alabama was my first time leaving home in a significant way. She told me later she had expected us to have a long conversation in the car reflecting on the past year and what awaited me in Alabama, where she had once lived for eight years. "I knew you would have an experience there unlike anything you'd had before. I thought it was going to make or break your interest in politics, seeing how this community you didn't understand interacted with each other, especially since it was still an uphill battle with Clinton." I slept nearly the entire drive.*

*We pulled into Birmingham, Alabama. She gassed up the car, and I dropped her off at the airport. When I walked into the Alabama state headquarters in Montgomery, it was January 8, the day of the New Hampshire primary.*

\*       \*       \*

## New Hampshire (Primary Day: January 8)

### January 4, 2008

*New Hampshire Average:* Clinton 39, Obama 27, Edwards 18
*National Polling Average:* Clinton 45, Obama 24, Edwards 14

*The New Hampshire primary has been around even longer than the Iowa caucus, though it currently comes second in the primary calendar. Much like Iowa, its political activists are used to being courted by presidential candidates, and the environment is unique. As with the other early states, the Obama campaign placed dozens of staff there and built a massive field organization.*

**Stephanie Speirs, Field Organizer, Rochester, NH:** Those five days between the Iowa caucus and the New Hampshire primary, all the polls in New Hampshire started to shift our way. We were in the midst of GOTV, and there was incredible energy while we sent dozens and dozens of volunteers out to knock on doors. Then we got a whole bunch of volunteers in from Boston and New York after the Iowa win, and they came in saying, "How can I help?"

When I had started out the summer before, my first house party had only two people show up. Toward the final couple of months leading up to the primary, the rallies started getting bigger, and it felt like we were seeing our theory of organizing manifest itself.

On New Hampshire primary day, we all slept in the office; then we were back at it in the morning, setting up for the first canvassers. GOTV revolved around having your list of neighborhood team leaders, checking in with them, checking with staging location captains, and making sure everyone was set up for every shift of the day.

**Greg Degen:** I was deployed to the volunteer headquarters in Chicago, where I watched the New Hampshire results come in. At this point we had had such a charmed existence. We had just won Iowa. The polling had changed over the past few days and now indicated that we would win New Hampshire. And then the momentum would carry us through Nevada and South Carolina, we would do incredibly well on February 5, Super Tuesday, and Hillary would drop out. That was the sense of how things would go in the five days between January 3 and January 8.

**Stephanie Speirs:** There was never any indication that we wouldn't win until the results started coming in. We had all gone to watch the returns together, assuming we would celebrate together. We kept thinking, "Oh, we're just behind 2 percent; we can get through this and more votes will be counted, and it will happen." And then the gap never got small enough.

**Lauren Kidwell:** As the evening wore on, it became clear we were going to lose New Hampshire. We were having a watch party at our St. Louis office, on the second floor above a bar. The mood in the room was so dark and sad. It was packed with people and getting very hot. Our state director, Mike Dorsey, climbed on a folding table to get the window open, and somebody across the room yelled, "Don't jump! It's not that bad!"

**Marygrace Galston:** I was standing in a room in Chicago where we were watching returns come in. Hillary won New Hampshire. Plouffe turned to me and said, "You're on a plane to Nevada tomorrow."
And I was like, "Oh, fuck."

**Stephanie Speirs:** There was a lot of speculation as we were watching the returns about why this was happening. Some offered the unfair and gendered argument that Hillary cried and got sympathy. My canvassers told me a lot of people at the doors said they didn't vote in the Democratic primary because they didn't think that Obama needed their help, so they voted in the Republican primary or switched their votes at the last minute. I heard that anecdote enough that I was a little shaken. Because in the New Hampshire primary, everyone can vote in either Democratic or Republican primary.

So going into it, it had seemed like organizing would win the day, but it turned out that organizing wasn't enough. And that was hard to stomach.

**Jon Favreau, Speechwriter:** It was shocking. We decided the thrust of the victory speech we had ready was, "Even if we win, the road ahead is going to be long and difficult. Not just to get to the nomination, not just to get the presidency, but even if we have the presidency." He wanted to convey that, so when we lost, the speech worked anyway. It's the speech that everyone knows with the only difference being that at the top it originally said, "Thank you, New Hampshire, for the victory."

> BARACK OBAMA [Speech Excerpt]: The reason we began this improbable journey almost a year ago is because it's not just about what I will do as president. It is also about what you, the people who love this country, the citizens of the United States of America, can do to change it.
>
> That's why tonight . . . belongs to the organizers, and the volunteers, and the staff who believed in this journey and rallied so many others to join the cause.
>
> We know the battle ahead will be long. But always remember that, no matter what obstacles stand in our way, nothing can stand in the way of the power of millions of voices calling for change.
>
> We have been told we cannot do this by a chorus of cynics. And they will only grow louder and more dissonant in the weeks and months to come.
>
> We've been asked to pause for a reality check. We've been warned against offering the people of this nation false hope. But in the unlikely story that is America, there has never been anything false about hope.
>
> For when we have faced down impossible odds, when we've been told we're not ready or that we shouldn't try or that we

*can't, generations of Americans have responded with a simple creed that sums up the spirit of a people: Yes, we can.*

**Stephanie Speirs:** There were key moments in that campaign where his speeches saved a lot of people and helped them move forward. That "Yes, We Can" speech was one for me. There was no alternative but to keep going.

**Greg Degen:** His concession speech became the very famous "Yes, We Can" speech. People were a little uplifted by that but still mostly disappointed. That night there was an all-staff midnight conference call with David Plouffe.

**Thomas Zimmerman, Field Organizer:** The whole message from Plouffe was supposed to be reassuring. "Don't worry . . . we have a plan." He almost had a tremble in his voice.

**David Plouffe, Campaign Manager:** My message that night was, "We have a plan. This definitely was not part of the plan. But we've got two states coming up, Nevada and South Carolina, and we've got great organizations in the states after that." Because of them, I was confident. I don't know how much I was trying to convince myself or everybody else.

**Thomas Zimmerman:** Then he closed with, "Let's go win this fucking thing."

**Greg Degen:** "Let's go win this fucking thing." I was sitting in the bathtub, listening to this conference call with the campaign manager talking about how we were going to "win this fucking thing." But it was still dawning on me that there was a fucking thing to win.

**Jon Carson:** You've got to understand, the idea of a drawn-out primary—that had not happened in such a long time. People viewed it as, "Someone wins these early states and rolls into the nomination." After we lost New Hampshire, people didn't know what to think. That conference call with Plouffe was the first moment people were waking up to what this might be like.

**Greg Degen:** I was trying to understand what this would mean and also how I could be a part of it. Because I knew I needed to be a part of it. The next day I went and said, "I'd really like to be part of this deployment to Nevada." I felt it was very important that I arrive by when the campaign expected me to get there, but they didn't give me enough time to drive two thousand miles. So I drove almost a hundred miles per hour across the desert in a Nissan Altima, in the middle of the night. I was so tired that I was seeing things on the highway that were not there.

\*   \*   \*

### Nevada (Caucus Day: January 19)

**January 10, 2008**

*Nevada Average:* Clinton 38, Obama 34, Edwards 18
*National Polling Average:* Clinton 38, Obama 31, Edwards 16

*Over the next two weeks, I would receive text and email updates from Iowans who had arrived in Nevada. No matter where you ended up, it was becoming clear how different every other state would be compared with Iowa.*

**Marygrace Galston:** I experienced this firsthand when I was on the Kerry campaign, so I know what it's like to leave Iowa. You feel like a hero—you won, and then you go to a state where they have been working for months and haven't received anything near what you did. Haven't seen the candidate much. Don't have materials. Don't have printers. And all of it is because of you. These people have had to do a lot with nothing, because Iowa got all the resources.

It wasn't that you weren't welcomed. They were excited to have trained staff. All of that knowledge and information was going to be super helpful in the states that came next. Everything was going to be faster with less information, less money, less materials, and you were also working with staff that may or may not hold some resentment toward you about the fact that you took all the money and attention for so long.

You realize pretty quickly that they're not going to have a parade in your honor—you have to hit the ground running.

*Unlike Iowa and New Hampshire, Nevada had never been an early state before. The turnout for 2008 ended up being ten times what it was four years earlier, a reflection of how much the state had come to matter. The politics of Nevada were different as well. Gaming industry unions held significant political power, and since the caucuses would take place in the middle of a workday, nine "at-large" caucuses were scheduled in several casinos.*

**Greg Degen:** I got to Nevada nine days before the caucus. When I was in Iowa, it was two organizers who were covering thirteen precincts. When I got to Nevada, I was paired with this organizer, and he was responsible for forty-eight precincts.

But I was struck by the culture difference between the voters. In Iowa, the people that we were trying to get to go to the caucus were very highly informed, very highly engaged, and expected to see the candidates themselves. And in the rest of the country, people had a more reasonable expectation of how much they were going to be able to meet presidential candidates. So the intensity of the conversations was far lower.

**Maggie Thompson, Nevada Field Organizer:** Nevada wasn't used to being an early state. It really was like the wild, wild west. There was a lot of anxiety about how a caucus was going to work, because the state traditionally had some of the lowest voting and volunteer rates in the country. People didn't know what the word *caucus* meant. Some of the union dudes we dealt with were like, "I'll show you my caucus."

Nevada's such a big state—the average turf was massive. On top of that, the party created "workplace caucuses," which were nine locations on the Vegas Strip where casino workers could caucus during their shift instead of having to go back to their neighborhood. As an organizer, my job was to take this different model of community organizing—workplace unionization organization—and apply it to an electoral campaign. Instead of being a neighborhood on a map, my "turf" was six casinos, and all of the workers at those casinos were my responsibility.

**Esther Morales, Nevada Field Organizer:** I was on the "at-large" team, and our turf was casinos. So our job was to try to identify volunteers and leaders in the unions. Many leaders of the Service Employees International Union (SEIU) were backing Edwards, so we had to be creative. For example, the employee entrances are underneath casinos—workers walk in, and they show a badge. We would scour these casinos for ways to get into the underground cafeterias. One time

I got dressed up in a suit and walked into the employee entrance. The guard was like, "Hey, can I see your badge?"

I was like, "I'm just a consultant for HR," and he let me through. We would always find these employee cafeterias and hop from table to table—without fail, ten to thirty minutes in, we would get kicked out by security. Then we would come back and do it all again.

We would try to go out to the casinos at 2:00 a.m. We would wait for workers to change their shifts, and we would try to talk to them on their way out. There was one area that I could get to where the employees took their smoke breaks. I don't smoke cigarettes, but I was like, "Today, I'm going to smoke cigarettes." I met this union leader who invited me to his house. Of course, I was a little freaked out, but Maggie came with me, and he ended up becoming one of our volunteers.

**Maggie Thompson:** The hostesses at casinos were good connectors. The iron workers were amazing. They're known to be a bit wild. There was one guy with the big iron workers local in Vegas—I went to pitch him on working with us. He always carried a loaded gun, and when I sat down across from him, he set it on the desk on its side in the holster facing my direction. He was like, "What can I do for you?"

**Esther Morales:** My greatest volunteer was Joan, a woman who was seventy-nine years old and a poker dealer. She would work all night, finish her shift around 8:00 a.m., and then come to the campaign office and volunteer with me. We would try to make calls between 10:00 a.m. and noon, and then she would take me to the casinos she worked at until I got kicked out.

She had incredible stories about Vegas in the old days. Her daughter didn't go to college, and she had lost her husband. She felt lonely, and I think she really believed in Barack Obama and wanted opportunities for her daughter. She was Filipina and loved the fact that he was a person of color.

**Maggie Thompson:** On the day of the Nevada caucuses, I went to my casino workplace caucus, and all of these folks in the casino caucuses were shift workers. A lot of them were in their uniforms. The lines were long. People started saying, "Oh my God. I have to get back to my floor for my shift." The way it was set up, it was not an inclusive process.

It wasn't, "This is democracy, and this is me getting to talk with my neighbors and friends." It was tense and chaotic and really, really

anxiety inducing. I somehow got stuck next to one of the Clinton law-
yers at the Bellagio caucus site. When it became apparent that we were
going to lose that location, he said, "This is for Iowa."

**Greg Degen:** At my caucus site, there were eight hundred people in
a high school gymnasium. The person who had been designated by
the party to run the meeting did not know the rules. The only person
who was there who had been at a large caucus and seen how it was
supposed to run was me, because I'd been in Iowa. So I went up to the
party official and helped them work through the paperwork, and at a
certain point, I was just running the caucus. A professional staffer for
one of the campaigns. Far from neutral. The party official welcomed
my doing this, because the disorganization was so high.

There were other stories from across the state about how other
campaigns were trying to close the doors early. It was the opposite of
Iowa. It didn't give you a lot of faith in the process.

**Maggie Thompson:** It was a complete mess. Some of it was because it
was the first time the party had ever run a caucus. That afternoon after
it was all over we all went back to the office and were so angry.

We did win the delegates in Nevada, because while we got absolutely slaughtered in Vegas, we ended up winning the rural areas.

\*    \*    \*

### Alabama (Election Day: February 5 . . . except Mobile County, January 30)

#### January 23, 2008

*Alabama Polling Average:* Clinton 43, Obama 28

*Shortly after arriving in Alabama, I was sent to Mobile, where I learned
the county had scheduled their voting day a week before February 5,
to avoid conflicting with Mobile's annual Mardi Gras celebration. This
should have been a signal to me that the nuances of local political culture
would shape our approach moving forward.*

*In Mobile, I attended a local county Democratic Party meeting,
where Joe Reed was on the agenda. Reed was a legend in Alabama. As a
young man, he had gotten involved in the civil rights movement. In 1968,
he became one of the first Black people from Alabama ever to attend a*

*Democratic convention, before establishing himself as one of the most powerful political leaders in the state. He controlled an organization with active chapters in nearly every county that was considered vital for turning out Black voters.*

*Reed had endorsed Senator Clinton, and his remarks at this public meeting would later be quoted in the Mobile Bay Times: "Nothing, nothing, nothing, nothing's more important than beating the Republicans. It's much easier for a Black to be for Obama than for Hillary Clinton, but I'm for this country first. I'm for someone who can beat the Republicans. I believe I know who the Republicans would rather run against, and it's not Hillary."*

*More than any specific remark, the subtext of his speech—one he amplified in press interviews—was that Barack Obama was unlikely to be elected president because of his race.*

*Five party officials spoke that day. All pledged their support for Hillary Clinton and asked to be elected as her delegate to the Democratic convention. There was one speaker for the Obama campaign: me.*

*I cited the fact that Alabama was my birthplace (I lived in Auburn till I was six) and "rediscovered" a long-lost southern accent. My three-minute speech stressed Obama's opposition to the war and my experience seeing his appeal firsthand in Iowa. "Race is no longer a barrier to election," I brashly declared. "If he can win in Iowa, he can win anywhere."*

*Prior to Alabama, my conversations about race had with voters been private, one-on-one, and—given the demographics of my turf in Iowa— almost entirely with white liberals who lived in racially homogenous communities. "I'm pretty sure anyone who won't vote for him because he's African American isn't voting Democrat anyway," I would say when the subject came up, and that was usually enough to move on.*

*Looking around that room, reflecting on the speakers, it began to dawn on me that this remained an open question.*

*    *    *

## South Carolina (Primary Day: January 26)

### January 20, 2008

*South Carolina Average: Obama 38, Clinton 27, Edwards 19*
*National Polling Average: Clinton 41, Obama 33, Edwards 14*

*The results in Nevada reflected an emerging theme of the primary— much like the electoral college, it was a contest not for votes but for* delegates who would be elected to the Democratic National Convention and ultimately determine the Democratic nominee. Nevada was considered a split decision. Clinton had more people show up, but because of how Obama's supporters were distributed in the caucuses, he came out one delegate ahead.

As the campaign became increasingly competitive, the remarks about other candidates cut deeper. Obama's team ran a radio ad saying, "She'll say anything, and change nothing . . . it's time to turn the page." The head of Black Entertainment Television, a prominent Clinton supporter, was forced to publicly apologize for saying, "As an African American, I'm frankly insulted that the Obama campaign would imply that we are so stupid that we would think Bill and Hillary Clinton, who have been deeply and emotionally involved in Black issues when Barack Obama was doing something in the neighborhood that—and I won't say what he was doing, but he said it in his book—when they have been involved." It was the second time in a month that a major Clinton surrogate had referenced passages about Obama's teenage drug use in Dreams from My Father.

All of this put more pressure on the team in South Carolina. Both the Obama and Clinton campaigns had invested significant resources there, and since (as he never tired of reminding people) John Edwards had grown up in a South Carolina mill town, he pledged to fight hard.

South Carolina was the only early state with a significant African American population. As I read the coverage about South Carolina from Iowa, a running theme over the past year had been that many older African American political leaders endorsed Senator Clinton, partly a reflection of her and former president Clinton's long-standing relationship with the state. Bill Clinton devoted significant time to campaigning there in the lead-up to the primary, and election press coverage explicitly referenced race more and more. This reached a head when President Clinton appeared to belittle the Obama campaign's strength in South Carolina by saying, "Senator Clinton and Obama are getting votes, to be sure, because of their race or gender, and that's why people tell me that Hillary doesn't have a chance to win here."

It was in this environment that organizers from Iowa first met their colleagues who had been working South Carolina since spring 2007.

**Yohannes Abraham:** I drove down with Mike Blake from Iowa to South Carolina. We showed up at the HQ in Columbia, and there was a sign saying "Welcome, Iowa Heroes." From there, I got sent to Orangeberg, where a woman named Elizabeth Wilkins was the regional field director, and I worked for her.

**Elizabeth Wilkins, Orangeberg, SC, Regional Field Director:** Once the focus shifted to South Carolina, people came from everywhere. I remember being very grateful for Yohannes, because he knew what he was doing. We didn't see each other very much, because I was like, "Great, I trust you. I am going to send you very far away, and you just need to do this yourself," because my turf was very large.

I had seven of the poorest, most rural, Blackest counties in the state. The way things worked there historically was that you paid the local political boss, who had people they controlled. So the traditional model, which we rejected, was you paid them, and they got those people to the polls to vote for whomever they were supposed to vote for.

It was super different from New Hampshire or Iowa, where people feel like they have a special place in the civic life of the country. South Carolina felt like a place where many ordinary people did not see themselves as agents in the process. People were not used to being asked directly what they thought about who to vote for. Our biggest foe was not another candidate. It was some combination of apathy and the existing political system.

**Yohannes Abraham:** It was a different set of norms and expectations in rural South Carolina. There was also a different organizing model. Until arriving in South Carolina, I assumed that the only way to do X, Y, or Z was the way Mitch Stewart or Anne Filipic or Paul Tewes taught me.

**Jeremy Bird, South Carolina Field Director:** Yohannes showed up from Iowa in his "Des Moines: Hell Yes" shirt, and I was like, "No, no, no, no. Here, you're going to have to pray before you kick off a canvass, man."

**Yohannes Abraham:** As a young organizer, you don't realize that your experience is just one possible style. You had to make that adjustment when you went to a different state.

**Chris Wyant, South Carolina Data Analyst:** In South Carolina, we believed we were building toward something where volunteer leaders, members of the community who were from South Carolina, were going to take real responsibility for turning out their community. To do that, we spent months developing relationships with people and giving them the skills to build their own relationships. These volunteer leaders, when all was said and done, weren't even knocking doors themselves on Election Day. They were directing their own teams of volunteers.

That was the dream. How we got there was through one-on-one conversations and house meetings where you spent two hours going around a room with people sharing their personal stories, talking about what issues they cared about. Of the thousands and thousands of house meetings we did across the state over the course of nine months leading up to January, the average size was twelve people. That structure meant that so much of our voter contact was in the last month.

**Jeremy Bird:** We weren't actually talking to very many voters at all in the early months. Our best organizer would have five to seven one-on-ones a day, meeting with thirty to forty people a week as opposed to calling four hundred people a night. The whole theory was you build up your volunteer base early, and you develop those volunteers into real leaders. We spent time building deep relationships with people, making sure our organizers knew all the barbershops and beauty salon owners, knew the pastors in each of the churches.

We had these people at house meetings, and unlike Iowa, the candidate wasn't in the house. It was our organizer, with a video of our candidate, talking about how you get involved.

**Chris Wyant:** Political elites in South Carolina, people sincerely trying to help us, were like, "That's just not going to work. There's not a culture of that, and that's not something that you can turn on overnight. The best way to win this is to pay people in certain communities to turn out the vote."

We totally rejected that thinking and entirely focused on finding and engaging volunteers. For five or six months, that did not translate into substantial voter contact.

**Jeremy Bird:** That was a different way of approaching politics than had been traditionally done there—you weren't turning organizers into basically telemarketers or taking just a handful of people who are supposedly the connected elites and letting them decide which campaign gets blessed in that county.

The other thing we heard over and over again from people—especially older African Americans and younger white volunteers—is that this was the first time they had seen a campaign put together a racially diverse volunteer team in some of these places.

At one Democratic Party event, somebody introduced me to one of the state representatives who had endorsed Senator Clinton. He basically patted me on the head and was like, "I love what you guys are trying to do—getting young people and African Americans who haven't voted before. It's really great for the state long term that you're trying, but you know that's not going to happen."

I thought about that conversation forever—the smugness of it but also the history behind it. That history was hovering there the entire year. I remember on our first day of action, there was this big fear that people weren't going to show up, because the traditional consensus was that poor Black people in South Carolina don't volunteer.

**Nicole Young, Columbia, SC, Field Organizer:** I joined the campaign on May 13, 2007, two days after college graduation, and deferred law school. It seemed really insane to my parents. I am a Black woman from a working-class family, and they were worried that if you took time away from school, you would never go back. It was like, "You're going to not go to law school to go work for this man who's not anywhere close to winning?" Because at that point Barack Obama was completely unknown and really, really far behind the polls.

**Lauren Champagne, Charleston, SC, Field Organizer:** You have to remember, in South Carolina, in the beginning, they had no idea who Barack Obama was. First, everybody knew who Hillary Clinton was. Then, for the Black community in particular, there was deep, deep concern that he would be killed. You're talking about people who were adults and young children during Jim Crow, during the civil rights movement, when our leaders were dying. They said, "If we make him the first Black president, we're essentially setting him up for assassination." It was widespread.

**Yohannes Abraham:** In South Carolina, I didn't spend a ton of time talking about race. It was subtle. You heard people express concerns about his safety, and you heard people say stuff like, "*They're* never gonna let him win," with the *they* being undefined but also assumed. Most of the voters and volunteers I dealt with—their willingness to believe in the prospect of this candidacy wasn't expressed in explicit terms.

**Michael Blake, South Carolina Political Outreach:** When I was in Charleston, I saw the Old Slave Mart, where slaves were auctioned. It wasn't just talking about the history. You saw it. You saw that, and you started to think, "This is bigger than an election. This is about fulfilling a promise that seemed impossible for so many people."

**Lauren Champagne:** My whole family is from South Carolina. I went to high school and college there. Being an African American, this was all very personal. My family lived through Jim Crow, lived through the Voting Rights Act. They understood what it meant not to have the right to vote. I had family members that never participated in politics at all that were knocking on doors. A lot of that was because of that history and because they understood they had the opportunity to be a part of electing the first African American president. That was a huge thing.

That was something that we constantly communicated to people in the community. It wasn't just, "Vote for him because he's Black." I used to tell them, "Vote for him because he's the best candidate and he's qualified. But know that he is standing on the shoulders of the giants that fought for us to have the right to vote and the right to be seen as fully human. His election would be a huge testament to that struggle."

**Elizabeth Wilkins:** It was different from the more center-stage thing that played out in Iowa and New Hampshire. I think we had a narrative for ourselves that we were doing something for South Carolina that was going to last well beyond January 2008. Like, our mission wasn't just to win the primary for Barack Obama but to put in place an alternate political structure. In South Carolina I did not feel very connected to the rest of the campaign. I felt way more connected to our field director and felt like South Carolina was our own little bubble.

It felt like what we were doing was unproven, untested. It was arrogant in some ways because we were walking into South Carolina and disregarding the advice of South Carolina politicos, including the ones who were rabidly pro–Barack Obama but thought that we were going to ruin things.

There was something about being in the first really Black primary state for a Black candidate that made it feel like we were doing something special when it came to race and self-empowerment in America. It was different from—not more special than, just different from—convincing white people in Iowa to vote for him. Convincing Black people to believe in themselves enough to vote for him felt like a different project.

**Nicole Young:** We had more Black organizers in South Carolina than any of the early primary states. And part of the reason why is, early on, Jeremy realized that having a lot of young, enthusiastic white people from out of state was really not going to connect with people on the ground. They needed people from South Carolina—they needed people who were Black—because the questions that we were getting about things that were holding people back from supporting Barack Obama were deeply grounded in race.

Black voters' number one concern was that this man was going to be assassinated. Because they did not believe we lived in a country in which white people would elect a Black man, and if he got close enough, someone would not kill him. Thinking about people in the South who'd watched all of their great hopes, all of the people who had led transformative change in this country on behalf of Black people, be murdered, it totally makes sense. White organizers got those questions too, and they had to learn how they were going to talk about it as white people. But I think there was a lot of comfort when we as Black organizers were like, "Hey, those are our concerns too. We're fighting anyways, because we think this is the right candidate for the job, and we believe that he will make it. And he will not only win but live to govern."

**Lauren Champagne:** When they said, "We're afraid he's going to die," I'd be like, "This man is highly educated. He knows his history. He knows what happened in the past, and he still has the courage to run. All he's asking you to do is have the courage to vote." That usually worked.

**Nicole Young:** As Black organizers, we shouldered a lot of the burden of that. We were able to be translators, to speak directly to the concerns, because those were concerns we had had ourselves or had to discuss with our family. It's just a different thing than white organizers who were coming in with "hope and change." They had to adjust and be able to address the fears and concerns of a lot of Black voters.

**Lauren Champagne:** We started by going into the homes of leaders in the community or into barbershops in spring and summer of 2007. The goal was to organize on a grassroots level. Then eventually those community members that had house parties or let you into their barbershop would become your leaders and run their own campaign office out of their homes or their businesses.

**Nicole Young:** Early on, I cold-called Mrs. Bennett, this eighty-six-year-old woman on my list. I was expecting to get a "commit" or "no commit" for Barack Obama, because eighty-six-year-olds typically don't volunteer. We stayed on the phone for super long, and she really wanted to meet me. We had a one-on-one at her apartment and talked for hours.

**Annie Corine Bennett, Columbia, SC, Volunteer:** I said to Nicole, "Whatever you need me to do, I'll be happy to do it. This is a day I have lived for, to see a Black man run for president."

I had never had any dealing with politics before. My grandmother was a slave. She had twelve children. My mother was a schoolteacher, and my father was a farmer at a time when you had to go to the back of the bus and there were always signs for "Negros" and signs for "Whites" at drinking fountains. I came through all of that and had an opportunity to work for somebody who was trying to bring the country together—I felt that was what Obama would do. Reading his flyers and hearing him speak, seeing Michelle—I just believed in him.

So I started.

**Nicole Young:** I expected maybe I could convince her to come do a couple of phone calls. But she wanted to do anything she could for Barack Obama. At our first big canvass, I gave her a small turf. She came back an hour later and was annoyed with me. She had finished it and was like, "It was too short. I want a bigger packet."

Every week she would come, and she'd have twenty supporter cards. She had gone to church, to her senior yoga class, to the grocery store and talked people into committing for Barack Obama. She would get voters registered. She just was killing it, and her story was so amazing. For her to be such an active and vibrant volunteer was really beautiful and touching. She was so kind and loved everybody. She epitomized what we were trying to do.

**Lauren Champagne:** We built those relationships for nearly a year. It was beautiful. I would go into the homes of people who had never voted—people forty, fifty, sixty years old who had never registered to vote. Those people became like family. Barack Obama brought you here, but it's us, the community—that's the reason why you stay and you volunteer. That model basically turned these unpaid volunteers into campaign leaders.

Once we did all that, Iowa showed them he could win. We had done a lot of the hard work to show this was the guy you should vote for. Once he won Iowa, that was the last piece we needed, because they saw he was able to win this predominantly white state.

**Nicole Young:** The night that Iowa happened, it was one of the most emotional nights of my life. Even though I was working a hundred hours a week for this man, I still wasn't sure we could do it. Iowa proved that we could.

**Chris Wyant:** Iowa Night was incredible. The whole campaign had pinned so much on it, and our strategy in South Carolina was built to capitalize on that energy. There was an incredible volunteer, Mrs. Bennett, who'd come in pretty consistently from the beginning.

**Jeremy Bird:** She was walking away from the TV, tears flowing down her face. I remember hugging her, and she was like, "I just can't believe it. I can't believe white people voted for him."

**Nicole Young:** I think it is hard for people in America, especially white people in America, to think about how recent slavery is. We're not that far from it. And the idea that there was this living, breathing person whose grandmother—whom she remembers—was an enslaved person, working to elect the first Black president, seeing him win the Iowa caucus, and then helping him win the South Carolina primary . . . it's mind-blowing.

**Chris Wyant:** Seeing her in our office crying when he won Iowa, having believed enough to work on behalf of his campaign for months but then, still, to be overwhelmed with emotion by what had happened, you could see with her and so many others, both staff and volunteers, that it went from "Maybe this thing could happen" to "We can really do this."

The reaction to New Hampshire was also incredible in that the next day, we had far more volunteers than we did the day after Iowa. New Hampshire happened, and it rocked people, but the next day they were like, "OK, we've got to work even harder, because yes, we can do this, but no one's handing it to us. It's in our grasp, and we have to work our tails off to do it."

**Jeremy Bird:** In the final weeks, we did a big GOTV training where we brought everybody together. It was just electric—the energy and the talent. You look at this room of hundreds of volunteers who had dedicated hundreds of hours of their time to this campaign and knew the scripts, knew their communities, had developed other leaders.

And you think back to when we first got there and people said, "No one's even going to volunteer for you; that's not how it's done here." That's when it felt like we'd really built something. We had gone deep into the barbershops and beauty salons, deep into the churches, deep into the HBCUs, and done thousands of house meetings. And all those people were going to run their own staging locations on Election Day.

**Lauren Champagne:** In the final weeks leading up to the South Carolina primary, we had hundreds of people flooding into our offices. The organizers from New Hampshire showed up, but then all these people from different parts of the country came in to help.

**Stephanie Speirs:** In South Carolina I was shocked how much easier it was to talk to people about Barack Obama in Orangeburg compared to New Hampshire. People in Orangeburg were so excited to talk about Barack Obama, and it was a pleasure to organize an area where people seemed receptive to this presidential candidate, compared to New Hampshire, which lacked a certain level of diversity.

**Jeremy Bird:** I remember being on a call after Nevada where they said, "If Obama spends all this time in South Carolina, we have to win it big, because otherwise it will reinforce a national narrative that he can win the African American vote but can't win white voters."

That was a big fear we had: if we blow out the African American vote at 80–90 percent but we get 5–10 percent of the white vote, then there's a whole narrative that isn't good for the campaign. That was the thing: we couldn't just win by five points; we needed to blow it out.

And the only way to blow it out was to get 20–25 percent with white voters.

**Chris Wyant:** I don't remember Saturday, January 26, Election Day in South Carolina, very well. It all unfolded in the way that it was supposed to. The only thing that was memorable was when the returns started coming in. We knew we were going to win at that point, but to win by twenty-eight points was unfathomable. The turnout was unfathomable. We had all sorts of different turnout models. Nothing close to over half a million people.

**Lauren Champagne:** When the returns started coming in, it was a decisive victory. Within five minutes of polls closing, we got this huge announcement that he won. I was crying. The volunteer that was with me was crying.

**Jeremy Bird:** The thing that really struck me was how historic it felt when I was walking in Columbia to the victory rally.

**Jon Favreau:** The audience started chanting, "Race doesn't matter! Race doesn't matter!"

**Jeremy Bird:** Everybody was talking about it backstage like, "Did they start chanting that? What the hell?" Not sure I totally agree with the chant, but it was cool.

> **From:** David Plouffe
> **Sent:** Saturday, January 26, 2008 7:19 PM
> **To:** #Staff-SC
> **Subject:** Back on track
> You guys hung the moon tonight—and picked up the whole campaign. And I would submit, the whole country. You built something people scoffed at—a real field organization—and dealt with as an intense week of politics as many of us will ever go through.
>
> Savor it—you just played an enormous role in shaping the future of our country and world.
>
> And kicked the ass of some who were sorely in need of a lesson.
>
> On to Denver.

**Nicole Young:** The next morning we had a final internal staff rally at the Columbia office. Mrs. Bennett came. I thanked her, and we cried. She had been on stage the night before at the victory rally. I remember her telling me, "Thank you for bringing me into this and making me a part of it."

My volunteers, especially in South Carolina, I hold those people deep in my heart, because the same way they would credit me for making them organizers, they made me an organizer. Before then, I was just a really enthusiastic twenty-two-year-old. But they taught me how to organize. How to talk to different groups of people and appeal to what people needed in order to feel included in the campaign.

And I'm grateful for Mrs. Bennett because, at eighty-six, she showed me a template for how you can continue to be engaged and can continue to be active. It doesn't matter how old you are—if this is something you're passionate about, you can find the energy and the time.

My mom was there, and my little brother, who was eight years old, was with her. And she was like, "It's really amazing this thing you did." That was really cool, for my mom to witness it.

I had never been on a campaign before, so I didn't understand that you wrap up and go on to the next state. I ended up going to six states and one territory over the whole campaign. You began to recognize who had done campaign cycles before and who was brand-new to this. The people who'd done it knew that you pack up and go, and us newbies were like, "We don't just bask in the afterglow of our twenty-eight-point victory?"

Bam in S.C. Landslide. Bill Can't Boost Hil as Barack Racks Up 55% of the State's Vote. He Lands 8 in 10 Blacks, But Rally Cries "Race Doesn't Matter!"
—New York Daily News, January 27, 2008

Kennedy Chooses Obama, Spurning Plea by Clintons
—New York Times, January 28, 2008

Obama Sets Fundraising Record: $32 Million in One Month: Campaign Drew 170,000 New Donors in January
—USA Today, February 1, 2008

Candidates Mobilize as Race Grinds On; Deadlocked Democrats Brace for Long Run; Clinton Seeks Cash, Obama Needs Latinos
—Wall Street Journal, February 6, 2008

Obama Claims Delegate Lead
—Politico, February 6, 2008

Central Texans Jam Caucuses in "Record-Shattering Turnout" Caucus: Campaigns Accuse Each Other of Rule Violations
—Austin American-Statesman, March 5, 2008

Clinton Beats Obama in Texas and Ohio; McCain Clinches Republican Nomination; Democrats Now Look to Pennsylvania
—Washington Post, March 5, 2008

The Origin of Obama's Pastor Problem
—Time Magazine, March 20, 2008

Obama on Small-Town PA: Clinging to Religion, Guns, Xenophobia
—Politico, April 11, 2008

Obama Angers Midwest Voters with Guns and Religion Remark: Comments Seized on by Hillary Clinton, Who Hopes to Turn Voters Against What She Classes as Obama's Revealed "Elitism"
—Guardian, April 14, 2008

Obama Strongly Denounces Former Pastor: Candidate Calls Wright's Recent Comments "Wrong and Destructive"
—NBC News, April 29, 2008

# 9

# LIVING OFF THE LAND

*February–May 2008*

### February 1, 2008

*National Polling Average:* Clinton 45, Obama 36

W*inning South Carolina by a huge margin seemed to unleash a wave of national support. My friends from Iowa were scattered across twenty-two states for the February 5 contests ("Super Tuesday"), and we would excitedly email each other about new endorsements.*

*Caroline and Ted Kennedy: "WHAT THE F? TED KENNEDY??!?!!?!?! Could you have pictured this ever happening back in the fall?"*

*Entertainers: "What's your fantasy? I was just asked to vet Ludacris. He wants to do an event for us in ATL."*

*Athletes: "A member of the US Ski Team just walked into our office and is making calls! Yes, he is cute."*

*Toni Morrison penned an open letter endorsing Obama. Robert DeNiro pledged his support at an event in New Jersey. Maria Shriver and Oprah opened for Obama at a Los Angeles rally. On January 30, John Edwards dropped out of the race, and we started targeting his supporters to switch to Obama. There was a sense that the entire country was waking up to a fight we'd been waging over tiny pieces of turf for a year. And now, half the states would have their say.*

*When I went to bed on February 5, the outcome of that day wasn't clear. Clinton had won big states like California and New Jersey, and expectations for Obama were low. But when I woke up on February 6, I was shocked to find that we were leading Clinton by a dozen pledged*

*delegates. As results had come in from smaller states, many of which
had higher African American populations, like Alabama and Georgia,
or held caucuses, like Idaho, Minnesota, and Colorado, our margin of
victory was so large that it canceled out Clinton's narrower big state wins.*

*Unlike the early states, where our focus had been wins that would
reset the media narrative and drive momentum, the primary became a
competition for delegates to the national convention. Because each state's
delegate apportionment system was unique, Obama had taken a lead
by strategically concentrating on high-delegate regions. Though half the
states had yet to vote and the remaining primaries were spread over the
coming four months, for the first time since Iowa, I was cautiously optimistic we might win the nomination.*

**Jon Carson, Voter Contact Director:** It very quickly became this mul-
tivariate battlefield with all these different dates we were keeping in
mind. There were states that we were probably going to lose, but the
top, overarching primary goal was to win the most delegates.

So we didn't think we had a chance to win the state of New York,
but we thought there were a couple of congressional districts in Brooklyn we could win, so we sent staff to New York.

From the very beginning, it was like this incredibly complicated
chessboard. It wasn't this linear thing. It wasn't, "We all go to a February 5 state, and then we go to a February 12 one."

**Michael Blake, Political Outreach Staffer:** I did Minnesota, Ohio,
Mississippi, Pennsylvania, Indiana. I was going everywhere. We had
ten months to build in Iowa. Going some other place, you might have
three weeks, and you had to maximize the moment.

**Lauren Kidwell, Regional Field Director:** The year of 2008, I didn't
have a home. I didn't have my name on a lease anywhere. Everything I
owned was in my car.

**David Plouffe, Campaign Manager:** Some of the later states were definitely more do-it-yourself. My message to people was, "Well, you've
got to figure it out. This is going to be more lean, and you're going to
have to lean a lot more on your volunteers."

**Jon Carson:** For redeployments, the first and most important thing
was who were going to be the leaders in each of these states. It gave

us an opportunity to train people up. And then I would give them a certain amount of staff to take with them. I would connect them with the team of super volunteers that had been created on the ground. And then we invented the concept of the stipend worker. You can pay someone up to $600 without considering them an employee. So we would tell people, "You've got this number of stipend workers allotted. Just send us their names." A lot of people got picked up by the staff and brought to the next state.

We were giving them the framework to go out and to hunt and kill whatever they needed. They would get an office up and running two days after they arrived in a city, all using in-kind forms and stipend workers.

*As the primary continued after February 5, there was an election nearly every week. My deployments began to follow a routine. Upon arrival in a new state, between a dozen and one hundred organizers would be trained on the local mechanics of voting. Was it a primary or a caucus? Did they have early vote or same-day registration? Were delegates elected by congressional district or statewide? A local surrogate would offer insight into the state's culture and relevant recent political history. After a night in the capital, you would ship out to your assigned turf and meet local volunteers who had been organizing for months with little direction from headquarters. Sometimes they would have opened their own office, printed their own buttons, and set up a local website, all with their own resources. You would live in a supporter's basement or guest room. Your job was to build on the work that predated you.*

**Pat Hynes, Northern Virginia for Obama Volunteer:** The Obama campaign was the first time I really got into politics. It's crazy, because I think of myself as a thoughtful, hardheaded voter. I try not to get into being a fan. But I think I was at that point where—like a lot of people—you keep voting, but you don't believe in very much anymore. You lose that sense that anybody in politics is speaking for you or to you or gives you hope that maybe what you think is important could actually happen. I guess I was at that point without realizing just how pessimistic I had become.

Then, here comes this guy. Barack Obama was speaking about hope. He was brilliant and engaging. He says what you want people to say. It had been so long since I'd felt at all hopeful.

**Yohannes Abraham, Field Organizer:** Pat Hynes was one of the "Northern Virginia for Obama" stalwarts. What was really cool about Virginia was, without a staffer having set foot in the state, particularly in northern Virginia, there was a highly developed, highly organized volunteer network. They had assigned volunteer leadership, they were running regular canvasses, they were running regular phone banks, and they were running regular visibility events at community gatherings.

When I arrived in town, one of the key volunteers organized a meeting for me and the local volunteer leadership. Despite some of the rhetoric, we had a top-down mentality as a campaign in the early states—and during my first meeting with the Virginia volunteer leaders, I had a sense that these guys really knew what they were doing. My job was to facilitate, provide them with resources, provide them with universes to knock, but they had a lot of the actual organizing already done.

**Pat Hynes:** My daughter and I didn't know what we were really doing at first. We knocked on every door in our neighborhood. And this one woman wouldn't even come to the door. She looked through the window and said, "Who are you here for?"

We told her, and she said, "No way!" There was tons of that, and it was hard, but you got a little desensitized to it.

Throughout 2007, I tried to do something every week. And I didn't always meet that goal, but at some point the OFA online tools allowed us to set up house parties and connect with people—some of them two blocks away, but they were people we didn't even know. I set up a group called NoVA for Change, and there were all these groups using the OFA tools across northern Virginia—we set up house parties, we did phone banking, we did a lot of voter registration, and we really got to know each other. That was the value of those nine months before the first staffer came.

**Yohannes Abraham:** They built an operation that was every bit as good as the staff-driven one, and they did it on a volunteer basis before we got there.

**Jon Carson:** We sent a ton of the South Carolina staff up to Virginia and Maryland for February 12. Maryland takes top prize for the most hyper-organized volunteer group that had their act together long before staff ever showed up. We sent Jeremy Bird there for the primary. He called me up first thing when he got there and said, "I'm in

Maryland. I'm in this giant room. There are people calling through lists everywhere. And they just told me this is one of six operations like this they have going on across the state right now."

**Jason Waskey, Maryland for Obama Volunteer State Director:** Maryland didn't get any paid staff until after South Carolina. By then, we had half a dozen offices. We had three thousand identified volunteers. We'd find someone and say, "You're supporting Obama? Great—you're now the deputy vice captain of Dorchester County." We really built that sense of empowerment; volunteers had titles and were making business cards. It was a total rogue operation we were running, but nobody cared enough about Maryland to tell us not to.

**David Plouffe:** I think that's an underappreciated part of the story. Minnesota, Idaho, Wyoming, Georgia, Mississippi—all these states where we ended up doing really well and winning massive delegate margins against Clinton, it was volunteers who set the stage. The folks who found each other on my.barackobama.com, used those tools, did offline events—they made it happen.

We would not have been the nominee without them, because they started before we had staff everywhere. They were identifying community leaders, and they were holding events. We wouldn't have been able to come in there four, eight weeks before and build an organization. The organization was there when staff arrived on the ground.

It was just heroic work. It's a great lesson to trust people and largely leave them to their own devices.

*Having grown up, gone to college, and worked in the same Iowa town, this was really my introduction to the rest of the country. In Fort Worth, Texas, our offices were in the town stockyards, flanked by an always empty Italian restaurant and airbrush T-shirt shop that catered to tourists. I spent three weeks there organizing voters for the Texas primary/caucus ("the Texas two-step!"), an electoral system that required our supporters to "vote" twice by returning to their polling place in the evening for the Texas caucuses. We lost the primary, won the caucuses, and had a net gain of five pledged delegates.*

*A week later I was in Mississippi (where the campaign sprung for hotels!), and after forgetting my suitcase in a Jackson Econo Lodge, I wore the same sweater, olive slacks, and rubber-soled loafers for four days straight. We arrived after the voter registration deadline and would drive*

*to heavily African American precincts to knock every door, not bother-*
*ing to print out walk lists. One low point came when I tried to set up a*
*small "Women for Obama" event along the coast for an out-of-state sur-*
*rogate. I arranged fifty chairs and purchased giant jugs of iced tea at the*
*local Walmart. The room was near empty, the jugs remained full, and the*
*event was a waste of everyone's time.*

*In Indiana I was placed in Bloomington, a college town, six weeks*
*before the primary. Voter registration was a priority; the campaign held*
*a massive free Dave Matthews concert on campus and made our office*
*the only ticket distribution point. Every person in line was asked a half*
*dozen times, "Would you like to register to vote? Would you like to volun-*
*teer for the campaign?" Our press team sent out the concert press release*
*just before Bill Clinton took the stage for his own campus rally. Students*
*started leaving his event to come to our office, leading* The Daily Show *to*
*award us "Dick Move of the Week."*

**Nicole Young, Field Organizer:** The most beautiful part of the campaign for me was getting to see the country that way. I worked in rural
South Carolina. My hometown, Virginia Beach. Suburban Pennsylvania. Urban Charlotte, North Carolina. San Juan, Puerto Rico. The
middle of nowhere in Michigan. Denver, Colorado. All of those places
are vastly different. My favorite thing when I got to each state was trying to figure out which issue paper was most relevant for this group
of people. Because it might be health care in this part of my turf, or it
might be veterans. It was an amazing way to get a pulse on the country.

**Megan Simpson, Field Organizer:** The best way to see a place is to
organize it, because you have to get to know every corner so fast. You
have to get scrappy and find the coffee shops to have one-on-one meetings or the best restaurant that might let you sit in the parking lot while
you steal their Wi-Fi. You're putting together walk packets and sending
volunteers out to knock doors, and if you don't know what the streets
that divide what neighborhood are, you're not going to get volunteer
buy-in.

When I would get to a new place, people were excited about
Obama, but they were also so excited to show off their community, tell
you about it and its history. They wanted you to love it as much as they
did. It connected me with different parts of the country that I would
never have gone to otherwise. This is going to sound corny, but it really
showed me that there's a lot that connects us.

From an organizer's perspective, you don't need to change your approach just because you're in a different place. You ask questions. You learn from people. If you ask the right questions, you can get a good look into not only the values of the person you're meeting but also the spirit of the community.

**Esther Morales, Field Organizer:** What continued to impress me time and time and time again were these people who gave everything during those three weeks or four weeks we were in a place. People opened up their homes and their lives to us across the country—everybody worked so hard to create the campaign that they wanted it to be, whether it was painting a mural on the Texas offices or bringing food or doing the hard canvassing and call work. But you always found people who were with you. There were constantly things that you could get done because you worked with a team—and when I say team, I mean both paid staff and volunteers—that had your back.

**Maggie Thompson, Field Organizer:** When we got to Dallas, this grassroots group set up a welcome event in a honky-tonk with a mechanical bull—it was like the bar from *Urban Cowboy*. We walked in, and there were six hundred people, a sound system, and live band. They brought us up on stage and introduced the twelve of us one by one. "This is your Obama team! Welcome them to Dallas!" It was like this rock star reception. They had organized this massive event with hundreds of people through Facebook and my.barackobama.com. We had a huge volunteer list right at the beginning.

**Nathan Blake, Field Organizer:** We had a rally in Jackson, Mississippi, in a basketball stadium. It filled up an hour before show time. The crowd was mostly African American. Before the event, the crowd started singing Negro spirituals and inserting Obama's name into the lyrics.

**Michael Blake:** I had never been somewhere where people were changing spirituals for an individual. Saying it was emotional was an understatement.

**Dean Fluker, Field Organizer:** It's in those parts of the South you really recognize what you're doing it for. To know that there are just so many large Black communities down there, and to be able to bring this to them, for me, meant the world.

**Megan Simpson:** I knocked on this woman's door in Hattiesburg, Mississippi. "Hi, ma'am, I'm Megan. I'm with Senator Obama's campaign."

She said, "Obama." Her eyes got super wide, and she said excitedly, "I'm going to wait until after school when my granddaughter gets home so she can go with me. It will be the first time I ever voted."

I said, "Wow, that's awesome. Do you know where you need to go?"

And she answered, "Where are you from, Megan?"

"I'm from Dubuque, Iowa, ma'am."

Then she pointed at a school and said, "Look right there. When I was in high school, kids your age came down here to make sure I could go to that school." There was a sign on her street that marked Freedom Summer. And she said, "I'm going to go vote. It will be the first time I do it, and I'm taking my granddaughter with me. Thank you for coming here, Megan, to help make this happen." And I left and started crying.

That was something so very different from what I was knocking on doors for. Until that moment I felt like for me there was so much personally at stake. I wanted my siblings to not have to work multiple jobs when they went to college. I wanted my friend to be able to have health care after coming back from serving in Iraq. And yes, I wanted to elect the first African American, but that wasn't what I woke up every day to do.

I felt like I heard so much talk in the press about Obama and whether the African American vote would turn out for him. You could feel how much it meant for her standing at that door. Until Mississippi I hadn't come across the intensity of what we were doing in that way.

**Jon Carson:** People did learn a lot by going state to state, but there was a pretty strong commonality. Like, Indiana compared to Mississippi are vastly different states culturally, but what they had in common was a whole bunch of Obama volunteers fired up. Something meaningful was actually happening in their states during a presidential race for the first time.

It's an art to be an organizer where there's lots of energy and lots of volunteers but very few staff. What was distinct about that moment in time that is so easy to overlook—the internet and Google were not back then what they are now. Today, it would be easy to just google "where's my caucus location?" That was not a thing back then. Tons of secretaries of state and local county offices didn't have all this readily available online. Or if they did, you would only be able to see it in a Word doc or something. So we pulled together the information on where all of these caucus locations were going to be and invented a caucus lookup tool.

I'll never forget sitting down and going through all this and realizing, "Wait a second, the entire city of Boise is one caucus site in the Taco Bell Arena?"

My favorite was, in Nebraska, the caucuses are not at the same time! Each county picked its location and its time. We would painstakingly put together these caucus location tools. Then our data guys had to build this backend machine that didn't really exist to help you look up your address and where it was. This was all new at the time, but insanely, there were many states where the amount of people who had used our caucus lookup tool was like 60 percent of the total caucus turnout.

Coming off February 5, we won eleven states in a row. But then we got to March 4.

*March 4 was the date of the Ohio and Texas primaries. There was a sense that a victory in both would lead Senator Clinton to drop out. But her campaign was tenacious—she won the Ohio primary by ten points and the Texas primary by four (though we won more delegates in the caucus), guaranteeing the slog would continue at least another two months.*

*Shortly after, the primary calendar entered a lull. It was seven weeks between the day Mississippi voted, March 11, and Pennsylvania's primary on April 22, followed soon after by Indiana and North Carolina on May 6. Most of the Obama organizers I knew fanned out across those three states, often on their fourth or fifth deployment.*

*It was around this time that clips began appearing in the news of Rev. Jeremiah Wright, who until the year prior had been Senator Obama's longtime pastor in Chicago, at Trinity United Church of Christ. Wright was more than just another religious leader—he had been a key character in Obama's first book,* Dreams from My Father, *and was credited by Obama for the title of his second,* The Audacity of Hope. *Wright had even officiated the Obamas' wedding.*

*Given that, when ABC posted a story on March 13 under the headline, "Obama's Pastor: God Damn America, U.S. to Blame for 9/11," it attracted immediate attention. Reporters had gone through old sermons of Wright, focusing on two in particular that had been delivered the week after September 11 and shortly after the invasion of Iraq in 2003. Two Wright quotes were played on loop:*

*After 9/11: "We bombed Hiroshima, we bombed Nagasaki, and we nuked far more than the thousands in New York and the Pentagon, and we never batted an eye . . . we have supported state terrorism against the Palestinians and Black South Africans, and now we are indignant. Because the stuff we have done overseas is now brought right back into our own front yards. America's chickens are coming home to roost."*

*And shortly after the Iraq invasion: "The government gives African Americans the drugs, builds bigger prisons, passes a three-strike law, and then wants us to sing 'God Bless America.' No, no, no, 'God damn America,' that's in the Bible for killing innocent people. 'God damn America' for treating our citizens as less than human. 'God damn America' for as long as she acts like she is God and she is supreme."*

*These were eventually boiled down to a clip that included only three words depicted as explaining Wright's long career and Obama's spiritual faith: "God Damn America."*

*Looming over the whole episode was the fact that the nomination was not sewn up. Though we had a small, stable lead in pledged delegates, getting the nomination also required the votes from a critical mass of superdelegates—Democratic Party elders and elected officials whose support was not tied to performance in any primary. Before Iowa, Obama had trailed Senator Clinton significantly among this group, but we'd been slowly making progress and seemed on track if we could make it through the remaining primaries without hemorrhaging support.*

**Jon Favreau, Speechwriter:** Reverend Wright was an existential threat to the whole campaign. I saw those sermons and was like, "What the fuck is this? Where did this come from? How did we not know about this? How is this the guy that the president wrote about in *Dreams from My Father* whose phrase 'audacity of hope' became the title of his book?"

**Tommy Vietor, Press Staff:** "God Damn America," that YouTube clip, was one of the moments when race went from subtext to text. That clip was plucked out, cut, edited, and disseminated like a missile designed to scare white people.

**Thomas Zimmerman, Field Organizer:** All of a sudden Reverend Wright's sermons went from just appearing in the news to coming up in every conversation I would have with people about Barack Obama.

It was rarely in the context of, "I can't vote for him because . . ." It was always, "Well, now he's unelectable because . . ." It was never that people themselves were upset about it, but more that there was a sense that now this somehow spiked the general election in such a way that any concerns about electability had been confirmed.

And I don't mean to cast motivations on individuals, but for some, there was a coded "I'm not comfortable with this. But I'm not willing to say, 'I'm not comfortable with this,' so I'm going to say, 'I'm worried other people might not be comfortable with this.'" People would never directly acknowledge their own discomfort. It was couched in something else.

**Bess Evans, Field Organizer:** Very few people overtly said to me in Iowa, "I don't think that he can be elected because he's a Black man." But many people said, "I don't know if he could be elected." I knew what that meant, even if they didn't finish the sentence.

But as we got further and further down the line after the Reverend Wright stuff, people were finishing that sentence: "I don't know if he could be elected because he is a Black man." People were very jarred by Reverend Wright, and that racism became more overt.

**Lauren Champagne, Field Organizer:** I remember at one point a white gentleman that I was calling said, "If I vote, I'm voting for Obama's white side." Another caller would be like, "You sound like a Black person. Call me back when a white person can talk to me about this."

**David Plouffe:** The fear was if we ended up losing basically every primary and caucus going forward—and the general election matchup showed us losing by ten and Clinton winning by ten—then as strong as our position was in the race, these superdelegates might say, "Hey, great guy, good candidate, but damaged goods."

**Greg Degen, Field Organizer:** I wasn't doing as much door knocking anymore at that point. I was organizing volunteers who were doing the door knocking. But the stories they would come back with—I didn't really know what to tell them because I hadn't had any experience hearing such overt racism out there. People hearing racial slurs at the doors, people being confronted by voters who were angry that there was a Black candidate who was running for president. This was the first time this really manifested itself for me. That was eye-opening and deflating, because I was experiencing something much uglier and harder to put under the rosy portrait that I had constructed of how this primary would go.

**Nicole Young:** If you're a white person, you've probably lived in mostly white places because in this country, we live in very homogeneous neighborhoods. You've never had to talk about race. I've had to talk about race my whole life. That's how race works in America. If you're a white person, you don't have to think about it very often. However, if you're a Black person, you do, in order to stay alive. Literally.

**Stephanie Speirs, Field Organizer:** One day I was knocking on doors in Pennsylvania, like any other day. I knocked on the door, and a guy answered. I said hi and did my spiel, and then he disappeared from the door. And I peeked in to see where he went, and then he appeared again, holding a shotgun aimed at my chest.

And he said, "I'm not voting for a Muslim. Get off my property."

I was torn between saying, "There would be nothing wrong with him, if he were a Muslim," and arguing, "He's not Muslim." I just didn't know which argument to make, and he shut the door in my face, saving me from having to say anything. I was so mad, because I thought, "These are the ignorant whack jobs that we have to deal with. These people give democracy a bad name. They give America a bad name."

It was a really crystallizing point in the campaign for me, because I had been so positively surprised by every experience I'd been thrown into thus far. I'd gone to some of the most conservative parts of the country and always found abundant generosity from people.

It taught me a lot about what democracy is. Later on, thinking back on it, I realized that democracy is not the triumph of the loudest majority. It is not the absence of oppression. Democracy means coexisting with people whose views you find intolerable and even defending their right to vote.

The beauty of being an organizer—the beauty of knocking on doors so many hours every day for such a long period of time—is that it teaches you almost to be immune to rejection. And you learn that the only way to do that job well is not to let each negative interaction get you down. So I did finish my walk packet that day. But I kept thinking about that moment for a long time.

**Lauren Champagne:** I think for many Black people, Reverend Wright was not a big deal because (a) we felt like his words were mischaracterized and (b) the commentary that was coming out of it betrayed the history of how Black people were treated in this country. You could go to any Black church and hear similar comments, not coming out of a place of hate but an understanding of the frustration and history. We didn't see it the way the national media made it out.

**Yohannes Abraham:** Jeremiah Wright hit when I was in North Carolina, and what I remember clearly one of the state leaders got on a call with all the regional field directors and basically said, "Look, our white support has zeroed out. The universe of white voters that we were looking to turn out—our support has collapsed." That was a scary moment.

**Nicole Young:** My turf in Pennsylvania was a little suburb right outside of Philly, which was really wealthy, mostly white. Some of our volunteers thought that they were living in a liberal bastion. And it really wasn't.

I heard the N-word more in Pennsylvania than in my five years living in South Carolina. Almost every day when I would be doing my calls, some person would tell me, "I'm not voting for that N-word." And yet my volunteers would be like, "Oh my God, you came from South Carolina. What is race like there?" That was always the conversation when I met new people.

In these cold calls, we weren't calling Republicans; we were calling Democrats or former Democrats. People who had been union members, voting for Democrats their entire lives. They didn't know I was Black but felt very comfortable on the phone telling me they weren't going to vote "for that N-word." I think that speaks partly to the level of disenfranchisement that white working-class voters were already feeling at that time. Not just economically, but specifically around race.

**Jon Favreau:** Obama decided, "I want to give a speech, and I don't just want to give a speech about Reverend Wright and what he said. I want to give a speech about race in America because I think what he said and who he is ties into a very complex history of race in this country." I think Obama always knew that he was not going to the presidency without addressing the complexities of race in America.

*BARACK OBAMA [Speech Excerpt]: Contrary to the claims of some of my critics, black and white, I have never been so naïve as to believe that we can get beyond our racial divisions in a single election cycle, or with a single candidacy—particularly a candidacy as imperfect as my own.*

*Race is an issue that I believe this nation cannot afford to ignore right now . . . we can play Reverend Wright's sermons on every channel, every day, and talk about them from now until the election, and make the only question in this campaign whether or not the American people think that I somehow believe or sympathize with his most offensive words. We can pounce on some gaffe by a Hillary supporter as evidence that she's playing the race card, or we can speculate on whether white men will all flock to John McCain in the general election regardless of his policies.*

*Against all predictions to the contrary, we saw how hungry the American people were for this message of unity. Despite the temptation to view my candidacy through a purely racial lens, we won commanding victories in states with some of the whitest populations in the country. In South Carolina, where the Confederate flag still flies, we built a powerful coalition of African Americans and white Americans.*

*The comments that have been made and the issues that have surfaced over the last few weeks reflect the complexities of race in this country that we've never really worked through—a part of our union that we have not yet made perfect . . . if we walk away now, if we simply retreat into our respective corners, we will never be able to come together and solve challenges like health care, or education, or the need to find good jobs for every American. . . .*

*There is one story in particularl that I'd like to leave you with today. There is a young, twenty-three-year-old white woman named Ashley Baia who organized for our campaign in Florence, South Carolina. She had been working to organize a mostly African American community since the beginning of this campaign, and one day she was at a roundtable discussion where everyone went around telling their story and why they were there.*

*And Ashley said that when she was nine years old, her mother got cancer. And because she had to miss days of work, she was let go and lost her health care. They had to file for bankruptcy, and that's when Ashley decided that she had to do something to help her mom.*

*She knew that food was one of their most expensive costs, and so Ashley convinced her mother that what she really liked and really wanted to eat more than anything else was mustard and relish sandwiches. Because that was the cheapest way to eat.*

*She did this for a year until her mom got better, and she told everyone at the roundtable that the reason she joined our campaign was so that she could help the millions of other children in the country who want and need to help their parents too.*

*Now, Ashley might have made a different choice. Perhaps somebody told her along the way that the source of her mother's problems were blacks who were on welfare and too lazy to work or Hispanics who were coming into the country illegally. But she didn't. She sought out allies in her fight against injustice.*

*Anyway, Ashley finishes her story and then goes around the room and asks everyone else why they're supporting the campaign. They all have different stories and reasons. Many bring up a specific issue. And finally they come to this elderly Black man who's been sitting there quietly the entire time. And Ashley asks him why he's there. And he does not bring up a specific issue. He does not say health care or the economy. He does not say education or the war. He does not say that he was there because of Barack Obama. He simply says to everyone in the room, "I am here because of Ashley."*

*"I'm here because of Ashley." By itself, that single moment of recognition between that young white girl and that old Black man is not enough. It is not enough to give health care to the sick or jobs to the jobless or education to our children.*

*But it is where we start. It is where our union grows stronger. And as so many generations have come to realize over the course of the 221 years since a band of patriots signed that document in Philadelphia, that is where the perfection begins.*

**Jon Favreau:** After that speech, he called me and said, "I don't know if I can become president giving a speech like the one I just did, but I also know that I don't deserve to be president if I'm too afraid to say what it is I really believe about race."

**Nicole Young:** All of the organizers in my office watched that speech together. It was deeply emotional for me. I had never heard a speech like that. That part where he talks about Ashley at the end still makes me bawl. That moment, I think, typifies why I feel so grateful to my volunteers. They made me an organizer. That moment—"I'm here because of Ashley"—is where a volunteer is making Ashley an organizer.

But the speech really was a lightning rod. When we'd go out and talk to voters after that, people were either incensed by it, thinking he was playing the race card, and really furious, or people were like, "Yes, yes, yes, more of that please." Pennsylvania was a tough state.

**Greg Degen:** The campaign produced hundreds of copies of huge printouts of the entire speech he gave on race to hand out to voters at the doors. And in the area that I was in, Indianapolis, our volunteers were really moved and excited about it.

**Elizabeth Wilkins, Regional Field Director:** The places that I was, we were always talking about race. I was only in very poor Black places. Like, *really* poor. The poorest parts of Baltimore, the poorest parts of Philadelphia, the poorest parts of Detroit, where, rural or urban, it doesn't matter who was running for president, people don't vote, and people feel totally disconnected from politics in their day-to-day lives.

When he did his race speech, he presented a balm to people that they needed after being so disenchanted and disillusioned with what politics was ever going to do for them. That we could have this man who was talking about race and talking personally felt soothing to so much of the angry apathy that we were confronted with in the places we organized. There was a rolling sense that those conversations got easier to have, even in the hardest places to have conversations at all.

\*       \*       \*

## Indiana and North Carolina (Primary Day: May 6)

### April 23, 2008

*National Polling Average:* Obama 50, Clinton 40
*Indiana Polling Average:* Obama 45, Clinton 45
*North Carolina Polling Average:* Obama 50, Clinton 42

*As the months wore on, I began losing all perspective on the world outside the campaign. In Indiana, I was promoted to a regional position and put in charge of ten people, and I had the chance to hire one of my oldest, closest friends. Years later, I would ask him about his memories of us working together. "My memories of that time are overwhelmingly positive," he said. "Also, you took the job so seriously that you sometimes treated people around you like shit."* Whenever I drove to an unfamiliar community, I would print out a page from Google Maps before leaving the office. My flip phone didn't connect to the internet, and GPS felt like an extravagance, so when I became lost (which was often), I would call friends and family in Iowa, tell them where I was, and ask for directions. I viewed them telling me where to drive as an acceptable way to keep in touch.

For that year, nothing—personal relationships, mental health, physical safety, my coworkers—mattered to me as much as the election of Barack Obama. And it was to my detriment as an organizer—the longer the campaign lasted, the harder it was to empathize with anyone who did not see the world the same way.

After we lost Pennsylvania, as the campaign grew more heated, Indiana and North Carolina came to be seen as the Clinton campaign's last stand. If we could hold the line in both, we would seal the nomination, but if we couldn't, it would raise questions about Obama's electability with superdelegates that might be impossible to overcome. It raised the pressure on everyone in the organization, many of whom had been at it for a year.

**Elizabeth Wilkins:** Those months between January and May, the campaign asked so much of us. To go from place to place and to leave it all on the field over and over and over and over again—it just seemed impossible.

I remember at some point getting angry, though not on behalf of myself. One of my best friends and I were both in Philly for the Pennsylvania primary. We were facing many of the same problems in really dangerous turf. Our canvassers got shot at and carjacked—those were things that we were dealing with on a daily basis.

He got so sick and went into massive credit card debt because the campaign was taking so much out of him. And I remember feeling really protective of him and other people—we were so depleted by the time we started the general because we had been asked to leave it all on the field so many times at the cost of our finances, our physical well-being, our mental well-being.

**Jon Favreau:** I woke up some days and thought, "I am in purgatory. I am going to spend all of eternity in a primary battle against Hillary Clinton with all my friends. It's just gonna be primary after primary. It's never gonna end."

**Ally Coll, Field Organizer:** We were asked to drive across the country a lot. After Iowa I went to Denver. Then Reno, Nevada. Then Nebraska. Then I drove to Columbus, Ohio, which was almost all the way back to the East Coast. My entire life was in my car, a hatchback station wagon, and the back seats were loaded with shit. I would go through these drive-throughs, and people would always ask, "Are you moving?" It felt unsustainable.

I got really sick in Ohio. They had put us up in a Days Inn that turned out to have a huge bedbug problem, and then we got moved to a Ramada Inn. Around that time I developed a 103-degree fever and couldn't leave my hotel room for days. My body just kind of gave up in mid-March. I had never worked on a campaign before, and I very much had the mentality in Iowa that it was a sprint to caucus day, because few people expected us to win. Then when we did win, and the turnaround was so quick, I ran myself completely into the ground between Iowa and Ohio.

**Greg Degen:** I was beyond burned out. I was coming apart at the seams. That is really my main memory of the rest of the primary. It was a slog. And the personal toll was not good. There were days where I would just drive around and cry. The day that we lost the Pennsylvania primary to Hillary by a very significant margin, I remember driving around and crying because I couldn't fathom working in more states. I thought it would never end.

**Elizabeth Wilkins:** My mom literally mailed me paper bags because I was having panic attacks. I thought I had the weight of the country on me 100 percent of the time. I think a lot of us did.

A lot was being asked of us. I felt at every stage so far out of my depth in terms of the enormity of what I was doing and how to do it. I think that a lot of the pressure on me came from being generally competent, but also Black and female.

I feel like I was supposed to be a part of this incredible success story, but I'm not sure I ever felt like a success. I was always running to try to catch up with the expectations that people had about the job that I needed to do.

This campaign committed to this massive investment in field, this massive civic engagement project. Everywhere that I went, I organized in almost exclusively low-income Black places. I think the campaign wanted to demonstrate to Black communities that they had a commitment to Black leadership.

I felt like when they found me, a competent young Black woman, they figured they had found a resource that they needed to deploy strategically to communicate those messages to the people that we were trying to organize. And there just weren't that many of us. Certainly not in field.

They needed Black organizers. I don't mean that in a bad way or that it was tokenism. I think that those were real commitments. They promoted smart, Black staff. But it was a campaign. It's not like campaign organizations are super good at thinking hard about how to train people and how to make sure that they're supported. It was trial by fire for everybody.

**Greg Degen:** I was deployed to North Carolina, my sixth state, in March. At this point I was no longer in touch with most of my friends and family. I would talk to them on drives across the country to the next state, but once I got to that state, they really wouldn't hear from me until after the primary was over.

When I got to the city that I'd been assigned in North Carolina, there was no supporter housing for me. That's when I hit my breaking point. And I left. I couldn't do it anymore. It was just too taxing. And I remember when I left, the shame I felt, and the guilt of not being able to do it anymore.

I went back to Chicago. Even though I had worked for nearly a year for the campaign, I still felt that I had failed, because it wasn't over yet and all my friends were still doing it. After four or five days, I was antsy to be back in it. Not more than ten days after I left from being so burned-out, I got myself another job on the campaign in Indiana. The primary became so all-encompassing that my personal life was erased. I was far from the best version of myself.

**Megan Simpson:** I got such a bad migraine I was in and out of the ER for a week. The doctors would attach me to an IV to get my fluids up because I was so dehydrated. They finally shot Novocain in my head to release the migraine. I physically made myself ill from not sleeping. I was told it was stress.

I cried a lot in the mornings because I was tired, and I was so angry. When I was in Laredo, I was at my worst mentally. We had volunteers whose teacher contracts were threatened if they went and volunteered for Obama. It felt real personal. And being tired, I just wanted Obama to be declared the nominee. Because I felt very passionately that the writing was on the wall and this should just be over and we should get to sleep.

**Tommy Vietor:** It was the worst. All the parts about Iowa that I loved—real voters, talking to them about real issues all the time, relatively positive, were gone. It became this awful slog where you were doing huge events, national media, planes take you everywhere. And you just fucking fought it out. It sucked.

**David Plouffe:** We had to start worrying about the general election, even though we weren't done with primaries. We felt pretty confident we were going to be the nominee. The Clinton-Sanders race in 2016 was like afternoon tea compared to Clinton-Obama. Things got pretty tough. Obviously Hillary Clinton attacked Obama's association with Reverend Wright. There was a moment where she sort of suggested maybe something could happen to Obama, bringing up memories of RFK. And some of their debates, they were just throwing haymakers at each other.

**Bess Evans:** It got really heated. It wasn't just about win or lose; it was about the hours that you had spent away from family, the birthdays you had missed, the weddings you had missed, all of the things that you had missed. The twenty-five pounds that you had gained, in my case—more for others. The hair that you had lost, for many of my male colleagues.

It was personal, and so you felt personal about the competition not dropping out. It was like, "Why are you coming for me?"

So Indiana wasn't just about fighting to win Indiana; it was working to win the whole thing. We thought, "If we can do it here, this is it."

**Greg Degen:** I was an organizer in Indianapolis. In early May, right before the primary in Indiana, which was one of the last states to vote, we had a rally in the city square in a park downtown with Stevie Wonder. I remember going to the event and seeing tens of thousands of people supporting Barack Obama.

During the previous event that I went to, I was on stage with him in Iowa. And all of a sudden I was looking over a crowd of thousands of people. It was this mass of humanity. And that was the moment, not when I thought, "Oh, he's going to be the nominee," but, "Oh, we launched something that is bigger than we ever imagined it would be.

And bigger than all of us." And in a way it felt like it was no longer just mine. It all of a sudden belonged to the country.

**Bess Evans:** On Election Day in Indiana, we had a bomb threat.

**Jon Carson:** Oh my God, I forgot about that.

**Mitch Stewart, Indiana State Director:** It was terrifying. A reporter emailed our communications director and said, "Hey, someone just called in and said there are bombs in three of your offices."

So we called the Secret Service. I was like, "Hey, I've got bomb threats in three of my offices. What do I do?"

The Secret Service guy said, "Well, are there a lot of boxes in your offices? A lot of strange or foreign boxes?"

I was like, "It's Election Day. There are literally hundreds of boxes in every single office right now."

He said, "OK, well, what you need to do is call the local police department. Have them come out, and hopefully they'll have a K-9 unit so that the dog can clear your office. If not, the police officers will do it themselves."

I then had to get on a conference call with all of our offices. It was the middle of Election Day, so there was tons of activity, no one was really focused, and I couldn't mute everybody on the phone. So I was trying to convey this really serious message, and people were screaming in the background, and I remember just screaming, "Everyone, shut the fuck up! I need to tell you something . . . Shut up! So listen. We got this threat. I need everybody to get out of your offices. Call 911. Explain that we need the police to come and clear your office."

But then this was where your reality became so skewed. I said, "But before you leave, make sure everybody takes every cell phone and call sheet out—keep calling as the police clear your office."

**Bess Evans:** I got off this call with Mitch in the office in West Lafayette, Indiana, and remember saying, "OK, we just got off a conference call. Our early exit polls say it is incredibly close and what is going to make the difference is getting everybody out on the doors."

That was the way to empty our office without freaking people out. I don't remember if we were advised to say that. We did not tell people that we had a bomb threat.

It was incredibly scary. But at the time, I thought, "Yes, I will tell people to go knock on doors. That sounds exactly right. The benefit of this bomb threat is that more people will be on the doors."

Then I called my mother and said, "Mom, if you see that there are bomb threats to Obama offices in Indiana on the news, I don't want you to freak out. I'm not in an office. We've evacuated our offices." And obviously my mother freaked out.

**Jon Carson:** That was kind of a theme of the entire 2008 primary. There were bricks thrown through campaign office windows. There were some crosses burned. There was some really nasty racial shit that happened. And the campaign never talked about it.

But we all didn't have cell phone video cameras at the time either. Staffers didn't have Twitter, and reporters weren't reading Facebook; it was the last time in politics that you could actually control information at that level. Nowadays, if a racial slur had been sprayed on the field office, there's no way that it wouldn't be on CNN, because even if the campaign didn't lift it up into the dialogue, it would just happen.

*The night of the Indiana primary, the election was too close to call until midnight. Though Senator Clinton won by 2 percent, in the end, it didn't matter. Obama had blown out North Carolina and kept it close enough in Indiana that Tim Russert, widely considered the leader of the political press corps, went on NBC to declare, "We now know who the nominee is going to be, and no one's going to dispute it."*

*As I left Indiana, a volunteer said to me, "Now we start preparing for the general."*

*"Good luck," I thought. "Indiana is way too conservative to be competitive in the general election."*

*There was another month of primaries left, which included several episodes that stoked each candidates' supporters' suspicions: Senator Clinton claimed Obama's support among "hardworking Americans, white Americans, is weakening again," which would make it hard to win a general election; a well-known Chicago priest made national news by mocking Clinton's voice from the pulpit of Obama's church and pretending to cry; Senator Clinton had to apologize for telling a South Dakota editorial board, "We all remember Bobby Kennedy was assassinated in June" in defending her decision to continue her campaign.*

*None of it changed the dynamics of the race. On June 3, the day of the last primaries, Obama gained a majority of Democratic convention delegates, ensuring his nomination. Four days later, Senator Clinton, the first woman ever to seriously contest the presidency, announced her withdrawal from the race.*

HILLARY CLINTON [Concession Speech Excerpt]: *I want to start today by saying how grateful I am to all of you. To everyone who poured your hearts and your hopes into this campaign, who drove for miles and lined the streets waving homemade signs, who scrimped and saved to raise money, who knocked on doors and made calls . . . who lifted their little girls and little boys on their shoulders and whispered in their ears, "See, you can be anything you want to be."*

*The way to continue our fight now, to accomplish the goals for which we stand, is to take our energy, our passion, our strength, and do all we can to help elect Barack Obama, the next president of the United States.*

*On a personal note, when I was asked what it means to be a woman running for president, I always gave the same answer—that I was proud to be running as a woman, but I was running because I thought I'd be the best president.*

*But I am a woman, and like millions of women, I know there are still barriers and biases out there, often unconscious, and I want to build an America that respects and embraces the potential of every last one of us.*

*You can be so proud that, from now on, it will be unremarkable for a woman to win primary state victories, unremarkable to have a woman in a close race to be our nominee, unremarkable to think that a woman can be the president of the United States. And that is truly remarkable.*

*To those who are disappointed that we couldn't go all of the way, especially the young people who put so much into this campaign, it would break my heart if, in falling short of my goal, I in any way discouraged any of you from pursuing yours.*

*Although we weren't able to shatter that highest, hardest glass ceiling this time, thanks to you, it's got about eighteen million cracks in it and the light is shining through like never before.*

*Life is too short, time is too precious, and the stakes are too high to dwell on what might have been. We have to work together for what still can be. And that is why I will work my heart out to make sure that Senator Obama is our next president. And I hope and pray that all of you will join me in that effort.*

Are Democrats Destined to Lose After an Eight-Year Republican Presidency?
—CBS News, June 3, 2008

**Obama Claims Nomination; First Black Candidate to Lead a Major Party Ticket**
—New York Times, June 4, 2008

Angry Clinton Supporters Start Rallying for McCain Online
—Wired, June 4, 2008

**Clinton Ends Campaign with Clear Call to Elect Obama**
—New York Times, June 8, 2008

Fox News Refers to Michelle Obama as "Baby Mama"
—Associated Press, June 12, 2008

**Fox Apologizes for Calling Michelle Obama a "Baby Mama"**
—New York Magazine, June 12, 2008

From Across Region, 10,000 Rally for Obama; Democrat Launches Next Stage of Campaign, Meets with Clinton
—Washington Post, June 16, 2008

**McCain Attacks Obama for Opting Out of Public Financing**
—CNN, June 20, 2008

Obama's Paid Staff Dwarfing McCain's
—Boston Globe, July 20, 2008

# 10

# UNITY

*June–September 2008*

**June 8, 2008**

*National Polling Average*: Obama 47, McCain 44

With Hillary Clinton's concession, Obama became the de facto Democratic nominee, earning him the right to face Republican senator John McCain in the general election. When I was a teenager, McCain was embraced by much of the political press as a maverick politician, exactly the sort of person you hope runs for office. McCain had spent five years as a prisoner of war in Vietnam and endured torture after refusing offers from his captors to be sent home before other American prisoners. In the Senate he had passed a landmark campaign finance reform law and seemed genuinely committed to ethics reform. He had become a household name during an underdog campaign for president in 2000, unexpectedly winning the New Hampshire primary before having his hopes crushed by George W. Bush in South Carolina. Growing up in my liberal college town, I would regularly hear Democrats say in casual conversation, "If John McCain ran again, I'd definitely look hard at supporting him."

But in the years since his first campaign, McCain had embraced conservative orthodoxy in pursuit of the Republican nomination—courting extreme white evangelical endorsements, championing the Iraq invasion, and emerging as an enthusiastic supporter of George W. Bush's agenda. The week Hillary Clinton conceded, there was an all-staff call with Obama where he laid out the stakes for the coming year.

BARACK OBAMA [Speech Excerpt]: I hope that all of you understand your achievement. I've often said in speeches that this is not about me. And I know sometimes it may come off as just a line, but I really mean it. This campaign has been about you and you guys discovering your collective ability to make history and move an entire nation in a new direction. And that is a remarkable feat . . .

Now, we also have more work to do . . . as I've traveled over the course of fifteen, sixteen, seventeen months and I've met people who are struggling—I meet single moms that don't have health insurance for their kids, or I meet guys who've been laid off of their job and entire towns that are basically dying because they've lost their factory—when you see those things, you really do get this enormous sense of obligation. We don't have an option now.

When we were at the beginning of this thing, if I'd lost Iowa, it would have been OK. One of the other Democrats would have emerged, and they would have carried the banner, and we would have joined their campaign . . . but because we won, we now have no choice. We have to win . . . because now, if we screw this up, all those people that I've met who really need help—they're not gonna get help.

So now everybody's counting on you, not just me. And I know that's a heavy weight, but also what a magnificent position to find yourselves in. Where the whole country is counting on you to change it for the better. Those moments don't come around very often, and here you are, five months away from having transformed the country, and made history, and changed the world. So we've got to seize it.

**Lauren Champagne, Field Organizer:** A lot of us we were told so often that it would never happen. Him sitting there in that room as the Democratic nominee, we proved them wrong. We took down this powerful political dynasty.

**Greg Degen, Field Organizer:** In the conference call, Senator Obama was saying that because we succeeded at winning the nomination, now we had to win because the whole country was counting on us. I was pretty tired and had been through eight different primary states. But I felt an obligation to finish what we had started.

**Stephanie Speirs, Deputy Field Director, Ohio:** What was at stake were the memories and conversations I had at the doors and the lives of my volunteers, who worked so hard because they wanted to see a better America.

I remember I knocked on a woman's door, and she sheepishly admitted that she hadn't eaten for days because she didn't get her Social Security check. The only thing she was eating was slices of white bread and confectionary sugar, to stay alive. She didn't have money for food, she didn't have anyone to take care of her, and she was so hungry but didn't have anywhere to go.

There was a guy that I talked to who had never gone to college but was so desperate to figure out a way to send his daughter to college so she could have a better life than him. These were the stories that drove me, personally.

**David Plouffe, Campaign Manager:** It was really important that there be a change in the White House. If John McCain won, he said we might stay in Iraq for a hundred years. Wouldn't have done anything on climate change. Wouldn't have passed health care. So the stakes were enormous for the economy, health care, foreign policy.

During that brutal period between the Pennsylvania and Indiana primaries, Obama said to his team, "I can handle not being the nominee. What I can't handle is being the nominee and not winning the presidency. We have to win. If we're going to be given this responsibility to be the party's nominee, we can't lose."

That's the pressure he felt. It's a pressure I felt, and I think we tried to make sure everybody on the campaign felt it. That this was not about making history. That this was about making sure we had a president who was going to do certain things as compared with their opponent who would do other things. That was what it was about—the agenda you set and the decisions you make as president. In the day-to-day execution of the campaign, we were very much focused on getting to 270 electoral votes, not thinking about the history.

*For seventeen months our campaign had been focused on winning primaries. But because most people do not participate in primary elections, the general election required appealing to a much larger universe. For Obama to reach the White House, he would need to unify the Democratic Party, bring Clinton supporters into the fold, register millions of new voters in swing states to fundamentally alter the electorate, and convince a sizable number of conservative independent and Republican voters to go against tradition and back a Democrat.*

*To do that, Obama reversed a pledge he had made during the primary to accept public financing of his campaign for the general election. This allowed him to spend an unlimited amount of money and hire thousands of staff to target fourteen states that George Bush had won in 2004, such as Indiana, North Dakota, Georgia, Montana, Alaska, and Missouri. The goal of all of this was to create as many paths as possible to 270 electoral votes on November 4.*

**Jon Carson, National Field Director:** We approached the general as though we were five points behind everywhere and drove every state hard, no matter how likely we were to win them. We never let ourselves believe we had it in the bag, and we had to keep it competitive in as many states as possible.

**Marygrace Galston, Campaign for Change Director:** The map was very different than it had been in the past. States like Indiana were on the list that had never been battleground states before.

**Lauren Kidwell, National Regional Director:** The map was super expansive. We even had people in Alaska. Our strategy was going after a really wide number of different paths to victory—so in my region, the Midwest, my battleground states were Wisconsin, Minnesota, Iowa, Missouri, North Dakota, and the Nebraska Second Congressional District.

**David Plouffe:** Field was essential. The only reason we targeted Florida was because we thought we had enough volunteers. North Carolina, same thing. Indiana, same thing. We made really important electoral college decisions about what we were going to target and our pathways to victory based on our organization.

**Greg Degen, Regional Field Director, Pennsylvania:** At that particular point in the campaign, there was a lot of jockeying and a lot of uncertainty as to where people were going to end up in the general election. A lot of us had either been promoted into managerial roles or expected to be promoted, and I remember a lot of phone calls to each other to try to relay this hearsay on who was going to be managing which states, which states were going to be the most important, what roles would be best.

**Lauren Kidwell:** There was a little bit of musical chairs to find your general election job. People had been plodding along from primary state to primary state, and the general election job felt higher stakes. There was a lot of stress around getting placed in the right role and location.

**Greg Degen:** Most of the organizers I worked with in Iowa went to North Carolina. I would have probably had a more fun experience had I just gone where the people I knew were. But at the time, I felt like it was more important to get the best possible job, so I took a regional field director position in Pennsylvania.

**Emily Parcell, Indiana State Director:** Tewes called me while I was on my honeymoon and asked whether I wanted to work for the general election, and I said, "Well, I'm working in Indianapolis either for Starbucks or for the Obama campaign." Because my husband was there.

There was competition among who was going to go to what state for several positions. Absolutely nobody wanted to be the state director for Indiana, and so I did it.

**Mitch Stewart, Indiana State Director:** I desperately wanted to be the state director in Virginia. They had somebody else in mind, and I think they offered the job to that person first, but because we didn't pay very much and the guy was more established, he was like, "Hey, I can't take this pay cut. I have a family. I have all this other stuff." So he turned it down, and then I was the second choice for Virginia, which I gladly took.

**Yohannes Abraham, Field Organizer:** Mitch called me up and basically said, "Hey, do you think you can handle being the Virginia field director?" I instantly said yes, and then from there worked backward and figured out how to actually do the job.

**Meghan Goldenstein, Field Organizer:** The night before I left Madison to move to Dubuque to be hired as a field organizer, I had this moment reading the hire letter and all the official paperwork where I thought, "Oh my God. I am not up to this." Because while I'd volunteered in several states, I'd never officially been a field organizer. As if I hadn't been doing all the work in all these different places. But it was this moment of, "Now it's real. People are going to depend on me, and I'm going to have all these volunteers." Looking back, I know now that young people, particularly women, constantly question their own qualifications.

*I was offered two positions: return to Iowa City, my hometown, or move to North Carolina, where my old regional director and many of my friends from the caucuses had ended up. North Carolina hadn't supported a Democrat for president since 1976, and Bush had won there by twelve points in 2004. There were rumors Obama was only targeting the state to trick McCain into spending money there, and we'd all move to Virginia around Labor Day. Plus, unlike Iowa, a crucial swing state, I assumed that even if we won North Carolina, we wouldn't have needed to for Obama to become president, since in that scenario he was probably winning lots of places. But in the end, it wasn't a hard decision. I wanted to finish the experience with the people I'd met at the beginning.*

*In North Carolina, I was assigned to Durham and Chapel Hill. In Iowa, I had been responsible for seventeen precincts and had been expected to identify 857 Obama supporters. For the general election, I was assigned a team of a dozen staff to cover six counties with hundreds of thousands of voters.*

*In my new turf, there was a group called Durham for Obama (DFO) that had been started on my.barackobama.com during the primaries and exploded into an organization of several thousand volunteers. Durham was one of the most Democratic counties in the state. It had huge voter registration goals, which would have to be met if we ever hoped to make North Carolina competitive. Unlike the primary, where you would arrive in a new place and often be the first official representative from the national campaign, in those early weeks, I got the feeling I was constantly being judged against organizers who had preceded me. It became clear these people— who had already won a massive victory for Barack Obama two months earlier—didn't need staff to tell them how to organize. DFO had strategically started to court key local supporters of Senator Clinton, embarked on a major local data initiative to identify where unregistered voters lived, and started asking volunteer leaders from the primary to recommit even more time in the general election. They just needed staff to not get in the way.*

*As organizers fanned out across the country in June, the early weeks of the general election were devoted to reconnecting with these grassroots volunteers, hiring organizers, and working with recruits from the new "fellows" program—hundreds of people who had signed up to travel to swing states and volunteer for free for over thirty hours a week through the summer.*

**Chris Wyant, Ohio Deputy Field Director:** After Obama lost the Pennsylvania primary in April, a dozen of us were sent to general election states and told, "Start building infrastructure. Don't make too much noise, don't get any attention from the press, and don't piss anybody off. The only things you can do are talk to volunteers and register voters. That's the extent of your work. Go forth and do good."

A really important piece of the work that we did in that interim period was that we interviewed and recruited and ultimately accepted hundreds of "fellows." They all started mid-June—three hundred full-time, dedicated, committed people working for free across the state.

**Greg Degen:** The Obama "fellows" program was basically the general election version of Camp Obama—it was an official-sounding program that had a goal of getting people to work for the campaign unpaid for the summer and then hiring a few for the fall.

**Howli Ledbetter, North Carolina Fellow:** A lot of the fellows were taking a break from professional jobs to come do this. It wasn't like this was our first gig. I had been working in New York at a public relations agency. But as the 2008 campaign heated up, I became obsessed with it. It was the only thing I read about. My hours at work were basically spent scouring the internet—I vividly remember watching the Obama race speech at my desk in New York and feeling like, "This guy is the guy."

I saw this email about the summer fellows program and looked at it as a way to scratch the itch. Then I got the fellowship in North Carolina. I had never even been there. But I showed up the first day, and a stranger picked me up at the airport and took me to a random house to spend the night.

The next day I went to this all-day training where you talked about why you were there. Everybody was different. Different ages, different backgrounds. But everybody had the same feeling: "We have to be a part of this—this is a huge moment, and it's really important." By the end of that first day, I was like, "This is not a six-week experience. I will stay as long as they'll have me."

**Chris Wyant:** A good percentage of those people ended up being full-time staff. There were a ton of people who got involved in the same way as I did with Camp Obama. They thought they were doing this for a summer and got hooked, and their lives are fundamentally different as a result.

**Howli Ledbetter:** In North Carolina, they sent us out across the state with two goals. One was to register voters, and the second was to hold a house party to recruit volunteers. I showed up at the house I was living in off MLK Boulevard on the outskirts of Greensboro. This single mom was my supporter housing. She sent her daughter to live with the daughter's grandma a few doors down, so I could live in her bedroom for six weeks. The room was hot pink. The bed was covered in stuffed animals that I had to take off every night. But that always struck me as amazing. It wasn't like she had an extra room. She kicked her daughter out so I could live there for six weeks.

When we got there, there was huge resistance from some of the party people, most of whom had strongly supported Hillary in the primary. We spent a ton of time on direct outreach to prominent Hillary supporters, who also happened to be most of the people who were active in Democratic politics in the county. We had meeting after meeting talking about everything that happened, including how in the primary an Obama field organizer had upset them.

Then, on the other side, there were women who had been strong Obama supporters in the area during the primary. One was hugely helpful to us, was happy we were there, helped give us the lay of the land, especially of the African American community—whom we needed to reach out to, which restaurants we needed to go to, which church we needed to go to. She was super helpful. Then there was another woman who told activists in the African American community that my white colleague and I were actually Hillary supporters, working to undermine Barack Obama from the inside.

She really wouldn't believe us. It was hard, because she was turning off people who were very active in the primary, who had supported Barack Obama, from working with us.

Eventually, Chris Lewis, who was the head of the North Carolina field program, came down and met with us and her. We all had a meeting where he was like, "I am the boss of all of these people, and they really work for us. Please stop telling people they're secret Hillary spies." That was a rough few weeks.

**Marygrace Galston:** The new volunteers were the people that were actually doing the work. They were signing up other volunteers. They were signing up new voters. They were registering people to vote. The volunteers were the ones that were knocking on doors and making phone calls and hopefully organizing themselves out of volunteer jobs. That allowed an organizer to basically just manage.

The infrastructure on the ground was the volunteers. It wouldn't have happened without the new people, because it allowed everybody to register more and more people to vote.

**Howli Ledbetter:** Canvassing to register voters was never as successful as just going to places where lots of people were. When we got to Burlington, we registered a lot of Democrats at one Walmart. The other Walmart, you registered a lot of Republicans. People were pretty racist, and they were very upset that white girls were working for Barack Obama. They would say, "Do your parents know what you're doing here?"

**Leonard Williams, Alamance County, NC, Volunteer:** I went over to Burlington one Saturday afternoon and met Howli. That girl was on a warpath, so I joined in with her. You hear a lot of stuff about people from California, but I never heard anyone say a negative thing about Howli.

Alamance is a very conservative county. I did a little bit of registering voters, but not a lot because that wasn't my thing. My thing was going out and knocking on doors. Howli got me so involved I made my house a staging location. I had some telephone lines run in—Howli had college students coming here and making phone calls.

I liked Obama because I thought that he knew what it was like to reach out to young folks and people that never had a chance—he's a smart guy, had gone to Harvard, but he could relate to us at the street level. It had nothing to do with race. It's just that the guy was good. He could get up and talk, and a lot of what he talked about made sense. Most of the people who worked from my house were Caucasian. It was a good mixture.

**Chris Lewis, North Carolina Field Director:** We knew we didn't have enough regular voters to win North Carolina, so we spent the first three months trying to change the electorate. If we could get over 180,000 new registrants, then we were in the game.

**Howli Ledbetter:** In the early days of the general election, we would stand in parking lots from morning to night. It was physically hard to stand for that many hours. It was very hot in North Carolina, and I don't tan, so I was slathering on sunscreen. But it was more emotionally hard—every day, you felt like you were learning things about our country that were really upsetting, which made the work of electing Barack Obama feel more important. I had a lot of naïve notions, and every day a sledgehammer was taken to them again and again.

People did not know their rights. At the time in North Carolina, as long as you were not on parole or probation, even if you were a felon, you could vote. So we spent a ton of time trying to educate people and let them know that that was the law. I met dozens of men—young African American men particularly—who hadn't voted for years because they thought they couldn't. I remember vividly sitting in somebody's house with prescription pill bottles everywhere. The husband couldn't get out of bed—they had a hospice bed in the living room—and I was trying to talk to him about why they should vote. It was a very up close and personal view of suffering.

That's the thing about being a field organizer. You are the first line of defense. The questions you get aren't just, "What is Barack Obama going to do about X?" It's, "If I vote for him, how does my life change?" And in a lot of cases, their lives were not changing. You had to have real conversations, like, "It's for your kids—if he's elected, he cares more about education, and hopefully the schools will be better funded. But for you, middle-aged woman in the gas station, who's living in poverty, probably not a ton is changing." So you tried to be honest with people but also explain why it's still important to vote, and to vote for Barack Obama. It was dozens of those conversations, every single day. That was the hardest part.

Also, you lost all fear for your own personal safety. Now, looking back on it, the amount of cars I got into with total strangers to talk to them about why they should vote was insane.

*Each state had different priorities. Because there had been a competitive primary nearly everywhere, very few communities were starting from scratch. In Durham and Chapel Hill, North Carolina, we devoted a lot of effort to registering new voters. In more conservative regions, the focus was on persuading regular voters to support Obama.*

**Megan Simpson, Southwest Montana Regional Field Director:** I was the regional director for southwest Montana. With a lot of the people that we were talking to at the door, the first question wasn't, "I'm out here knocking on doors for Barack Obama. Do you support him?"

It was, "Hi, I live in this community. I'm talking to voters today about the upcoming election. What issues matter to you?" And then we pivoted into, "Well, this is why I'm out supporting Barack Obama."

We taught our volunteers how to weave their personal reasons for supporting Obama to help connect with voters on the issues. If we got issues that people cared about, we had volunteers who wouldn't do anything but write personal handwritten letters to the voters with the issue one-pagers on where Senator Obama stood. And then they would follow up with phone calls saying, "Hey, did you get my letter? Can we talk about it more?"

**Nicole Young, Western Michigan Regional Field Director:** I was in a really conservative region in Michigan where all of these super right-wing Christian groups had a big presence. And so we would get this question a lot about Obama being "pro-abortion." That was how it was always framed. They don't talk about being "pro-life." They talk about you being "pro-abortion."

One of my volunteers was like, "I'm with you. I'm a Catholic. I have the same concerns. I care a lot about abortion. But you know, I care about someone's right to live, not just from the moment of conception, but until their natural death."

And she's like, "Barack Obama supports making sure that we are doing everything we can to improve people's quality of life so that they are not dying early in this crazy war. And until we can guarantee that everyone has a right to a full life, then we can't hinge our whole vote on this one thing."

It was so good. No one gave her that talking point, and I shared it over and over again with volunteers.

**Jon Carson:** Creating a permission structure for independents and some Republicans to be able to vote for a Black guy named Barack Obama—that happened at the doors. What we realized out of focus groups was that it wasn't that the health care message worked at the doors. It wasn't his economic argument that did it. The message that we were delivering at the doors was, "Whoa. Look at that. There's somebody from my town, one of my neighbors, standing at my door saying that they are voting for the Black guy. Wow. I guess maybe I can do that too." That was the message.

When you build a giant field operation, half the impact you see is on the lists. But I have always believed the other half of the impact is these volunteers, excited, feeling like they're a part of something and talking about it at the work break room, or talking about it in the church basement over coffee, talking about it in the grocery store parking lot, and creating that permission structure by having this army of excited people. That was our theory.

**Janice Rottenberg, Hamilton County, OH, Field Organizer:** One of my volunteer leaders got really stoked on the idea of making yard signs that said, "Another Terrace Park resident for Obama."

I was like, "Yard signs are stupid, man." I spent a couple of one-on-one meetings trying to talk him down from the yard signs, but he kept coming back to it.

He'd be like, "I want to do an overnight drop to shock people. Nobody in Terrace Park thinks that there is a single Obama supporter. They'll be shocked when they see fifty or sixty of these signs go up."

Finally, I gave up. It may have been one of the coolest things that we did over the course of the campaign. It wasn't because I could say, "We won a vote today," but it gave my volunteers so much more confidence. As silly as it was, seeing fifty yard signs go up helped them feel like they could go out and knock doors in their neighborhood, because they knew there were at least fifty or sixty people who thought like them. It's the only time I ever liked yard signs. It made them feel like they were part of a movement.

*There was no way to hit the voter registration and persuasion goals being asked of us without growing our organization. Unlike during the primary, in which our volunteers all supported Obama over other Democrats, in the general election, we were working for the Democratic nominee, which meant we had to integrate our operations with the long-standing local Democratic Party apparatus and try to reactivate volunteers from Hillary Clinton's campaign. This was much easier said than done, given how heated and personal the primary had become for each candidate's supporters.*

*To make sure no one missed the point, Hillary Clinton and Barack Obama held a joint rally in the tiny town of Unity, New Hampshire, less than a month after her concession. Remarkably, given the name, each had received 107 votes there during the New Hampshire primary, making it neutral ground for two former rivals to appear together for the first time.*

**David Plouffe:** What was remarkable to me was that when we began to try to make peace after Senator Clinton conceded, at the principal level they were pretty calm about it. They had known each other. It still took a while for the staff blood to cool down. You spend a year and a half trying to decapitate your opponent, and then you turn around, shake hands—it's a hard transition. I think both Hillary Clinton and Barack Obama led the way in modeling good behavior.

One of my mantras was, "We have to welcome Clinton volunteers with open arms." That may mean listening to them complaining about things we said.

**Chris Wyant:** There are eighty-eight counties in Ohio. Overwhelmingly those counties went for Hillary, and overwhelmingly those Democratic Party county chairs—many of whom had been engaged in the 1990s and built relationships with Bill Clinton—had supported Clinton.

Some of them were not supportive. Wanted nothing to do with us. We were probably a little naïve, because we figured, "OK, some bad blood. People didn't want us to win, but the primary's over. Time to move to the general against John McCain." People operated on their own timeline. In a lot of cases, it was months before people became meaningfully engaged.

**Carrianna Suiter, Ohio Regional Field Director:** After he secured the nomination, we got a lot of staff in Ohio from the Clinton campaign. We had been through a really, really rough primary, and in many cases, there were staff who had been in the same states working against each other who were now working together on the same campaign. That was hard. There was anger and frustration left over from grievances we all felt, and all of a sudden we were supposed to function like this seamless machine.

**Jeremy Bird, Ohio General Election Director:** In Ohio it was a big project to get both staff and volunteers who had worked for Hillary. Early on it was certainly something we were very worried about. The primary had gotten really heated.

**Brynne Craig, Ohio Deputy Field Director and Former Clinton Organizer:** When I walked in on my first day, my background on my computer was an image that said, "I Love Being Black and Working for Hillary Clinton," because if you were a Black person not supporting Barack Obama, it was hard during the primaries. I opened up my laptop, and the person next to me was like, "Get that shit out of here."

**Jeremy Bird:** I hired Jackie Bray to be our field director in Ohio, which was not an uncontroversial thing among the team. I had worked with her in '04 and knew she was very good, but I also knew that it would send a big signal and attract other Hillary organizers, which it did.

**Jackie Bray, Ohio Field Director and Former Clinton Organizer:** I was so grateful for this opportunity, but I underestimated the transition. Two sets of insults drove me crazy. The first was that the Clinton organizers "couldn't organize." There was this assumption that if you could draw a big crowd, you were a good organizer. No, the hardest thing as an organizer is when your candidate can't draw a big crowd and you *still* draw a good crowd.

The other thing that got under my skin and has stayed with me was that there was a significant underappreciation of misogyny and sexism. We've learned so much both as a party and as a nation that it's hard to remember that, back in '07 and '08, some of the Obama team got away with saying that Hillary wasn't being hurt by sexism. And that was so maddening.

There was this idea that those of us working for Hillary didn't believe in her but just thought she was going to win. In 2007 I got offers from Obama and Edwards and Hillary, and I picked Hillary because I remember my mom saying, "God, wouldn't it be amazing to see that?" So the idea that we weren't in it for the right reasons was insulting.

**Brynne Craig:** When we got to Ohio to start the general election, people seemed to have forgotten that Hillary Clinton won Ohio in the primary. She won Ohio because she had a really good organizing team, but that seemed lost. The idea that we could have outorganized them somewhere, anywhere was lost. So we ended up having to prove we knew what we were doing all over again.

**Jackie Bray:** When I arrived for my first day on the job in Ohio for Obama, there was a team of Obama organizers there already. One of them said to me, "Our friend was supposed to get your job."

I said something like, "Well, I hope that I'll come to earn your respect."

And then I remember looking in the mirror, thinking, "You're going to have to be perfect." It took a long time to get to a place where the team could respect me, although I think they eventually did. But that happened throughout the summer.

I remember a field organizer coming up to me and saying, "Would you like me to teach you how to tell your story?"

I thought, "Are you fucking kidding me?" I had just been hired by the Obama campaign to be that person's boss's boss's boss. And more importantly, I wouldn't have been hired in the first place if I wasn't a great organizer. But this person couldn't see that because we had been on opposite teams in the primary.

*The Democratic National Convention marked the end of the summer and helped force everyone to come together. Hundreds of Clinton and Obama delegates from each state would travel to Denver and spend four days on national television celebrating Barack Obama and Joe Biden, who had been selected as Obama's vice presidential nominee.*

*The convention was also a local organizing opportunity. We scheduled house parties throughout the four days as a way to recruit new volunteers and draw the attention of voters who might just be tuning in to see the Obama family for the first time.*

**Greg Degen:** In Pennsylvania, we were still doing the normal business of the campaign during the convention. We didn't take any time off, but we did watch the major speeches. And I vividly remember watching Michelle Obama's speech. Her poise and her grace. It was so satisfying to watch someone who had been given a raw deal by the press at certain points during the primary have this moment. It was also the first night of the convention. I was a registered independent at that time, and the Democratic Party always seemed like a staid political organization. So to see her as the first Obama to claim the mantle that week was a moment where I was feeling like, "Wow, we really took over the Democratic Party."

**Marygrace Galston:** Paul and I flew out three days before the convention. We were in charge of running the boiler room, which manages the run of show. It was a contentious primary, so there were a lot of Clinton delegates that were going to vote for Hillary. So there was a plan—they'd go through the states alphabetically until we got to

Illinois. And then Illinois was going to yield the floor to New York, and Hillary Clinton was going to walk out to the New York delegation and ask for a unanimous vote.

So Illinois yielded to New York. Hillary Clinton came out. Everybody was all excited.

*HILLARY CLINTON: Madam Secretary, on behalf of the great state of New York, with appreciation for the spirit and dedication of all who are gathered here. With eyes firmly fixed on the future in the spirit of unity . . . let's declare together in one voice, right here, right now, that Barack Obama is our candidate . . . I move that Senator Barack Obama of Illinois be selected by this convention by acclamation as the nominee of the Democratic Party for president of the United States.*

**Marygrace Galston:** She asked for a unanimous vote. And all of a sudden, Barack Obama was our nominee.

**Sue Dvorsky, Johnson County, IA, for Obama Cochair:** When she came out and delivered the votes by acclamation, I remember watching it with tears pouring down my face. Her grace, her grit—there was so much respect, so much affection for her. She was big enough to absolutely, honestly say, "I want the people who supported me to support this candidacy."

**Jackie Bray:** Hillary Clinton gets nowhere near enough credit for her behavior after her concession. She hit the campaign trail and told us all to go.

**Brynne Craig:** She even had pins for volunteers saying "Hillary Sent Me."

**Meghan Goldenstein:** When I came back to Iowa during the general election, there were a lot of people who had caucused for Hillary and weren't automatically excited to support Obama. The reconciliation work in Iowa that summer consisted of a lot of outreach to people who had been Hillary supporters. Iowa Hillary supporters were some of the earliest and most committed people. And much like us, those people went to other states. They phone banked. They went to her events. They held house parties to raise money for the campaign. So when she conceded, that was not nothing for them. People who had followed her for so long didn't have as much of a chance to get over their own feelings. Had the situation been reversed for me, it would have been really hard to be excited about her as a candidate.

*The final night of the convention was Obama's acceptance speech. It was set outside in a football stadium; seventy-five thousand were expected to attend. We had house parties planned across my region to watch. It was August 28, 2008, the forty-fifth anniversary of the March on Washington.*

**David Axelrod, Chief Strategist:** The night of the acceptance speech at the convention happened to be the forty-fifth anniversary of Dr. King's "I Have a Dream" speech on the mall in Washington. The date was set long before Obama was the nominee.

**Jon Favreau, Speechwriter:** We thought it was wise to be subtle about it. We thought that saying, "And on this day, we all remember Martin Luther King gave a speech, and now here I am . . ." would be like hitting people over the head. So we had this nice ending: "Forty-five years ago, Americans gathered on a mall, and they heard a preacher say . . ." He didn't even mention King, but the whole day was heavy with that. We were sitting in a hotel room in Denver when Obama went through the speech for the first time.

He got to the part about King at the end, and he stopped and choked up. He was like, "This has never happened to me before giving a speech." And he went into the bathroom for a minute to collect himself. He told us that the gravity of what was about to happen, accepting the nomination, hadn't hit him yet until that moment.

**Elizabeth Wilkins, Michigan Field Director:** When it became officially clear that Barack Obama had the nomination, my mom called. She started crying. She was really emotional. She was supportive from the beginning, but that was a moment where she expressed to me, "As much as I wanted to, I really never believed that I would see this day." She was in her late sixties at the time and had grown up in segregated public housing in the South.

**Patricia King, Elizabeth Wilkins's Mother, Washington, DC, Resident:** I grew up in public housing in Norfolk—segregated, rebellious Virginia. There was a poll tax. I was still in school in Norfolk when

Prince Edward County public schools were closed for five years. It wasn't clear that I was going to graduate from high school the year I graduated, which was 1959. So having lived through all of that, having felt totally disempowered, I never thought I'd see the day.

**Elizabeth Wilkins:** To hear her talk vulnerably about her childhood and how far we'd come, it brought home to me what we were doing. Many of the public moments on the campaign felt like they passed me by. That was one of the few where I thought, "This is intergenerational history. This is changing what people think is possible in this country."

**Thomas Zimmerman, Field Organizer:** In your day-to-day, you didn't feel like you were a part of something that was of great historical significance. But at that moment, you realized you had been.

**Megan Simpson:** We were sitting at a pizza place in Bozeman, Montana, with our volunteers. Everyone was there, excited when they announced him and he accepted the nomination. One of my organizers and I were sitting in the back of the room, holding hands. When he got up on stage, I started crying.

One, it was recognizing the historical moment. But two, it felt like, "Wow, we did it." It was such a long primary and so drawn out that it didn't feel like it was real until that moment. It had been over a year of work, but it felt worth it, and I was so proud.

**Thomas Zimmerman:** The next morning in Chicago, I turned on the TV and saw breaking news announcing the Republican vice presidential selection. There'd been all this prep, a whole campaign built around how whomever they picked was "the next Cheney." CNN teased the rollout, and I remember immediately being like, "Who's Sarah Palin?"

*The morning after Obama accepted the nomination, John McCain announced Sarah Palin as his running mate. Palin was virtually unknown to the public, having been elected governor of Alaska less than two years earlier. But in the aftermath of her selection, she was heralded as a "fresh-faced maverick" who would boost McCain's chances. She was only the second woman ever to be nominated for vice president, and Clinton supporters I knew tended to view her selection as a cynical move by Republicans to win their support, despite her extremely conservative positions.*

*Palin immediately started drawing bigger crowds than McCain. She had no problem launching extreme personal attacks against Obama, and five weeks after her selection, she accused him of "palling around with terrorists." There were reports from her rallies that spectators would shout "kill him," "terrorist," and "treason" when Obama was named from the stage. Less than a month before Election Day, McCain held a town hall meeting where he said, "Senator Obama is a decent person and a person you don't have to be scared of as president of the United States." The crowd booed in response.*

**Greg Degen:** The first event with Barack Obama, Joe Biden, Michelle Obama, and Jill Biden was in my region, the day Palin was picked. No one knew who she was at that point, so that was a big part of the conversation leading up to the event among people attending. People were concerned that she could be a real game changer.

**Yohannes Abraham:** Post-Palin announcement you felt a weird energy. There was a nasty and dangerous element to the discourse. Safety of my staff became something that was on my mind in a way it would not have been prior.

**Meghan Goldenstein:** The Hillary ladies had been tough nuts to crack up to that point, but after the Palin announcement, it was like magic. They were so offended by the idea that John McCain had selected a woman whose résumé paled in comparison to Hillary's and who stood against everything Hillary stood for. They were offended that John McCain thought that that pandering would earn their votes.

**Janice Rottenberg:** I remember distinctly the day they chose Sarah Palin. Hillary supporters walked into our office like, "I'm absolutely not doing this. We can't have this guy be president. This is insane. This is pandering."

**Jackie Bray:** In Ohio, an Obama regional director for Appalachia called the Ohio headquarters and said, "There are these women that just showed up. They're old, they brought their own chairs, they brought us all food, they brought red pens, they're refusing to use our blue pens and our black pens, but they're making calls. Hundreds of them. Where did they come from?" And Brynne and I were standing in the back sort of laughing, going, "Those are our people."

**Brynne Craig:** The Hillary army had arrived. And to the Obama team's credit, they stayed.

**Chris Wyant:** It wasn't until a little bit after Labor Day where you felt like everyone came around—at least everyone who was ever going to come around. The stakes were getting more real, as they do after Labor Day in every cycle. The Palin decision, Senator Clinton's convention speech, I think all of that compounded. You had to be in a dark place to not appreciate he was the nominee, and Senator Clinton was a real supporter.

A Pit Bull with Lipstick: Why the Smiling, Sudden, Relentless Sarah Palin Should Scare Democrats

—Slate, **September 4, 2008**

**Republicans' Enthusiasm Jumps After Convention; McCain Edges Ahead; Palin Speech May Be a Factor**

—Gallup, **September 8, 2008**

Central Banks Band Together to Slow Economic Collapse; Senator Obama Gains Lead in Poll of Polls

—Finance Wire, **September 18, 2008**

**Obama: "Help Main Street" as Well as Wall Street**

—CNN, **September 19, 2008**

57% of Public Favors Wall Street Bailout: Obama Seen as Better Able to Address Crisis

—Pew Research, **September 23, 2008**

**McCain Suspends Campaign, Shocks**

—U.S. News & World Report, **September 24, 2008**

Palin: Obama Began His Political Career in Terrorist's Living Room

—CBS News, **October 5, 2008**

**Barack Obama Called "Terrorist" at Republican Rallies as US Election Campaign Turns Nasty**

—Telegraph, **October 10, 2008**

Campaign Amid a Crisis: Market Collapse Has Frozen Presidential Contest in Place: Polls Indicate Obama Keeps His Edge as Americans Are Worried About a Tanking Economy

—Houston Chronicle, **October 12, 2008**

**Excitement, Frustration as Early Voters Brave Long Lines**

—CNN, **November 3, 2008**

# 11

## FINAL SPRINT

*September 2008–January 2009*

### October 8, 2008

*National Polling Average:* Obama 49, McCain 44

*W*hen *I started learning about politics, I read somewhere that Labor Day marked the beginning of campaign season, the idea being that only in the final eight weeks leading up to Election Day do the voters you need to reach tune in to the race. By Labor Day, 2008, 569 days had passed since I attended the first Obama rally in Iowa. It was hard to relate to anyone just now starting to pay attention.*

*There were still plenty of big moments remaining—including three debates between Obama and John McCain—but in my field offices, the final stretch of the election felt like a frenzied sprint of volunteer trainings, voter registration deadlines, midlevel surrogate events, and early voting metrics. I absorbed information about the outside world almost exclusively through two lenses: (1) How does this affect Barack Obama's election chances? (2) What will volunteers need to say about this to voters?*

*Throughout the general election, our message to voters about John McCain had been simple: "John McCain equals George W. Bush's third term." But shortly after Labor Day, I started to see a subtle shift in the campaign talking points as the economy took center stage. For several months, the United States had been sliding into a recession, one I had not realized was happening in real time. But in September it overwhelmed all other news as multiple banks went bankrupt or required massive federal bailouts to stay open. On the eve of the first presidential debate, John McCain announced he was suspending his campaign to go to Washington so that both parties could "meet until this crisis is resolved." The resulting negotiations at the Bush White House—where McCain and other Republicans were depicted as disorganized, unengaged, and overly reliant on boilerplate conservative talking points—received wall-to-wall coverage. The week's events were widely seen as a pivotal moment that demonstrated Obama could handle a crisis as president.*

*Despite the media attention, this swirl of activity in Washington had little effect on my life. We continued to build neighborhood volunteer teams, call voters, and knock on doors—in the field, that was our entire focus.*

**Lauren Kidwell, Regional Director:** As an organizer in this campaign environment, you're obsessed with the day-to-day news and the talking points that go with it, because it's relevant to your job and to what your staff will say at the doors. But you don't have time to actually follow it.

**Nicole Young, Western Michigan Regional Field Director:** In Michigan, the economy tipped the scales dramatically for us in the general election. My region was really a bellwether because it was already on the way to recession. I had never seen so many foreclosed houses in my entire life. I didn't have any kind of understanding of what was coming. There was nothing in my background that would have made me think, "Well, that probably indicates that we're on the way to recession." It was just head down. Looking at a foreclosed house, I'd think, "We're talking about the economy here" and reshuffle my position paper to talk about jobs before knocking on the door.

But I think the states where I heard the most violent language about race were these places that were eventually going to be really hard-hit by the recession. There was a younger organizer I worked with—a very sweet, Jewish white man from a family committed to social justice. He and I went out one day in rural Michigan and did voter registration together. While we were there, someone screamed at him he was a "N-word lover."

He was shaking, so we had to have a conversation about that. I, a Black woman, had to comfort this young white man more than once about the terrible racist things people were saying to him.

Looking back, I recognize the ways in which those things were tied to job insecurity. At the time, I didn't realize it in that way. I didn't know that economic anxiety can further radicalize racial anxiety. I just thought they were hella racist places—which they also may be.

**Lauren Kidwell:** I distinctly remember the day that McCain erred in saying that "the fundamentals of the economy are strong," but I really didn't realize that our economy was collapsing around us. I wasn't following the degree to which real people were losing their jobs, which is so crazy to think about when the first thing I did in the morning was read the news clips. I knew what was going on, but in this cocoon of my all-consuming job, it was all through the lens of "What does it mean for my organizers today?"

I did notice how Nevada's housing crisis affected our ability to organize. Las Vegas is always a fairly transient place, but given the degree to which the housing crisis was already hitting that part of the country, we started noticing that our walk lists were garbage. It was rare to find a person at the door who matched the name on our list, and we were coming up on a lot of abandoned homes.

*As the election became more all-consuming, I would tell myself I needed to be at work until midnight, never getting a full night's rest. The cycle perpetuated itself to the point that I could waste hours each day just staring at my computer screen. Leaving the office one morning, I realized I had left my campaign Blackberry on the roof of my Toyota and backtracked along the highway to find it scuffed on the side of the road. The danger of running between speeding cars did not register in the moment. There was another night I fell asleep driving home and woke up in the middle of a pitch-black, empty highway, the car miraculously having come to a complete stop. Confusing time spent at work for productivity, I took a perverse pride in ignoring the rest of my life.*

**Howli Ledbetter, Burlington, NC, Field Organizer:** There was no outside world. Everything was work: registering voters, cutting turf, canvassing. The campaign isolated you from everyone you knew who wasn't doing it and bonded you with the people you were doing it with. So your life was split totally in half. There were all these people you knew before the campaign who were very important to you and whom you used to see all the time and cared about.

There wasn't time for people who weren't on the campaign. With the people you were working with, it felt like, "We're in this together. They're the only people who really understand what it's like." I had never had a job like that before, and it happened instantly. It was like a sliding door. I had one life, and then that ended, and the new one was all-consuming. I was in a very serious relationship in New York that ended in flames. There wasn't one person I knew on the campaign who had a relationship at the beginning and still had that relationship at the end of the campaign.

**Chris Wyant, Deputy Field Director, Ohio:** It's all a blur. I gained thirty pounds over the course of nineteen months. I remember debating how long I should leave work to go to my brother's wedding and struggling with feeling like I needed to stay.

**Carrianna Suiter, Regional Field Director:** I felt deep personal pressure to spend every moment of every day doing something that would positively impact the election. And every moment I wasn't working, I felt horrible. The closer we got, the more it terrified me that I wasn't doing enough. It felt like life-and-death. There was a real emotional and physical toll that work had on me. At the end of it, my physical health was in shambles. I was not taking care of myself, eating bad food, not sleeping, smoking too many cigarettes, and drinking way too much caffeine, which combined with lack of sleep had real implications for my health.

I hit my limit ten days before the election, when I totaled my car on the highway. I'd been ignoring the fact that the brakes were getting harder and harder to engage, and I couldn't stop in time. A volunteer came and picked me up after my car was towed. She said, "You need to go to the hospital," because I had all of this neck pain and back pain. And I remember thinking, "No, I've got to go to the office. I'll just take a day off after the election."

She had kids in college a few years younger than me. At a certain point, she said, "No, you need to go, and I'm going to take you because I would want someone to do this for my child." She took me to an urgent care ER.

Those moments of self-care that in any other job would've been a no-brainer didn't feel like an option. Not because anyone was telling me it wasn't an option—it was all internal pressure to work all the time.

**Meghan Goldenstein, Field Organizer:** Life doesn't stop while you're doing stuff like this. My aunt passed away two weeks before the election. While she was in hospice, I went home to see her for two days. I remember sobbing in the office about how I felt like leaving Dubuque was putting the campaign at risk—which, of course, in retrospect, was not true and sounds extremely self-centered. But the campaign made you feel like you were indispensable to your volunteers and your team.

The thing we kept saying was that John Kerry had lost Iowa by five votes per precinct in 2004. That was the mantra. "Five votes per precinct." And the idea that you might step away just felt like, "Well, what if it's those five votes?" I haven't been many places where it feels like everything you do is that momentous.

**Cathy Bolkcom, Le Claire, IA, Volunteer:** Beth Wehrman, who was one of our Le Claire leaders, got pancreatic cancer in 2007. Obama took a personal interest in her—he called, checked in on her. Beth was a worker bee, and as she got sicker and sicker and less able to work, she was very, very, very, very sad, because she wanted to be out there, knocking on doors and making phone calls.

**Sara Sullivan, Beth Wehrman's Daughter:** The day that all of us found out she was sick, she just went right back in to the campaign office. This was one of the big things in her life. The local caucus organizer, Tripp Wellde, was a really close friend of hers.

**Cathy Bolkcom:** Obama came back during Labor Day weekend in 2008 to do an event at the fairgrounds for undecided voters focused on small business owners. Beth was in the hospital, and she insisted that she was to come to the fairgrounds for the speech, so she was there in a wheelchair. She was not well. It was a very emotional time.

Beth was discharged and told there was nothing more they could do for her, so she went home to die. Her house was on my route to and from work, so I took to stopping by. We were not really tight friends. But I've found that when somebody's dying, sometimes their friends go away because they're not sure what to do or they don't want to impose. The four young adult daughters who were all there caring for her at home told me she looked forward to my visits because she wanted to hear about the campaign. So I'd go by every day, and I'd fill her in. She was so bummed out because she couldn't door knock and she couldn't make phone calls. She so wanted to live long enough to see this man elected president of the United States.

We organized an event, "Beth's Day of Action." And I was able to say to her, "You've got to let this go. You can't knock doors. But we're going to take one day and we're going to knock on more doors and make more phone calls than you could possibly have done during that time." In the end, a hundred people showed up to knock on doors in Beth's name on a Saturday in October.

I don't know how many nights I went over and they said, "We don't expect her to live through the night." And the next morning, I'd go over, and she was still there. She just wanted to vote. Finally, absentee balloting started, and the ballot came to her house.

**Leah White, Precinct Captain and Beth Wehrman's Daughter:** When that ballot showed up, it was symbolic, and it was very meaningful to all of us. I really do think that her passion and her drive about that gave us more time, because she really, really wanted to stick around and see it through.

**Sara Sullivan:** That was really monumental in her being able to let go. We didn't know what she was waiting for, quite honestly, and after she voted, she passed away.

Barack called my dad and asked if there was anything that he could do. He said that my mom was one of his best volunteers. I remember my dad being very surprised that Barack had taken the time to call him and realizing what a big impact my mom had.

*       *       *

*As Election Day grew closer, all of our efforts turned to early voting. People tend to think of Election Day as one day, but in several states, early and absentee voting allowed you to cast a ballot a month in advance. In states like Florida, Ohio, Iowa, and North Carolina, stressing the convenience of this became a huge part of our pitch to supporters.*

*Having caucused in Iowa, the first vote I ever cast for Barack Obama was at an early vote site in Raleigh one week before Election Day. I waited in line for an hour outside a suburban branch of a public library. Since so much of my time over the past few months had been spent talking to volunteers or convincing people to register, I had rarely been around ordinary citizens whose only connection to Obama would be visiting a voting booth during the general election. Watching the other people in line, overhearing their conversations, I had a palpable sense that history was unfolding, even if the outcome remained uncertain.*

**Tony Rediger, North Carolina Early Vote Director:** Early vote was a huge priority in several states. North Carolina had what they called "one-stop early voting," which meant even if you were unregistered, you could show up to the polls, register, and vote at the exact same time. So Election Day wasn't just one day; it was several weeks.

There was some hesitancy among our supporters about early voting. There was just a lack of trust and the idea that by voting outside Election Day, your vote might not be counted. We had to really work to show that not only was this a safe way to vote but that it was what the Obama campaign wanted you to do.

To encourage early voting, we required every organizer to hold a certain number of early voting events in their turf. Souls to the Polls was a big program in which we encouraged churches to go en masse after worship. In some high-target areas, we had major surrogates hold speaking events right next to early voting sites, and everyone who showed up would be told "go vote right now." In true North Carolina fashion, one organizer put together an early vote pig pickin', where they set up a pig pickin' across from a polling site. There were hundreds of events like these across the state.

So by the end of October, two million people in North Carolina had already voted, the majority of whom we thought were Obama supporters. Every day the Board of Elections released the list of who had voted, which meant every day we could cross all of those people off our list and focus only on those who had yet to turn out.

**Ava Hinds-Lawson, Sunrise, FL, First-Time Volunteer:** I voted early. It was Florida. I took every possible ID that I had. I remember I took my driver's license, I took my nurse's license, I took my work ID, I took my passport, I took everything with me because I was like, "There is no way they're gonna stop me from voting today." I took my mom. My mom was in her eighties, and she was ecstatic. Normally she voted by mail, and this time, she wanted to go to the polls. The idea that we might actually see a Black president in our lifetime—we wanted to be in the room where it happened.

I actually fell in love with Michelle first. Listening to her talk. The idea of a Black first lady was very appealing, and she was not just any Black first lady. She was educated, very, very knowledgeable about what she was talking about. I thought she was powerful and would be a powerful image for girls—for young Black girls, as a matter of fact, to see somebody like them in the White House. She was very real, and the fact that she was a working mother—when I would listen to her talk, her struggles sounded like my friends' struggles.

I thought of girls I know, especially Natalie, my daughter, because I remember when Natalie was younger, she was almost always the only Black girl in her gifted class, and it was a struggle coming up. Coming from Jamaica, we've had our struggles—it was something that we felt that we had a duty to make happen.

**Carrianna Suiter:** The pleasure wasn't necessarily even having the first Black president. It was being able to even cast that vote. It felt like such an emotional thing for many of the voters that we talked to. Regardless of whether he won or lost, that moment was historic.

**Stephanie Speirs, Ohio Deputy Field Director:** The historic nature of his candidacy was partially about race. But it was also, it seemed, about the inspiration that he was able to infuse into the election that people hadn't felt in a really long time.

By that I mean, I had volunteers who had never voted in their entire lives, and yet they were canvassing every day for Barack Obama. These old grandmas would come in from their canvassing shift and ice their knees, because they shouldn't have been walking. I had a woman who had Parkinson's and couldn't go door-to-door, but she would sit in our office for eight hours a day and write postcards to people in her town, trying to convince them to vote for Barack Obama, because it was her way of contributing. I was so lucky to witness stories like that, every single day.

That was my real-world manifestation of the historic nature of this candidacy. And it wasn't really explicitly discussed on a day-to-day level in terms of race. I know that the media made that the main manifestation of the historic nature of the candidacy—and I believed it to be part of it. But what I thought was really historic was the way he could inspire so many different kinds of people to believe in a common cause. That's what felt like we were part of a movement.

**Megan Simpson, Southwest Montana Regional Field Director:** I started Election Day with my family, who were volunteering back in Iowa, calling when they got up to start their staging location. Everyone was yelling, "I-O-W-A, Barack Obama All the Way!" All of them told me they loved me and were excited to talk when polls closed.

**Lauren Kidwell:** I woke up around 4:00 a.m. Pacific time. On Election Day, if you've done your job right, there's not much for you to do except be stressed and clamor for information. I remember being prepared to deal with long lines, but it wasn't an issue in Nevada. The day was kind of unremarkable.

**Yohannes Abraham, Field Organizer:** We were nervous wrecks that day. Every objective criterion pointed to us being in a position to win. But you just never know, particularly given the historic nature of this candidacy.

**Tommy Vietor, Press Staff:** In the back of your head, you have people telling you about the "Bradley effect," and you think of the people who said they'd vote for an African American candidate when maybe they really wouldn't. You're thinking about all the things that could go wrong and all the ways polls could have been off.

I knew we were up in states. I knew the financial crisis pulled the bottom out from under McCain, because he didn't know what the fuck to do. And so intellectually I felt really good, but emotionally I was a basket case.

**Jason Waskey, Maryland Field Director:** In the general election, Maryland shipped as many people as we could into Virginia and Pennsylvania to knock on doors and set up twenty-three call centers across our own state. On Election Day, the very first person I called was an older African American woman in West Philadelphia.

I said, "Ma'am, I'm calling to remind you that today is Election Day. Your polling place is . . ." and she let me go on.

Then she said, "You sound like a very nice young man. I want you to know that I've been ready for this Election Day my entire life. I was the first person to vote in my precinct this morning."

That was the moment where I really felt the history that we were making. What a good first call to make.

**Joe Cupka, Indianapolis, IN, Regional Field Director:** On Election Day, Obama did one campaign event, in Indianapolis, Indiana, where I was the regional. I get a phone call: "Joe, the senator's going to be at the UAW hall in Wayne Township for an unannounced stop."

I went out to the front of this UAW hall, and Reggie Love, the senator's traveling aide, got out of the car, came up, and gave me a big hug. I was wearing an Indiana sweatshirt. I had a white stocking cap on. I had a month-long beard. I looked absolutely wrecked after twenty-one months of campaigning.

Slowly getting out of the car after him was Barack Obama. He made eye contact with me and said, "Big Joe."

He had met so many more people since Iowa, but he remembered who I was. That melted me. I said, "Sir, every minute of this has been worth it."

And he said, "Let's go win this thing."

**Ava Hinds-Lawson:** Election Day, I was knocking on doors. I had never done this for another candidate before, and I was really passionate. I remember this elderly white man using a cane—I knocked on his door, it was almost five o'clock in the evening, and he was so upset. He was like, "I am not voting. I am not going."

"Why?"

"The place that I voted for years—I went over there, and they told me that I was supposed to go vote some other place. I am not going back." Then he saw who I was campaigning for, and he said, "I was going to vote for your guy."

I said, "You still can!"

He said, "Well, I'm not going to."

I was not having that. I took him in my car, drove him to the polling station, had him vote, and took him back home.

**Meghan Goldenstein:** Polls in Iowa were open until 9:00 p.m. Those last days, you had out-of-state people volunteering, and people were leaving early so they could get back in time to be in Grant Park. I cannot tell you how many volunteers asked, "Are you guys coming to Grant Park?" We'd say, "No, we're staying here until polls close—we don't get to just sneak out at five o'clock!"

**Kal Penn, Surrogate and Out-of-State Volunteer:** If you were an early surrogate, you got an invite to come to Grant Park for a victory celebration on election night. I was very appreciative, obviously, to be included in an invitation like that. But the first thing I thought was, "Well, what happens if we don't win? Am I really going to be cool with myself if I'm in Chicago with everybody getting drunk, watching us lose?"

Florida was still a toss-up. So I went down to Gainesville, to the University of Florida, for three days of GOTV. It was cool to see a bunch of people who shared that belief that, like, hey, we should probably be knocking doors until the last possible second. We got rocks thrown at us by some college Republicans on Election Day, which was very classy.

**Ava Hinds-Lawson:** On election night, we all went over to my cousin Richard's house, and we were gonna have a watch party—there were about thirteen of us glued to the TV. It was such a high. We had champagne. We had wine. We had a cake. We made a party out of it.

**Stephanie Speirs:** We were waiting, and we were waiting, and we were waiting. And someone screamed, "Oh my God, Fox News is calling it." And someone said, "Turn it to ABC; it might not be real."

**Bess Evans, Field Organizer:** Watching results come in, I remember exactly where I was standing when I heard Brian Williams say, "It's 11:00 p.m. on the East Coast, and we have news . . . "

> *BRIAN WILLIAMS [NBC News]: It's 11:00 p.m. on the East Coast, and we have news . . . an African American has broken the barrier as old as the republic. An astonishing candidate, an astonishing campaign, a seismic shift in American politics. You are looking at the forty-fourth president of the United States. The celebrations begin at 11:00 p.m. on election night. Let's listen to Grant Park in Chicago.*

**Stephanie Speirs:** And then the whole room exploded.

**Thomas Zimmerman, Field Organizer:** You heard cheers coming out of Grant Park, ricocheting off the buildings all around you. The whole city erupted in shouts. Everyone was so excited and emotional; everyone was hugging. You had all these people on the barrier crying and waving flags. On the cityscape they'd written "USA" across the buildings in lights.

**Jon Favreau, Speechwriter:** You could see this sea of people all the way up Grant Park. This incredibly diverse crowd cheering, crying. Every kind of American you could imagine. It was amazing . . . it was amazing.

**Michael Blake, Political Outreach Staffer:** I was running through the halls of the Renaissance Center in Michigan, saying, "We won! We won!" I remember jumping onstage, leading the chant, "Yes, we can! Yes, we can! Yes, we can!"

**Marygrace Galston, Campaign for Change Director:** In Virginia, I went behind the big screen and cried. My sister called me, and I cried. It was emotional and exciting. It was perfect. It was the greatest achievement of my life, other than having my daughter. Barack Obama winning the presidency was a culmination of so much work and money and blood and tears from everybody, and we helped put him in office. We changed the world that night.

**Lauren Kidwell:** In Vegas, we had our party at a casino. Just after the election had been called, I was walking around wearing my "Let's go win this fucking thing" T-shirt. You would see one crowd of Obama people run into another crowd of Obama people, and cheers would go up. It was jubilant. In the casino, there were people cheering, hugging, high-fiving, laughing. And gambling.

*I watched returns come in at a restaurant down the street from our Chapel Hill office. When Obama crossed 270 electoral votes, Andrew, whom I met at the first Students for Obama meeting in Iowa and later hired as a North Carolina organizer, hugged me. "Thanks for calling me," he said as we wiped away tears.*

*The room was packed with celebrating volunteers. We walked outside and heard this roar start to build down the road. Thousands of students had rushed onto Franklin Street, as if UNC had just won the Final Four. We walked to the intersection. Some students recognized Andrew and hoisted him on their shoulders. He crowd-surfed through the street to chants of "O-BA-MA! O-BA-MA!" Traffic stood still, and a boom box blasted Obama's victory speech.*

**Jon Favreau:** He came to public life as a community organizer and believed deeply in that, and he wanted to build a movement that was about organizers and activists and ordinary people believing that they could actually change the world. That was a central thesis of his candidacy. So it felt obvious that on election night, as he claimed victory, it would be the victory of all the people who signed up to knock on doors and make phone calls and believed.

> *BARACK OBAMA [Speech Excerpt]: I will never forget who this victory truly belongs to—it belongs to you. I was never the likeliest candidate for this office. We didn't start with much money or many endorsements. Our campaign . . . was built by working men and women who dug into what little savings they had to give five dollars and ten dollars and twenty dollars to this cause. It grew strength from the young people who rejected the myth of their generation's apathy; who left their homes and their families for jobs that offered little pay and less sleep; from the not-so-young people who braved the bitter cold and scorching heat to knock on the doors of perfect strangers; from the millions of Americans who volunteered, and organized, and proved that more than two centuries later, a government of the people, by the people, and for the people has not perished from this earth. This is your victory.*
>
> *What began twenty-one months ago in the depths of winter must not end on this autumn night. This victory alone is not the change we seek—it is only the chance for us to make that change. And that cannot happen if we go back to the way things were. It cannot happen without you.*

**Lauren Champagne, Field Organizer:** We all just burst into tears, particularly the minorities in the room, because to see that happen was something we couldn't describe in words, but we all felt it so deeply.

As a dark-skinned Black woman, you're always told that you're not attractive, or you're not valued, or you're not smart. Every year in school, no matter how well I did, I was told I shouldn't go into the honors classes. Because you are African American, you are "less than." You can't be the Disney princess. You can't be the president.

And to have this man do it and do it in such a graceful fashion, in a dominating way—that was amazing. The front page of our student newspaper was me and my best friend from law school embracing with tears streaming down our faces.

**David Axelrod, Chief Strategist:** Election night played out exactly as Obama said. All over the world, people were looking at the

United States differently, and there were all these young people of color who were in disbelief and joy over what had happened. He really foresaw what that night would be like.

**Marie Ortiz, Marshalltown, IA, Precinct Captain:** I never thought it was actually going to happen until that night. I just didn't think America was ready for that. No matter how far we'd come, we still had a long way to go. When he won, my great-grandma was the first person to call me. That brought tears to my eyes because she said, "I can't believe it . . . I never thought it would happen in my lifetime."

My kids, her great-great-grandchildren—she says she didn't think it would happen in *their* lifetime. And I sat down and thought about it, all the stuff that she did. And she lived to see that day. So I thought, "My kids—we helped make history." No matter what anybody says, we helped in our own little way, in Marshalltown, Iowa, make history.

**Dean Fluker, Youth Vote Director, North Carolina:** It was a really surreal moment, being surrounded by all that excitement. In Raleigh, I walked down the street late that night and saw all these people I did not know, also celebrating. Because at that point it was all so personal to us. We'd put eighteen months into this. And you think you know everybody, or at least they all know you. But to see these people in the street I'd never seen before, who were also so emotionally invested, that was a really cool moment I'll never forget. Because we were a part of something that was so much larger than anything I had an inkling of.

**Thomas Zimmerman:** Day to day, there wasn't this sense that you were making history. The story felt like this huge national moment, but the work in front of you was so all-consuming you rarely had the space and time to make that connection. It didn't fully sink in until Grant Park.

**Maggie Thompson, St. Paul, MN, Regional Field Director:** We went to the watch party in this big hotel in downtown St. Paul. I felt relieved. I was not a screamer and jumper. I felt like every cell in my body sagged, and I was so tired but overjoyed.

I left the party and stopped at my favorite campaign restaurant, Hardee's. I pulled into the drive-through, paid for my chili cheese fries, and drove into a parking spot. I thought, "I'm going to sit here for just a minute and eat my cheese fries."

I woke up the next morning at 8:30 a.m. My car was still running, my doors were unlocked, and there was an unopened, congealed tray of chili cheese fries in my passenger seat. I had twenty-two missed calls. I had slept there the whole night.

**Vera Kelly, Davenport, IA, Volunteer:** I didn't go to sleep at all. We were up all night long. And then I said, "Well, I'm going to the inauguration."

**Yohannes Abraham:** The next day, I woke up, and my parents had gathered every newspaper they could get their hands on. Reading the headlines the next day, seeing the pictures, you felt like you were a part of something really, really special. The other people in your life validated that. There's a lot of intrinsic satisfaction, a lot of external validation.

**Greg Degen, Regional Field Director, Pennsylvania:** It wasn't until I saw the images of people from around the world celebrating that the historic nature of what we had done dawned on me. Being so young, and having had no prior experience in politics, I had no appreciation for how American politics is something that the entire world follows and feels invested in. So to realize that we had lifted the hopes of not only millions of Americans but millions of people around the world felt amazing and made me realize that what we were involved in was much bigger than our country—it was about the direction the entire world felt like it was going in.

**Ava Hinds-Lawson, Sunrise, FL, First-Time Volunteer:** You felt like a new day was dawning. Like something new was happening. And I knew that he could not have won with just the votes of Black people in America. I knew that a substantial amount of white America voted for him too.

**Nicole Young:** The next morning, the first thing I did was call my little brother, who was nine years old. I was like, "Matthew, do you know who won the election?"

He was like, "Duh, Barack Obama." As if there was no question in his mind. Then he told me he had a school election the day before, and somebody had voted for McCain. But he was like, "But I knew that Barack Obama was going to win."

For me as a Black woman, it was beautiful to know that my nine-year-old brother was never going to doubt that a Black man could win the presidency.

**David Plouffe, Campaign Manager:** The history of it didn't dawn on me really until the next day. Then you started to see some of the video from around the world, and some commentary on it. We were just trying to win the presidency. We weren't trying to make history.

*Nearly seventy million people had voted for Obama, more than any candidate for president in American history. He ended up flipping nine states Bush had won in 2004, en route to earning 365 electoral votes. Even Indiana, which I had thought an impossible reach, ended up in our column.*

*By Wednesday evening, copies of the* New York Times *were selling for $400 on eBay as images of celebration rolled in from across the world. Kenya declared a national holiday; "Histórico!" read front-page headlines in Peru, Portugal, and Panama. Nelson Mandela published an open letter congratulating the president-elect: "Your victory has demonstrated that no person anywhere in the world should not dare to dream of wanting to change the world for a better place." Our office filled with volunteers looking to reminisce and souvenir hunters I had never met.*

*The week after the election was one long, rolling goodbye. Our Chapel Hill volunteers hosted a party, where I hugged the local retired women who made the operation run and offered vague promises to keep in touch. Durham for Obama, which in less than nine months had grown from an online grassroots group to an eleven-thousand-person volunteer organization, was already planning to pivot to local issues. I printed up farewell presents for each organizer at Kinko's—a photoshopped map of their turf inside a six-dollar Walmart frame, showing Obama had won North Carolina by 14,177 votes and comparing the turnout from 2004 to that of 2008. At the bottom was the quote from Obama's victory speech about the volunteers and organizers to whom his victory belonged. When I paid for my copies, the Kinko's associate, who looked to be in his midforties, said, "First time I voted for president, man," and smiled.*

*Soon after, the North Carolina staff had a farewell gathering that brought everyone in from across the state and eventually migrated to our apartment. I ended the night eating cereal out of a box with my hands and softly singing Usher's "Love in This Club" until I fell asleep midchorus, surrounded by now-former colleagues. Saturday, I cleaned the stacks of unused Obama stickers out of my back seat, threw away the three inches of trash that had accumulated since June, and headed west toward Iowa.*

**Megan Simpson:** My office was packed up, and that's when it hit me: "I don't know what I'm supposed to be doing now." Because for a year and a half, you had goals, and you had places you had to be. And then all of a sudden you didn't have to do anything.

I decided that I wanted to do a road trip. I drove out of Montana with another staffer, and I went to Arizona for a couple of days. We stopped at the Grand Canyon. We drove through Utah and saw Zion National Park. Drove through Idaho. I felt a little lost, because I didn't know what I wanted to do next. "Should I go back to school?" I wondered. I had a lot of decisions that I didn't want to make.

**Meghan Goldenstein:** I went back home. I got really sick, because it's what your body does when you haven't slept in forever. Somehow you stay healthy through adrenaline and then crash when everything's over. It feels like the world has stopped around you, because you're so used to the relentless pace.

There were some people that went straight to Georgia, because there was a special election for the US Senate that was going to happen four weeks later. I remember being so jealous because they were still riding the train. I wanted to be doing that. But it would have felt like running away from people that I had already put on hold for too long.

**Nicole Young:** I remember watching David Axelrod saying, "It's like the end of the TV show *M.A.S.H.*, where you've been at war this whole time, you loved all these people, you've done this thing together, and you're really glad to be going home, because the number one thing you want to do is go home. But then also you know you'll never have this moment again. You'll never be with these people in this way again. And you kind of don't want to go home, but you have to go home."

That perfectly explained every feeling I had, which was this deep, deep absence of purpose, of community, of shared passion and vision for the world. I found myself missing so many moments afterward. I missed the thrill of going state to state and being able to be like, "I'm the Obama girl." Like I'd walk into a local Democratic meeting or a union meeting, and they'd be like, "There's the Obama girl." I missed that. I missed my volunteers. I knew we could never re-create that moment, and I felt the loss immediately.

**Pete Rouse, Obama Senate Chief of Staff:** 2008 was unique, in terms of what it was like to be part of an effort of that magnitude, with those stakes. It's an amazing example of talented, dedicated individuals— from field organizers to the most senior people in the campaign— sublimating their own egos and their own personal goals and needs to the greater cause. I'd never been part of anything like that before, and I'm sure I won't be again.

**Janice Rottenberg, Hamilton County, OH, Field Organizer:** After the campaign was over and I went back to school, I used to call into freeconferencecall.com just to listen to the music because I missed the campaign so much. I was so confused about what I was supposed to do now that I was a college kid again and not an organizer. I was eighteen. For me it was life changing that somebody had said to me, "You seem to be pretty good at this." And I thought this could be a thing I keep doing.

**Lauren Kidwell:** There was a conference call with Plouffe and President-Elect Obama, who got on and said something like, "Thank you all. Come to Washington. There will be a spot in my administration for anybody who wants to work for me," which didn't turn out to be true. He wasn't trying to make false promises, but I think we were all naïve to the realities of how few slots there were going to be. We could have done a better job setting expectations.

**Howli Ledbetter:** I didn't know what I was going to do. I kept getting sick after the campaign. My personal life was in total shambles. I'd broken up with my boyfriend in New York. I'd started dating somebody else in North Carolina, who was about to deploy to Iraq. There was this feeling when the campaign ended, like, "Of course everybody's going to the White House. Put your résumé on change.gov; they'll call you any minute." I lived on my girlfriend's couch in San Francisco and started applying for jobs after it became very clear we weren't all getting jobs at the White House.

**Yohannes Abraham:** There were multiple moments over the next couple weeks where I'd catch myself getting emotional about what had happened. It was another weird time because it had been eight years since the last Democratic president. It had been sixteen years since the last Democratic inauguration.

There was no road map, like if we win, I wanna do *X*, or if we win, I wanna do *Y*. Almost nobody had that clarity of vision because we had been focused on the mission. For the first time in a year and a half, you had to ask, "What do I wanna do with my life?"

**Kal Penn:** I resumed my job on a TV show, so I had something to go back to. I remember thinking, "I just spent a year going to more than half the country telling young people they should vote for a guy for the following reasons. Shouldn't I help execute these promises?"

**Maggie Thompson:** When we started looking for jobs, the economy had just collapsed. It was depressing because we had just gotten off this amazing experience, but a lot of our parents were losing their savings. It was a rough time in addition to the more existential question: "What do I do now?"

**Yohannes Abraham:** It's a hard pivot from being a part of something historic and huge to worrying about a paycheck. You had to very quickly figure out how you were gonna pay your bills.

\*        \*        \*

*I arrived back home and watched the Obama transition play out over television. The economy was losing eight hundred thousand jobs per month, and Obama's appointments seemed designed to stress unity and stability in the wake of a divisive predecessor. There were early Obama endorsers named to key posts, but nearly every rival from the primary who had not become engulfed in scandal was given the chance to serve in the cabinet. Former Iowa governor Tom Vilsack, who had dropped out of the race two weeks after Obama's announcement and become Hillary Clinton's top Iowa supporter, was named secretary of agriculture. Bill Richardson was briefly named secretary of commerce before withdrawing due to an ethics investigation. Joe Biden ended up as vice president.*

*The biggest surprise was Hillary Clinton's appointment as secretary of state, followed closely by the reappointment of George W. Bush's secretary of defense. "I am a strong believer in strong personalities and strong opinions. That's how the best decisions are made," Obama said. "I will welcome vigorous debate inside the White House, but understand I will be setting policy as president. The buck will stop with me."*

*Slowly, an Obama presidency was starting to take shape. These appointments, Bush's unpopularity, and the historic nature of Obama's candidacy turned his inauguration into a bipartisan moment of celebration—counterprogramming to the worst crisis since the Great Depression. When I landed in Washington, DC, three days before his swearing-in, the commercialization of the Obama brand was everywhere: Hennessey cognac released a limited edition "44" label, Pepsi redesigned their logo as an homage to the Obama O ("Yes You Can!"), IKEA had built a replica Oval Office in its Union Station store ("Change Begins at Home"), and street vendors hocked Obama condoms.*

**Ava Hinds-Lawson:** I couldn't wait to get to DC. I bought my ticket for the inauguration before he even got the nomination—for me, my mom, my husband. I bought tickets for everybody. A lot of people that I knew were going. We were bursting with excitement. The plane was half full with people who were headed to DC for the inauguration, so it was a party atmosphere—there were people on the flight chanting, "Yes, we can! Yes, we did!"

**Meghan Goldenstein:** On Inauguration Day, I got up at 5:00 a.m. The metro was packed. We layered up in seventeen layers of clothing. Everything felt momentous and exciting again. Like, "This is historic. How lucky are we to be here to be part of this?"

There was a line to get onto the metro at Bethesda. The trains would come, and they were all standing room only. Your platform was full, and you packed on.

**Jan Bauer, Story County, IA, Democratic Party Chair:** For me, and I think for a lot of people, the fact that he was African American just didn't matter. Of course, we, the folks that were saying this, were not African American. I was oblivious to it, you know? For me, it was just winning the caucus for a guy I truly believed in.

Well, of course, it's hugely important. It took the inauguration for me to wake up. I was amazed at just how many people were so energized by the fact that he was the first African American president. The city was alive. It was electric. I was sitting in a section near the Tuskegee Airmen. That was really powerful.

**Annie Corine Bennett, Former South Carolina Volunteer:** It was a feeling that I cannot describe. It was cold. It was cold, but I was so happy to be there. It was a beautiful day.

**Michael Blake:** I was on the bus with the King family on our way to the Capitol. I was silent out of respect. I didn't know what to say. When we pulled up, MLK III turned to us and said, "Thank you." I just teared up.

You got up to the Capitol, and it was chaos everywhere. We were trying to figure out where to go stand. We stood up on the platform and looked out. I saw this endless sea of people.

**David Axelrod:** It's a cliché to say "a sea of humanity," but there were people as far as the eye could see. It was astonishing. You couldn't move in the streets of Washington leading up to the inauguration without running into crowds of people who had come from all over.

**Lauren Champagne:** You had all these people descend on DC from different walks of life. As President Obama was speaking, my friend and I were just outside of the gate and could hear the speakers. We ended up right next to this couple we had never met, and we started crying and hugging each other. That was the joy. Euphoria. There was no fighting. People were happy. They were just randomly hugging each other and chanting and crying and excited. Every race, color, creed, whatever. It was beautiful.

**Nicole Young:** "We did that." That was the refrain in my brain the whole day. Even when my feet were going numb and I put hand warmers in my shoes and we were standing in the freezing cold. Being able to be in that crowd and watch that man be sworn in as president was just amazing.

**Elizabeth Wilkins, Michigan Field Director:** I was in the purple ticket tunnel of doom. But everybody was so happy that I didn't really care. I just wanted to be a part of it. We got out of the tunnel, but we couldn't get into the gate, so I ended up too far away to see or hear well.

I was with a friend, and we could have been super disappointed, but there was an older white couple that had an old-school transistor radio. We huddled around this little radio and were a part of the crowd. I loved it. All of these people had traveled from all over the country because they were so excited about this moment, and we were there together.

It was the first time over the course of the campaign I felt like, "I'm just a citizen of this country, and I get to be a part of the public narrative, and there's something amazing about that."

*I had two purple tickets for the swearing-in, which made my friend and I one of 1.8 million people trying to get through security to the National Mall. Stuck in our assigned tunnel entrance that would become known informally as the "purple ticket tunnel of doom," we eventually gave up and walked around the parade security perimeter. Thirty minutes before Obama's swearing-in, we found space to stand just in front of the World War II Memorial, nearly two miles west of the Capitol. I watched Obama's inaugural address on the jumbotrons surrounding the Washington Monument. When he finished, a man near me turned to a stranger and asked their name. "I want to remember who I was standing next to when I saw this," he said.*

*We had planned to line the parade route, but the crowd was too overwhelming. We slowly made our way east along the National Mall, across the highway, past the Capitol, and to the room I had rented for the weekend. When we finally arrived, CNN showed the Obamas in their bulletproof review stand, watching the inaugural parade.*

**Steve Dunwoody, Former Field Organizer:** The parade went on so long there weren't enough people in the parade box behind the president and they needed to make it look full, so they asked me and a couple others to sit there, acting like we were guests.

When the military came down the street, Barack was turned around talking to someone, and the chairman of the Joint Chiefs of Staff gave him a little elbow nudge to say, "Mr. President, military is coming down the street." Barack turned around to return the salute. That was such a moment for me.

**Melvin Shaw, Former Iowa Caucus Precinct Captain:** I didn't go into the office that day. I remember watching the inauguration on CNN and watching President Obama and Michelle walk down Pennsylvania Avenue. Watching him walk down the street and seeing the throngs of people and hearing some who didn't think that he could win now remarking about how historic it was.

I felt ownership because I had participated. I hadn't just gone into a voting booth and cast a ballot, but I was actually telling folks throughout the campaign why they should make a switch. I had moved from being inactive to being an advocate. So Inauguration Day was euphoria. It was "We made it." I walked taller. I'm not kidding. I walked taller the next day. Because I felt as though I identified with President Obama. I felt as though he were a common man. Some say it was because he was Black, but that's not it. I felt taller because I thought the country would be different for my child. I truly did.

**Cathy Bolkcom, Former Iowa Volunteer:** After the election, we were talking about how we weren't going to Washington for the balls. We decided we should have an inaugural ball here in the Quad Cities. So I signed contracts for a ballroom at the River Center for dinner for hundreds of people. We had two bands. We had big-screen projector TVs that I got a guy to donate in exchange for a table. It was fifty dollars a ticket for dinner and dancing and the whole nine yards. The night of the ball, we had to turn people away, because we were full at 525 people. It was full-out formal.

**Kal Penn:** I took my parents to the Southwest State Inaugural Ball. I remember it being such a scene, because it wasn't just the campaign alumni; it included all these old school DC people who were more interested in taking their picture and networking than celebrating the moment. It was everything about politics that I didn't like.

**Ava Hinds-Lawson:** The day after inauguration, we went and drove by the White House and were like, "He's situated. We're happy. We're glad."

I felt proud that I helped make it happen. I volunteered. I'd never done near anything like that before, but I was proud that I was able to go out despite all my fears and all my trepidation and knock on doors to say, "We gotta do this." I was not fearful at all doing that. Now I would be. And prior to it, I might have been.

For my little male cousins, the really young boys—there were four of them at the time—I made a binder memorializing the campaign, election, and inauguration and gave it to them. I told them that they could add to it as his presidency went on. I still have all the newspapers. I have every magazine cover that they were on. I can't afford to forget that era.

*The final inauguration event was the one I most looked forward to: the staff ball. Every campaign staffer was invited to the DC Armory hall for a thank-you party. Jay-Z was the headliner. Arcade Fire opened in front of a banner that declared "Renewing America's Promise." I screamed along to every song they played.*

*"This is the funnest party I've ever been to for a bunch of people who just lost their jobs," lead singer Win Butler said.*

*"Ninety-nine problems, but a Bush ain't one," Jay-Z rapped.*

*"If I'd known how good you guys were, I'd have never gone to Iowa," Joe Biden said when he took the stage.*

*For the first and only time, this group of people were together in the same room, celebrating the accomplishment so many had thought impossible. Walking through the hall, I kept recognizing alumni from different primary states. Many friends walked over to meet David Plouffe, connecting a face to the intense, hyper-disciplined, disembodied voice that had directed our lives for nearly two years via conference call.*

**David Plouffe:** By inauguration weekend, the history really had sunk in.

Because I was mostly in the headquarters in Chicago during the general election or on the plane, I didn't meet most of the staff out in the states. So the night of the staff ball I had hundreds of conversations with people, and they largely would be, "Hey, I'm Chris, and I worked in Pennsylvania."

I'd say, "Where in Pennsylvania?" They'd say the town and the county. For the most part, I could remember the result and congratulate or say, "You kept it close," or would ask them to tell me about the volunteers.

"I was in Asheville, North Carolina." "I was in Fort Myers, Florida." "I was in Laconia, New Hampshire."

Walking through that hall for a couple hours and meeting everybody, hearing their stories, was so incredibly powerful. It was one of the more meaningful nights of the whole enterprise for me. There it was. *That* was the campaign. All these young kids who had gone to different places in the country—a lot of them for the first time— experiencing these communities, making it happen.

**Bess Evans:** I remember going to the staff ball and thinking, "Who are all these people? This was much bigger than I even thought." Because you sort of rolled with people that you knew—we never did an all-staff get-together before that staff ball.

So I remember seeing Thomas Zimmerman and that Iowa crew. And there were a lot of tears. Every picture I have of that night has me with mascara running down my face.

**Thomas Zimmerman:** The staff ball was like a constant parade. You're walking through this darkened room and keep bumping into people. You bump into people from Iowa, and then you bump into people from Chicago. There was an element of it like when you watch the end sequence of a movie where they run through the text of where everyone went.

**Lauren Champagne:** It just seemed like a family reunion. People you collected and met during different primaries all gathered together. That was the best thing, being able to celebrate with all the people you met along the way.

**Kal Penn:** They asked me to introduce Plouffe, who was then going to introduce the president. Backstage in this hallway at the staff ball, there were thirty tactical assault team guys who rolled in heavily armed. There was a little buffer, and then the Secret Service guys in suits show up. Then I saw the boss, and I was like, "Holy shit."

That was the moment when I realized all of those individual people who thought, "I want to vote because my student loans are too exorbitant" or "I lost my cousin in Afghanistan" or "I don't have health insurance"—all of those individuals added up to electing this guy. And now he was the president, with everything that comes along with that. It was a really sobering visual.

You work on a campaign early enough, everybody is just a human. You know all the staff. And then you cut to this surreal moment where what you have the opportunity to do and represent for your country is so much bigger. That image, that contrast—I remember feeling simultaneously very proud of the work that we had done and very humbled by what was about to happen over the next four years.

**Lauren Kidwell:** The last event of the inauguration was President Obama thanking the staff. He'd always identified with us—he'd been a community organizer when he was in his twenties, and you really felt that come through in that speech.

**Meghan Goldenstein:** Apart from having this three-day trip to DC, some of us were in kind of a dark place. As somebody who was there that night feeling very uncertain about what my next steps were going to be—knowing I was off this train and worried there wasn't going to be a chance to get back on—it was great to be back among all your people. But it also highlighted the extent to which a lot of them were already doing new things in DC or in their own states. It's easy to feel like you're the only one who's like, "OK. Well, I'm going to go home and go back to living with my mom when this weekend's done."

I was in a place where I wondered if this would be the most amazing thing that I did with my whole life . . . and it was over.

**Greg Degen:** The day before inauguration, I turned twenty-one. So at the staff ball, I was excited that I could now finally drink with my colleagues after having spent a year and a half watching them drink without me.

It was a very uncertain time for a lot of the staff. I had to go back to college, so I didn't expect to have a job, but expectations had been a bit mismanaged for how likely it was going to be that people would work for the administration. It's weird to be twenty and feel like you've done the most important thing that you might ever do. I remember thinking a lot about that Bruce Springsteen song "Glory Days," about middle-aged people who only talk about the time they won a high school baseball championship. I remember thinking, "Is that gonna be us? Because we're already doing a lot of reminiscing about the Iowa caucus, and it's only been a year."

There was this lingering question: "What can we do that would ever be so important again?" And at that staff ball, Barack Obama answered that question by giving a speech about how to think about the next step.

> BARACK OBAMA [Speech Excerpt]: So many of you are at the start of your careers . . . take the spirit, the culture of this campaign, and keep applying it not just to campaigns. That sense of possibility that you guys can do anything. That you can reimagine the world. That you can lead—not by trying to manipulate your way, or push somebody else out of the way, but instead lead through the force of your example . . . I just hope that you carry that with you everywhere you go. Because that's what America

*needs right now. Active citizens like you who are willing to turn toward each other, talk to people you've never met, and say, "C'mon, let's go do this—let's go change the world."*

*For the rest of your lives, cling on to that essential thing about you. What made this campaign special was you. And don't let anybody forget that. Don't let anybody take that away from you! Because I promise you if everybody in this hall is willing to keep doing what you guys did over the last two years, then I'm optimistic about America. I may make some mistakes, but you'll set me right. And after I'm out of office, then you'll set the next person right.*

**Meghan Goldenstein:** To have him say, "You don't all have to do *this*. You're going to continue this work. Not just in DC, not just if you work for my administration, not just if you run for office." The nature of that quote was essentially, "I believe in you, and you can continue to carry the same principles to whatever spaces you're leading in."

That was really impactful. So much of his campaign was about sharing your stories and finding connections and realizing that your experience is valuable. Your view is unique, and yet you have more in common with people than you think, if you reach out and find connection.

I watched it enough times when I got home that some of those phrases stayed in my head. There were thousands of people there that night, but I would think, "He's talking about me. I'm going to hold on to this. There are plenty of days where I don't necessarily believe that this is true. But the president of the United States believes this is true. So I'm going to fake it until I make it."

**Bess Evans:** There wasn't an ounce of cynicism in me. I remember feeling, "We can take this and apply it to the rest of our lives." And yes, some of that has been broken down in me. But for the most part, I still truly believe that. We had proven all those cynics wrong. "They said this day would never come." They did. And it did.

**Greg Degen:** I had always felt like Election Day was the end. But this was the first time I realized it was the beginning. And in some ways, there is no beginning and end.

We're part of a continuum of Americans who are just trying to make their country better. This need to improve the country, this need to be an active participant in democracy—it never ends. I remember when Trump was elected, I had the exact same realization I had on the day after Obama's inauguration: "This never ends."

There is no perfect union. You just keep making it.

# EPILOGUE

*"This Never Ends"*

As I stood on the National Mall the week of Obama's inauguration, there was a sense of finality to the celebration. It felt as if we were witnessing the last chapter of a decades-long struggle and the birth of a new progressive era.

Congressman John Lewis—whose skull had been fractured leading the march for voting rights across Edmund Pettis Bridge forty-four years earlier—declared, "Barack Obama is what comes at the end of that bridge in Selma." Some conservatives said that Obama's ascent was proof America had entered a "post-racial" period. Democrats were on their way to a sixty-seat majority in the Senate, and there was speculation the Republican Party could be on the verge of elimination. Bill Clinton's former campaign strategist even published a book predicting Democrats would rule for the next four decades.

In the months and years that followed, I ran into campaign alumni at miniature reunions during GOTV or on the sidelines of Obama's second inauguration and heard about the paths they took after 2008.

Meghan Goldenstein finished the master's degree she put on hold to join the 2008 campaign and ended up working at a Chicago non-profit that teaches civic engagement to middle and high schoolers. Every four years since, she takes a new group to Iowa so they can witness the caucus process that had such an impact on her.

Stephanie Speirs became an entrepreneur. She started a Boston-based company that brings solar energy to low-income communities and says that her experiences as an organizer and a waitress are the two she draws on most in her current daily life as a CEO.

A few former organizers ended up back in Chicago, working for the United Way. Others went to law school. Or business school. Or divinity school. Some moved to San Francisco and worked for start-ups. Others became teachers and social workers. Several, like Megan Simpson, Michael Halle, and Ally Coll, dove back into campaigns and hopscotched across the country for years.

Still others, like Yohannes Abraham, came to the White House and helped pass legislation that expanded health care insurance to twenty million Americans, reformed Wall Street, and confirmed two Supreme Court justices. Appointees at federal agencies, former organizers like Esther Morales, implemented presidential initiatives that cut carbon emissions and supported clean energy. Hundreds more worked across the federal government to expand LGBTQ protections, spearhead criminal justice reform programs, reduce student loan debt, and prevent another recession.

The experience even led some to became media stars. Jon Favreau, Tommy Vietor, Dan Pfeiffer, and Alyssa Mastromonaco started podcasts or wrote books that offered platforms to shine spotlights on candidates and direct money to progressive causes.

Like most alumni, I hoped Obama's record and strong approval rating would help carry another Democrat into the White House to continue his work. And so, eight years after Obama's inauguration, in the lead-up to the 2016 election, I returned to North Carolina to volunteer for Hillary Clinton. Walking into a local volunteer office to get my packet, I could scarcely contain my impulse to scream at the field organizer training me, "I used to have your job!"

In North Carolina, I visited former volunteers who were still leading canvasses and organizing rides to the polls. For so many who volunteered for the first time in 2008, Obama's margin of victory had rewarded what little faith they had in politics. His success was proof that despite obstacles, fundamentally, the American system worked, and it was possible to accomplish something that had never been done before.

The election of Donald Trump, a reality television star whose political ascent in the Republican Party was sparked by his "investigation" of Barack Obama's citizenship, did serious damage to that faith. That he would win the electoral college with nearly three million fewer votes than Hillary Clinton only further laid bare the structural shortcomings of our democracy and all that remained undone despite the past eight years. In the weeks following Trump's election, I heard people talk of little else.

"Why didn't we focus more on state legislatures?"

"We need to plan an event that trains people how to run for office."

"How can we get volunteers in safe districts connected to flippable seats?"

This feeling of existential dread extended far beyond former organizers. A friend's uncle in Queens told me he was so shaken by Trump's election that he planned to dedicate all his free time and disposable income to taking back the House of Representatives in 2018. "That will not happen," I thought. "Gerrymandering makes it impossible."

Ten days before Obama left office, my wife, Fiona, another '08 organizer, and I flew to Chicago for the president's farewell address. The night was supposed to be a break—a nostalgic interlude in the face of looming disaster. But waiting for Obama to take the stage, I wondered whether his farewell would sound more like an elegy, as the accomplishments we gathered to celebrate were in danger of being washed away.

The speech began with Obama reciting the origin story I had heard so many times in Iowa: a directionless young man, looking to make a difference, who came to Chicago and found a purpose in organizing. He listed the greatest hits of his administration: passage of the Affordable Care Act, the Iran nuclear deal, marriage equality. But his words focused less on the past and more on the potential to meet the challenges ahead.

> *BARACK OBAMA [Speech Excerpt]: But that potential will be realized only if our democracy works . . . our democracy is threatened whenever we take it for granted. . . . It needs you. Not just when there's an election, not just when your own narrow interest is at stake, but over the full span of a lifetime.*
>
> *If you're tired of arguing with strangers on the internet, try to talk with one in real life. If something needs fixing, lace up your shoes and do some organizing. If you're disappointed by your elected officials, grab a clipboard, get some signatures, and run for office yourself. Show up. Dive in. Persevere. Sometimes you'll win. Sometimes you'll lose. Presuming a reservoir of goodness in others can be a risk, and there will be times when the process disappoints you. But for those of us fortunate enough to have been a part of*

*this work, to see it up close, let me tell you, it can energize and inspire . . . that faith I placed all those years ago, not far from here, in the power of ordinary Americans to bring about change—that faith has been rewarded in ways I couldn't possibly have imagined. I hope yours has, too.*

*Some of you here tonight or watching at home were there with us in 2004, in 2008, in 2012—and maybe you still can't believe we pulled this whole thing off . . . to all of you out there— every organizer who moved to an unfamiliar town and kind family who welcomed them in, every volunteer who knocked on doors, every young person who cast a ballot for the first time, every American who lived and breathed the hard work of change—you are the best supporters and organizers anyone could hope for, and I will forever be grateful. Because, yes, you changed the world.*

*That's why I leave this stage tonight even more optimistic about this country than I was when we started. Because I know our work has not only helped so many Americans; it has inspired so many Americans—especially so many young people out there—to believe you can make a difference; to hitch your wagon to something bigger than yourselves. This generation coming up—unselfish, altruistic, creative, patriotic—I've seen you in every corner of the country. You believe in a fair, just, inclusive America; you know that constant change has been America's hallmark, something not to fear but to embrace, and you are willing to carry this hard work of democracy forward. You'll soon outnumber any of us, and I believe as a result that the future is in good hands.*

Listening to the speech, surrounded by other alumni, I thought back to Obama's first campaign. Back then—when you sat alone at your computer to donate five dollars, or approached a stranger in a gas station parking lot to ask about voter registration, or knocked on a Republican neighbor's door—it rarely felt like you were making history. There had been no guarantee it would lead to anything. More than likely, it would end in an awkward conversation or door slammed in your face. But because millions of people I never met put aside their discomfort and took action, those moments added up to more than anyone ever could have hoped to accomplish on their own.

The morning after Obama left office, I stood on the National Mall with a clipboard to collect signatures for a candidate running for governor of Virginia.

"Hey there, are you all registered to vote in Virginia?" I called out to people headed to the Women's March.

As strangers signed my form, I asked what had brought them to the march. Each had a personal story, even if they didn't know how to articulate it. Some had been volunteers for Hillary Clinton, Bernie Sanders, or Obama; some had never voted before; some saw the march as totally disconnected from politics. The common thread was they wanted something to be different and realized they had a voice.

I didn't know whether that day would lead to anything. I didn't know that all across the country, hundreds of local organizers were putting on their own marches. Or that so many marchers would show up again, at congressional town halls, candidate recruitment forums, and neighborhood canvasses. Or that hundreds of thousands would return to where I was standing more than a year later, inspired by high schoolers to rally against gun violence. Or that my friend's uncle in Queens would prove me wrong and that so many women—the largest number in history—would fly to Washington for their own swearing-in as new members of Congress, less than two years after Trump's inauguration.

As with a decade earlier, all I knew for sure was that I and so many others wanted something to be different. We had seen the power of that before, which meant we could see it again.

So that morning, I held on to my clipboard and marched—one voice among millions, calling for change.

*After the 2008 election, organizers scattered in hundreds of different directions. Here's what some of the voices included in this book are up to as of fall 2019.*

### Yohannes Abraham

Yohannes went on to work in both terms of President Obama's White House and on his reelection campaign in 2012. He is now on the faculty at Harvard.

### Nathan Blake

Nathan worked on antihunger policy at USDA in the Obama administration before returning to Iowa in 2011. He lives in Des Moines, where he serves as Iowa's deputy attorney general for policy and works to raise three kids with his wife, Andrea.

### Jackie Bray

Jackie left the campaign lifestyle behind and now works in government. She still misses it, especially during election season.

### Lauren Champagne

Lauren is an attorney who currently resides in Washington, DC, with her husband and beautiful baby girl.

### Ally Coll Steele

Ally went on to serve as the field director for US senator Patty Murray's (D-WA) successful 2010 reelection campaign and Tim Kaine (D-VA)'s successful 2012 bid for the US Senate before leaving politics to pursue her law degree. After graduating from Harvard Law School, she joined the legal department of Hillary Clinton's presidential campaign and now serves as president of the Purple Campaign, a nonprofit organization she cofounded in the wake of the #MeToo movement to address workplace harassment.

### Brynne Craig

Brynne continued working on campaigns and issues that are important to her. Her love of spreadsheets continues.

## Joe Cupka

Joe is happily working only forty hours a week, these days for Eastman Music Company in Southern California. He lives with his girlfriend in Pasadena, has become one hell of a cook with all his free time, and enjoys doing yoga with Nobel laureates at CalTech.

## Greg Degen

After the Obama campaign, Greg went on to serve in various roles at the White House and at the US Agency for International Development. He has since moved to New York City and is currently completing a graduate program at Harvard.

## Steve Dunwoody

Since the campaign, Steve did stints during the first term of the Obama administration at the Pentagon, the Department of Energy, and the White House. He now resides in Los Angeles, California, working with organizations that champion diversity and social and environmental justice.

## Bess Evans

After serving eight years in the Obama administration, Bess now works in communications in the private sector on issues impacting communities at the intersection of corporate social responsibility, public policy, and human resources. She currently lives in Washington, DC, with her husband.

## Anne Filipic

Anne serves as chief program officer of the Obama Foundation. Previously, she served as president of Enroll America, a national nonprofit organization that supported the effort to enroll millions of Americans in health coverage made available through the Affordable Care Act. Anne is married to Carlos Monje Jr., who served on the 2008 Obama campaign policy staff. They met in Iowa in 2007 when Carlos came from Chicago to knock on doors and contact caucus goers. They have a son, Sebastian, and live in Washington, DC.

### Dean Fluker

Following the 2008 presidential campaign, Dean joined the Obama administration as a political appointee; he worked on President Obama's health care bill and First Lady Michelle Obama's Let's Move! Initiative against childhood obesity. Currently Fluker is a talent agent at United Talent Agency (UTA), where he represents artists including actors, writers, performers, and musicians.

### Marygrace Galston

Marygrace currently lives with her four-year-old daughter in Denver, Colorado. She is the executive director of Wildfire Contact, a voter contact firm owned and managed by Iowa Obama alumni.

### Rachel Haltom-Irwin

Rachel is the cofounder and executive director of Organizing Corps 2020. She is building the next generation of campaigners and the organizing force for the general election nominee to ensure Democrats can win back the White House in 2020.

### Anna Humphrey

Anna is a speechwriter at West Wing Writers, where she helps visionary leaders from fields as diverse as tech, consulting, academia, and entertainment in matching messages to moments. She lives in New York City and volunteers as a mentor for Girls Write Now, a nonprofit serving high school writers.

### Patricia Hynes

After starting a grassroots Obama group in the 2008 primaries, Patricia is now an elected member of the Fairfax County School Board. She teaches in Arlington and continues to be active in Democratic political organizing, though she finds her free time increasingly focused on organizing for climate action.

### Francis Iacobucci

After serving in President Obama's administration for seven years, Francis graduated from the University of Pennsylvania with a master's degree in social work. He works as a primary psychotherapist for an agency providing outpatient treatment for individuals struggling with eating and feeding disorders, body image, and comorbid mood and personality disorders. He and his partner live in Philadelphia, Pennsylvania.

### Lauren Kidwell

Lauren worked in the Obama administration at the Department of Health and Human Services and the Commerce Department. In between, she served on the 2012 reelection campaign as regional director for the Great Lakes and Mid-Atlantic region and earned a master of public administration degree from the Harvard Kennedy School. She was also a founding partner at 270 Strategies. In 2015, she married fellow Obama campaign alum Chris Wyant, and they live in Chicago with their son, Owen.

### Tyler Lechtenberg

Tyler spent all eight years in the Obama White House, primarily as a speechwriter for both President and Mrs. Obama. After the administration, he supported Mrs. Obama on her record-breaking memoir, *Becoming*, and is now a partner at Fenway Strategies, a speechwriting and communications firm.

### Howli Ledbetter

After the inauguration, Howli moved to Washington and spent six years working in communications for the Obama White House. Today she and her family live in the Bay Area. She still gets sunburned while knocking doors in nearby swing districts.

### Esther Morales

Esther spent eight years working for the Obama administration helping to make policy like the Affordable Care Act and the Clean Power Plan a reality. In 2018, Esther moved to Brooklyn and is hoping to work at the intersection of climate crisis mitigation, women's business ownership, and politics.

### Emily Parcell

Emily lives in Des Moines, Iowa, with her husband and their two boys. She is a co-owner and partner at the political consulting firm Wildfire Contact. In 2016 she served as an Iowa senior advisor to Hillary Clinton's general election campaign. In 2019, she rejoined the campaign world full time as a national senior advisor and states team director for Warren for President.

### Joe Paulsen

Joe went on to work in the Obama White House for eight years and is currently deputy chief of staff to President Obama. He lives in Washington, DC.

### Jamal Pope

After spending several years in the Obama administration, Jamal went back to school for an MBA. He has enjoyed working on teams with an entrepreneurial style similar to that of the 2008 campaign and appreciates reconnecting with some of his 2007–2008 campaign comrades each fall to play fantasy football. He lives in Atlanta.

### Janice Rottenberg

Janice is currently living in Des Moines, Iowa, where she is working on her fourth presidential campaign—this time as Elizabeth Warren's Iowa state director.

### James Schuelke

Following the Obama campaign, James worked for the White House's Office of Public Engagement and Intergovernmental Affairs. He then joined an educational nonprofit led by Dr. Jill Biden. Today, James lives with his wife in his native Ventura County, California, where he works as a community college administrator.

### Megan Simpson

Megan is working in Democratic politics to make sure every American has a fair shot. She is the Iowa state director for Governor Steve Bullock's presidential campaign.

### Carrianna Suiter Kuravilla

After the 2008 election, Carrianna spent nearly eight years working in the Obama administration. Shortly after the inauguration of Donald Trump, she decided to run for office herself and now serves as a member of the city council in Hyattsville, Maryland.

### Simeon Talley

Simeon is a small business owner and lives in his former turf of Iowa City. He cohosts the podcast *Political Party Live*.

## Maggie Thompson

After Nevada, Maggie worked in five additional states for the Obama campaign through the general election, including Texas, where she met her now husband, Trey, a fellow Obama organizer. After the campaign, Maggie moved to Washington, DC, where she served in the Obama administration and went on to be the executive director of Generation Progress. Today Maggie and Trey reside in Raleigh, North Carolina, where she is working for Senator Elizabeth Warren's campaign for president.

## Jaci (Urness) Friedley

Jaci is the director of public engagement for a wind and solar energy company. She is married and living in Minnesota.

## Shannon Valley

Shannon is completing a PhD in climate science at Georgia Tech in Atlanta. She hopes to combine that with her experience organizing on the campaign and communicating NASA science on Capitol Hill as part of the Obama administration to help build a world more resilient to climate change.

## Jason Waskey

Jason currently lives in Washington, DC, but still keeps a toe in Maryland politics. He launched his own consulting firm, focused on accelerating action on climate change, and founded the nonprofit Civic Nation. When not engaged with those two things, he can usually be found hiking.

## Chris Wyant

Chris is currently the deputy chief program officer at the Obama Foundation, where he helps oversee the strategy and operations for the foundation's various programs. Since the 2008 campaign, he has held a number of leadership roles in government, advocacy, nonprofits, and campaigns. He and his wife, Lauren Kidwell, an alum of Obama's 2004, 2008, and 2012 campaigns, are proud parents of Owen, who at one year old appears to be an organizer in the making.

## Nicole Young

After the 2008 campaign, Nicole went on to work at the US Department of Education, the White House, the College Board, and Bard

Early College in New Orleans. Nicole is currently an independent education policy consultant based in New Orleans.

## Leah White

Finally, Leah, whose time as precinct captain in Davenport was her first political volunteering experience, also volunteered on the 2012 reelection before taking a break from campaigns.

When asked about 2008, she said the following:

*My daughter was born during that time. I have pictures of me in my Obama shirt and my little pregnant belly. When we talk about that period, I tell her I'm proud to have been a part of it and explain why I was involved. I wanted to help make our country a better place for her. We're lucky to live in this country, but we can't take it for granted, and we have to be a part of helping make it better.*

*I haven't been directly involved in campaigns since 2012, but I have been active in my government. I'm involved in different ways now. We didn't have a Narcan law in Iowa. After a friend's brother passed away from a heroin overdose, I went up and lobbied on the hill in Des Moines for legalization of Narcan. And I hope that's the legacy my mom's left with me—to be active and to have a voice.*

*I feel like Barack Obama gave me a voice in my own government. Tripp and the people like him, they taught me how to use it.*

# ACKNOWLEDGMENTS

When I started recording oral histories, I wasn't sure where this project would lead. The fact that it became a book is a testament to the Obama alumni who agreed to share their stories. Nearly all the people included here opened doors to others, a reflection of the bond the alumni community retains more than ten years later. As one person with whom I had never spoken texted in response to a short-notice interview request: "A fellow field organizer from 2007 = whatever the fuck you need."

My parents, John Westefeld and Deb Liddell, and my sister Gina were a source of love and support (as well as transportation and lodging) for years as this endeavor with no obvious end kept me returning to the Midwest.

Colleen Lawrie, my editor at PublicAffairs, took a chance on a first-time author and shaped this manuscript in so many meaningful ways. When she shared a decade-old photo of herself in Pennsylvania as an out-of-state volunteer, I knew there could be no better collaborator.

Rafe Sagalyn, my agent, and Brandon Coward of ICM shepherded a proposal through countless revisions and offered sage advice over the past two years.

Jack Cumming agreed to jump in on short notice to get this book across the finish line. Scott Buchanan and Nathan Blake offered a place to stay in their respective towns, allowing me the chance to pack in three stops a day when passing through.

A group of friends—Kaylee Niemasik, Annie Reiner, James Schuelke, Maggie Anderson, Emilie Surrusco, Lauren Kelly, Kristin Avery, Mark Johnson, Saumya Narechania, Rachael Klarman, Hallie Schneir, Laura Updegrove, Soheil Rezayazdi, Howli Ledbetter, Laura Updegrove, Natalie Lawson, David Jonas, Dean Fluker, Shilpa Hegde, Ted Chiodo, Anuj Gupta, Ethan Yake, and Sam Slaton—were kind enough to read chapters, give advice, or suggest edits throughout the process. Brian Beutler and Jon Favreau's willingness to publish an excerpt at Crooked Media focused on Iowa made it possible for others to see what it could become. David Litt, Pat Cunnane, Sarah Hurwitz, Amanda Urban, Ken Auletta, Richard Reeves, Beck Dorey-Stein, and William Callahan offered advice from their own publishing experiences that proved invaluable when navigating unfamiliar terrain.

And it's safe to say that if not for Sean Williams, Kousha Navidar, Peter Slevin, Tony Rediger, Dan Pfeiffer, and Joe Paulsen—whom I can never thank enough for the crucial encouragement and support each provided in very different ways—you would not be reading this book today.

To my everlasting regret, I did not keep a journal during 2007–2008, so my reflections included here are drawn from old emails, notes, newspaper clippings, photos, and oft-told anecdotes I could confirm with a second source. What I hope shines through is my profound gratitude to the staff and volunteers who sacrificed so much to make the Obama presidency possible and to the president who lived up to the promises so many made on his behalf.

Finally, the best part of joining the Obama campaign was the person it led me to after it was over. My wife, Fiona, and I never crossed paths in any of the six states she worked in 2008, but she was the person I always hoped to find. This book exists because of her. That she made me a member of her family is what I'm most proud of.

# INDEX

**CHRIS LIDDELL-WESTEFELD** joined the Obama for America campaign in 2007 and went on to spend five years on the Obama White House staff. Since 2014, he has documented the story of the Obama presidency through oral history interviews. An Iowa native, he currently works as an oral historian in Washington, DC, where he lives with his wife and daughter.